Fighting and Writing the Vietnam War

Don Ringnalda

University Press of Mississippi
Jackson

The University Press of Mississippi and the author thank the following publishers for granting permission to reprint some material included in this book.

Some of the material that appears in chapters 1 and 2 was first published in *Journal of American Studies* (April 1988). Reprinted with permission of Cambridge University Press.

Some of the material that appears in chapter 3 was first published in *Western Humanities Review* (Summer 1986). Reprinted with permission of *Western Humanities Review.*

Some of the material that appears in chapter 4 was first published in *A Sourcebook of American Literary Journalism,* edited by Thomas Connery (Westport, CT: Greenwood Publishing Group, 1992). Reprinted with permission of Greenwood Publishing Group; and in *America Rediscovered: Critical Essays on Literature and Film of the Vietnam War,* edited by Owen W. Gilman, Jr. and Lorrie Smith (New York: Garland Publishing, 1990). Reprinted with permission of Garland Publishing.

Some of the material that appears in chapter 7 was first published in *Journal of American Culture* (Fall 1993). Reprinted with permission of *Journal of American Culture.*

Some of the material that appears in chapter 8 was first published in *Fourteen Landing Zones: Approaches to Vietnam War Literature,* edited by Philip K. Jason (Iowa City: University of Iowa Press, 1991). Reprinted with permission of University of Iowa Press.

Excerpts from the following poems are reprinted by permission of the authors. John Balaban's "After Our War," "For Mrs. Cam, Whose Name Means 'Printed Silk,'" "Dead for Two Years, Erhart Arranges to Meet Me in a Dream," "April 30, 1975," from *Blue Mountain,* published by Unicorn Press, 1982; "Words For My Daughter," "Crossing West Nebraska, Looking For Blue Mountain," "Walking Down Into Cebolla Canyon," from *Words For My Daughter,* published by Copper Canyon Press, 1991. D. F. Brown's "Coming Home," "Eating the Forest," from *Returning Fire,* published by San Francisco State University Press, 1984. W. D. Ehrhart's "Christ," from *Winning Hearts and Minds,* edited by Larry Rottmann, Jan Barry, and Basil T. Paquet, published by 1st Casualty Press, 1972; "Letter," "To Those Who Have Gone Home Tired," "The Invasion of Grenada," from *To Those Who Have Gone Home Tired,* published by Thunder's Mouth Press, 1984. J. Vincent Hansen's "Upon Entering a Montagnard Hamlet," "The Dark Forest," "Infrared," "Americans," from *Blessed are the Piecemakers,* published by North Star Press, 1989. Steve Hassett's "And what would you do, Ma" (untitled), from *Demilitarized Zones,* edited by Jan Barry and W. D. Ehrhart, published by East River Anthology, 1976. Yusef Komunyakaa's "You and I Are Disappearing," "Eyeball Television," from *Dien Cai Dau,* published by Wesleyan University Press, 1988. Walter McDonald's "Once You've Been to War," from *Carrying the Darkness,* edited by W. D. Ehrhart, published by Texas Tech University Press, 1989. Marilyn McMahon's "Wounds of War," from *Visions of War, Dreams of Peace,* edited by Lynda Van Devanter and Joan A. Furey, published by Warner Books, 1991. Basil T. Paquet's "Morning—A Death," from *Winning Hearts and Minds,* edited by Larry Rottmann, Jan Barry, and Basil T. Paquet, published by 1st Casualty Press, 1972. Bruce Weigl's "Song of Napalm," "Burning Shit at An Khe," "Monkey," from *The Monkey Wars,* published by University of Georgia Press, 1985.

Library of Congress Cataloging-in-Publication data on page 261

British Library Cataloging-in-Publication data available

CONTENTS

PREFACE

As many readers know, the literature about the Vietnam War has already received rather extensive critical attention, mostly from university presses. Philip Beidler has done two books with Georgia, and Vince Gotera, one. Susan Jeffords has published with Indiana, John Hellmann with Columbia, Thomas Myers with Oxford, Tobey Herzog with Routledge, and Owen Gilman, Jr., with Mississippi. Plus, there are critical anthologies with Bowling Green, Garland, and Iowa. [1] This does not even take into account interviews with authors, articles published separately in journals and books, special Vietnam issues of journals, numerous issues of the valuable journal *Viet Nam Generation*, or an ever-growing body of Ph.D. dissertations. Someone once said—and not altogether jokingly—that the pages written on this war would stretch all the way from the United States to Vietnam.

1. Philip Beidler's two books are *American Literature and the Experience of Vietnam* (1982) and *Re-Writing America: Vietnam Authors in Their Generation* (1991). John Hellmann's *American Myth and the Legacy of Vietnam* was published in 1986, Myers' *Walking Point: American Narratives of Vietnam*, in 1988. Susan Jeffords' study of gender and the war is called *The Remasculinization of America* (1989). Both Tobey Herzog's *Vietnam War Stories: Innocence Lost*, and Owen Gilman's *Vietnam and the Southern Imagination* were published in 1992. Vince Gotera's 1994 study of the war's poetry is called *Radical Visions: Poetry by Vietnam Veterans*. The Bowling Green anthology, *Search and Clear: Critical Responses to Selected Literature & Films of the Vietnam War*, edited by William J. Searle, came out in 1988. In 1990, Garland published *America Rediscovered: Critical Essays on Literature and Film of the Vietnam War*, edited by Owen Gilman, Jr., and Lorrie Smith. Finally, Philip K. Jason edited the 1991 collection of critical essays called *Fourteen Landing Zones: Approaches to Vietnam War Literature*.

So why *another* book? Because both the popular and the scholarly remembrances of Vietnam remind me of one of the classic scenes in war literature: Joseph Heller's Yossarian fastidiously treating Snowden's superficial hip wound, unaware of the evisceration held in by his flak jacket. Much of America's memory of Vietnam is focussed on the hip wound inflicted on the proud myths of the "City on a Hill." And sad to say, much of its energy is focussed on restoring those myths. Too often the radical wound goes unattended, perhaps out of collective and individual fear that it is beyond treatment. More often, however, this country's "flak jacket" effectively and insidiously protects its people from the sure knowledge that there even *is* a more serious, radical wound—namely, that America is inherently as malevolent and violent as any other nation on this planet, which explains why Richard Slotkin refers to it as a "Gunfighter Nation." America is not nearly as special as its people like to believe.

Nor was the war in Vietnam an aberration of the nation's behavior. The uniqueness of the war is one of the most powerful myths concocted by a national psychosis that seduces citizens into denying history or recalling it sentimentally. According to that myth, Vietnam was the one rotten apple in American history; the toxicity of the barrel itself goes undetected. Vietnam veterans seem especially susceptible to this pathology. In *The Wages of War* (1989), Richard Severo and Lewis Milford write, "If the soldiers of Vietnam thought there had never been a group of veterans so ignored, abused, and betrayed, it was not because they tried to rewrite history, but because they knew so little about it" (419). Speaking of Americans in general, they add, "It is unseemly for people so proud of their heritage to be so unaware of the dark side of it" (425).

The best Vietnam writers transcend the psychosis of uniqueness. In Emily Mann's play *Still Life* (1980), dysfunctional families and social institutions are viewed as basic training for Vietnam. In Peter Straub's novel *Koko* (1988), the antagonist reminds us that there is as much violence outside the average Milwaukee tavern as in a fire fight; inside the tavern there is a bit more. In his poem "April 30, 1975" (the date of the official end of the Vietnam War), John Balaban looks out at a generic American city and sees "scorching skies over a city at war." Often, however, even when critics of the war do point to America's abdominal wound, it's rather like, Now You See It, Now You Don't. Thus I argue that the collective American mind regarding the Vietnam War is like a cluttered attic, stuffed with sentimental memorabilia. Our creative writers and critics—I include myself—too often are like the person who cleans out the fire-trap attic, puts the stuff on the curb, but before the trash man arrives, moves half of the junk back up into the attic, incapable of parting with the perennial myths of Americana.

My book is atypical in several ways. It makes no attempt to "cover" Vietnam War literature. The writers mentioned in the opening paragraph have done this several times over. It is not, strictly speaking, a work of literary criticism; instead, it uses literary works as touchstones to engage in broader cultural criticism. Nor does it attempt to be representative (again, other books have done this). Rather, it attempts to offer an alternative voice—a dissenting one—to the monovocal one sounded by most of the war's writers and critics. That voice finds its verbal foundation in a two-word phrase frequently repeated by Philip Beidler: "sense making." One of the essential points of my study is that the last thing America needs to do with the Vietnam experience is make sense of it. Arguably this is the very reason we got into the war in the first place: we tried to make geopolitical confusion behave by force-tailoring it to the simplistic, arrogant myths of good and evil, saviors and sinners, democracy and monolithic world Communism, POWs and sadistic captors. In view of the continuous religious fervor with which the last adolescent dualism is clung to, we can see just how difficult it is to part with attic memorabilia. If it helps us make sense, it stays. But I reason that instead of making sense, we need to articulate the contours of *nonsense* that culminated in the war. This must be the epistemological starting point if America is ever to grow up and learn, as Paul Fussell puts it, the "power of facing unpleasant facts."

As the title of this book suggests, there is a link between the way America fought this war and the way it usually writes about the experience and its aftermath. I contend that this link is not merely metaphorical; on the contrary, the reason Americans fought it, the way they fought it, and the way they often write about it all stem from the very same failure of imagination, which in turn stems from this nation's righteous, sense-making rage for order and its perennial flight from the humility engendered by self-irony. Missing from most of America's remembrances of the war are the humble assumptions behind the title of poet Yusef Komunyakaa's book of Vietnam poems: *Dien Cai Dau* (1988), which in Vietnamese means "crazy in the head."

The foundation upon which *Fighting and Writing* rests is the final couplet of a poem called "In Broken Images," written by World War I veteran Robert Graves: "He in a new confusion of his understanding, / I in a new understanding of my confusion." Most of the Vietnam War fighting and writing refused and refuses to accept an understood confusion as a viable, satisfying option. Instead, the option pursued is an insistent objectivism that blindly equates human constructs with reality. Falling in love with sense-making conventions, the warrior and the writer try to create the illusion of understanding their understanding. In reality, however, because those conventions forcibly simplify and order the scabrous terrain of America's behavior in Vietnam and on previous frontiers, they result in solipsism, paradigm paralysis, and "a new confusion of . . . understanding."

This rage for order results in paradoxes. Because the fighter-writer is taken in by his own sense-making power-propaganda, his apparent strength turns into its opposite. The strength of his reactions to and memories of Vietnam's complexities is his weakness. "Knowing" too much, he actually knows too little. Ignorance masquerades as knowledge, caricature as reality. In its rage for order, America used its awesome technology to impose maps and geometry on a seemingly amorphous Vietnam. One of the principal agents of this imposition goes by the color orange. The defoliation and poisoning of the Vietnam landscape is not just *like* sense-making literary responses to the war; both actions issue from the same cultural imperative against disorder and defeat. In both cases, simplistic firepower replaces complex understanding, or understood confusion. Imposing the "technology" of toughminded realism (I-was-there-you-weren't-so-listen-up machismo) onto the Vietnam morass is a result of the same epistemological hubris that found it wise to destroy 25 million acres of farmland and 12 million acres of forest in a country (South Vietnam) smaller than the state of Missouri. On the literary front, that hubris forcefully illuminates the darkness of the war's evil with what GIs called "basketballs"—large flares used during the war to light up a square mile of terrain.

The tragic legacy of this artificial illumination is that it wastes the suffering. It wastes waste. It squanders the opportunity for America to grow up by recognizing that as in Vietnam, so throughout our history, "a major theme . . . has been a combination of hideous atrocities and protestations of awesome benevolence" (Chomsky, 294). On the other hand, instead of being squanderers of the suffering, the more visionary writers of the war are, as it were, scroungers working in the dark. Instead of sanitizing the war via the reassuring and alluring power of linear, mimetic narratives, the most alert, seeing-in-the-dark novelists, poets, and dramatists sift through the wreckage and offer up deconstructive, interrogative collages composed of unsettling juxtapositions. They make it a point to make more out of less. They are like the sculptor who welds together isolated pieces of junk to create tenuous new wholes—without obscuring the identity of the constituent junk. In *All Quiet on the Western Front* (1928), the narrator, Paul Bäumer, tells us that all the myths he had clung to were blown to pieces by the first bombardment. The Vietnam scroungers respect those pieces *as* pieces. Instead of denying they exist, they make use of them. To illustrate this scrounging process, I use as a leitmotif a scene from Jack Fuller's novel *Fragments* (1984). In it, a soldier named Neumann tries to rebuild a village dispensary leveled by a B-52 strike. Instead of ordering a shipment of new cement blocks from Quartermaster Corps, he mortars together the rubble itself. He doesn't finish, but by analogy he shows the responsible writer where to start and from what to build.

The central argument of my book is built on the assertion that writers who follow Neumann's example are those who write like the Vietcong fought, in other words, those who win by not losing, rather than those who lose by not winning. Whereas most of the war's "basketball" literature emulates the conventional tactics and strategies of the

U.S. military, the "scrounging" literature emulates the unconventional conventions of the guerrilla fighter: waste is used, not wasted; darkness is used, not artificially illuminated; the jungle chaos is explored, not defoliated; the illegitimacy of the guerrilla is a strength, not a weakness; conventional, linear trails in the jungle are deconstructed with metafictional booby-traps, not foolishly walked on, because as James William Gibson puts it, ". . . conventional paths [he also calls them "the old trails"] in search of war lead only to destruction of serious intellectual inquiry" (11).

The problem with "old-trail" literature is identical to "old-trail" warfare: neither is cognizant that the "trails" are potentially dangerous human constructions, not the "jungle" of reality itself. Believing his own propaganda, the fighter-writer unconsciously transmutes fiction into "essays" of reality, denies the truths of *conscious* fiction, and then enters a self-referential, self-prophesying, tautological trap. My book has three concerns: the trap, how it gets set, and how to escape it. Confronting all three of my concerns, Tim O'Brien's Doc Peret (*Going After Cacciato*, 1978) is one of the most fascinating fictional characters in all of Vietnam War literature. Vexed by the tautological trap, he counsels, in effect, the self-interrogations of metafiction. In another of the leitmotifs of *Fighting and Writing*, Peret warns us to pay close attention to how we look at the war, how we mediate it with our perceptual equipment: ". . . [o]bservation requires inward-looking, a study of the very machinery of observation—the mirrors and filters and wiring and circuits of the observing instrument. . . . What you remember is determined by what you see, and what you see depends on what you remember. A cycle, Doc Peret had said. A cycle that has to be broken. And this requires a fierce concentration on the process itself . . ." (247–48).

The writers who can teach us the most about any war are hybrids of Neumann, Peret, and the Vietcong. Blue-collar postmodernists, they can help us become "appropriately upset" (Egendorf) by making peace with the pieces made by war. Like Maya Lin's Vietnam Veterans Memorial, they show us that we can gain healing power from facing more than 58,000 "unpleasant facts." By eliciting thoughtful reflection rather than goose bumps, sentimental tears, and the reification of warrior nostalgia, they show us how to remember the war without conferring dignity on it. They can convince us that, myth-hungry, we "mended crooked" from the Vietnam War, and that we therefore need to get "broken up again" (Tesich). Most importantly, they exemplify that we're much better off scrounging than squandering.

ACKNOWLEDGMENTS

This book belongs to many people, without whom it never would have been written. I'm lucky to be a member of a supportive community of scholars, both inside and outside the University of St. Thomas. Over the last several years I've often arrived in the morning to find valuable Vietnam War material—reviews, articles, books—in my department box. In particular, two trusted colleagues and friends at the university, Michael Bellamy and Thomas Dillon Redshaw, have guided me from the start: Redshaw as the inspiration and the person who drew my attention to Peter Straub's "non-canonical" Vietnam novel, *Koko*, and Bellamy as the invaluable reader of every chapter and revision. Everyone needs an outside reader; everyone should be fortunate enough to have someone with Bellamy's knack for doing it.

Although I fear I have let her down, Lady Borton has never tired of reminding me "Don't forget the Vietnamese people." More than any other person, she has convinced me of the necessity to step outside my male, Western shoes. A Navy veteran of the Vietnam War, John Mitchell has been my check against academic isolationism since I started publishing in this area. A world-class debater and curmudgeon, he has done his best to keep me honest. I would like to think he has succeeded.

A special thanks to Stephen Fender, former editor of *Journal of American Studies*. It was he who patiently talked me through several rather inchoate drafts of a Vietnam War literary overview back in 1987. Most editors would have simply rejected the mess I first sent him. But he saw something I didn't. The resulting article, "Fighting and Writing: America's Vietnam War Literature," convinced me that I had something to say. Since then, Owen Gilman, Lorrie Smith, Philip Jason, Thomas Connery, and Vince Gotera have helped me immeasurably in their role as editors of anthologies in which my writing appears. I'm particularly indebted to Lorrie, who has never tired of offering her timely criticisms.

I am grateful to Seetha A-Srinivasan, the editor of this book, and the University Press of Mississippi. Like Stephen Fender, she truly is a writer's editor who recognizes and tutors potential, rather than merely oversees the production of books. Finally, my wife Jonelle, who often had better things to do, repeatedly indulged me by reading sentences, paragraphs, pages, and chapters—often on a moment's notice. I can never thank her enough for being my "in-house" editor.

Fighting and Writing the Vietnam War

ONE

Prospero Goes
to Vietnam

He is quick, thinking in clear images;
I am slow, thinking in broken images.

. . . . .

He continues quick and dull in his clear images;
I continue slow and sharp in my broken images.

He in a new confusion of his understanding;
I in a new understanding of my confusion.

Robert Graves

A familiar sight at the Vietnam Veterans Memorial (VVM) in Washington, D.C., is people tracing onto a piece of paper the name of a
relative or friend who was killed in Vietnam. Anyone who has visited
the memorial has observed this practice. On one hand, this gesture is
sadly poignant; likely it's even cathartic. On the other hand, it also
seems symptomatic of the perceptions many Americans hold of the
Vietnam War, whether in the 1960s or the 1990s: when we have the
name of something, we somehow also possess the thing named. Even
though there is obviously an enormous semiotic gap between that

symbol, etched in stone, and its object, long gone, the symbol nevertheless acquires a powerful ontological status. A traced symbol of a symbol on a symbol becomes reality. Whenever I witness this scene, I can't help asking myself, "just what kind of legacy is this reification of a purely human construction?"

It is difficult to know the thoughts of those people doing the tracing, and coldhearted to denigrate their actions. Although I will have more to say about the Vietnam Memorial in the final chapter, it needs to be stated at the outset that these actions, at the very least, seem to run counter to the design and spirit of Maya Lin's troubling and humbling black wall, one of the greatest postmodern "texts" to come out of the war. Because the VVM "begins" and "ends" on dates in 1968—the middle of the war—when the killing and destruction reached the most intense level, the memorial offers viewers who pay attention no entrance or exit. The "circularity" of the wall precludes closure as well as any pretense of "kicking the Vietnam syndrome." Therefore, any catharsis derived from the experience will at best be ambivalent, convoluted, and hard-earned. More likely, however, it will be misappropriated through denial or ignorance of the wall's treatment of space and time.

Conscious or not, these misappropriations represent a continuation of simplistic attitudes that got Americans involved in Vietnam in the first place, kept them there for more than a decade, led to their defeat, and culminated in thousands of literary memorials, including several hundred Vietnam War novels alone, many of which resimplify our relationship with time and history, symbol and object. In most of these novels, the symbol often replaces the object, and unexamined, unseen cultural and literary conventions tame America's jungle nightmare. As Frances Fitzgerald says in *Fire in the Lake* (1972), America tried to play the role of Prospero in Vietnam, deluded into thinking that it could translate the untranslatable, name the unnameable, map the unmappable, control the uncontrollable—all by falling into the trap of reification, that devilish habit of confusing human fiction with nonhuman reality. America reasserted thousands of times its superiority over nature by dropping unthinkable amounts of explosives and herbicides on the unruly nature of Southeast Asia. To use Prospero's word, America felt it could and must "nurture" nature. Our

4

nation felt it could and must name it with our own store of names to make it behave unambiguously. But in order to give it our name, we first had to try to erase the original one—"Nuoc Vietnam"—which literally means "water nation," a fluid nation of maddening genesis. In the end, however, it was the tenacious Caliban and the muddy waters of the Vietnam monsoons that erased, rather than traced, the name of America's Narcissus.

Written by descendants of Prospero, most Vietnam War literature tries to make America's experience with Nuoc Vietnam behave by smelting it down into traditional mimetic transcriptions. Refined out of these too-tidy narratives are the disturbing shapeless contingencies—both moral and epistemological—of the actual experiences. Rather than probe dark recesses, they trace surfaces. Implying a sense of controlled continuity and rational ordering, realism is a particularly inappropriate mirage in the context of America's Vietnam War. In fact, in *Culture and Imperialism* (1993), Edward Said argues that the only "appropriate" context for realism is a tautological, imperialist mind-set. One can infer from Said's argument that to "remember" Vietnam by means of war-story realism is to deny that we lost the war or that our cultural motives for fighting it were self-serving, ethnocentric, and racist. Wary of this complicity of writing and fighting, Tim O'Brien has always been less fearful that America will forget the war than that it will remember it simplistically, a concern he made public at a 1978 Vietnam War Writers conference at Macalester College in St. Paul, Minnesota. He had reason to be fearful. Since 1978 we've seen how adept America's memory is at editing out of its war in Vietnam the complexities and the threats to national order.

Even the military strategist Colonel Harry Summers (*On Strategy: A Critical Analysis of the Vietnam War;* 1982) recognizes that memory's editing job gives the delusion of traditional order: "Vietnam was not a canvas by Daumier or even by Degas. It was more an abstract by Dali or DeKooning" (241). Also employing the painterly metaphor, Steven Smith, author of *American Boys* (1975), says of one of his characters, "If he'd had some paints and canvas, he would've sat down in the goddam dusty road [in Vietnam] and started to work. He wanted a canvas as big as a football field or a wall a hundred yards long. The shape in front of him began to extend indefinitely, then became gro-

5

tesque. He could make *Guernica* look like a country fair by the time he was done. Crazy. Crazy" (162). Yet, despite the actual "canvas" of the war, many writers paint stories that are more reminiscent of Norman Rockwell on a rather bad day than of Dali or DeKooning. The twofold purpose of this study is, first, to discuss a handful of novelists, playwrights, and poets who successfully take on the role of literary Dalis; and, second, to show that in fact they are a mere handful among the hundreds who continue to "Rockwellize" the war.

Sense-making narratives of realism continue to display the will to superimpose the clarity of Rockwell over the ambiguity of Dali in our Vietnam experience. Two virtual footnotes in our military intervention in Vietnam exemplify this wilfulness. Harry Summers tells a story that made the rounds during the Nixon Administration:

> When the Nixon Administration took over in 1969 all the data on North Vietnam and on the United States was fed into a Pentagon computer— population, gross national product, manufacturing capability, number of tanks, ships, and aircraft, size of the armed forces, and the like. The computer was then asked *"When will we win?"* It took only a moment to give the answer: *"You won in 1964!"* (42)

Having fed the computer with data derived solely from a "traced" Rockwellian world, what other answer could one expect? If you begin with the epistemologically arrogant assumption made by America's "Best and Brightest," that, "If it doesn't have a solution it isn't a problem" (Baritz, 32), you can see how America readily and insistently saw Rockwell, "on a rather bad day," as its mentor. It still does. Granted, if one fed a computer with the "data" of the war's literature, the answer would be somewhat more consistent with the actualities inherent in the conflict; but that's like saying a yew is more like an elm than a bar of soap.

The second footnote takes us back to February 26, 1965, when President Johnson sent two Marine battalions to defend the vulnerable Air Force base in Danang. As Olson and Roberts say in *Where the Domino Fell* (1991), on March 8 they arrived,

> . . . as if it were Iwo Jima or Tarawa all over again, 3,500 troops stormed the beaches in full battle regalia, complete with M-14 rifles, landing craft, naval air support, amphibious tractors, helicopters, 105-mm howitzers,

M48 tanks, and 106mm recoilless rifles. But instead of a firefight, they encountered young South Vietnamese women waiting on the beaches with flowered leis to put around their necks. The smiling mayor of Danang welcomed the troops to his city. The marines clambered into trucks for the ride to the air base, and all along the way waved at thousands of school-children lining the highway and welcoming them. (129)

Considering the massive turmoil and killing that had been taking place in Vietnam for many years, this landing assault should have occasioned a worrisome what's-wrong-with-this-picture response from our leaders. The great "success" should have been unnerving. It was not. Why? Because our leaders, like the novelists and critics later, willed a previously successful tactical paradigm into a place where it did not fit. If they had been less entrenched in American Frontier and Manifest Destiny paradigms, and more entrenched in the history of warfare, say, between the Vietminh and the French, or the Vietnamese and the Chinese, Johnson and the Pentagon would have quickly surmised that the game here was not the one they were used to playing. Instead, Johnson celebrated the landing in igno-rance: "Now I have Ho Chi Minh's pecker in my pocket" (Olson, 129). Peculiarly "pecker-conscious," Johnson evidently believed that safekeeping this part of Ho Chi Minh's anatomy was feasible, having bragged that he had cut it off the previous August when the Tonkin Gulf Resolution sailed through the Senate, 88 to 2.

In actuality, the only thing Johnson possessed was a raging case of paradigm paralysis, a condition that, undiagnosed throughout the course of the war, repeatedly prevented Americans from appreciating what kind of war they were in. Ethnocentric to the end, the American leadership was insistent upon imposing the American Rockwell on the Vietnamese Dali. And it did so in a spirit of arrogance. I say "to the end," because even as the war was drawing to a close, Dr. Henry Kissinger's *American Foreign Policy* (1974) displayed an unquestioning fidelity to American (and Western) paradigms: "A scientific revolu-tion has, for all practical purposes, removed technical limits from the exercise of power in foreign policy" (54). In *The Perfect War* (1986), James William Gibson disagrees with Kissinger's solipsistic commit-ment to imposing a Newtonian worldview on Vietnam: ". . . he claims that the West knows reality and the underdeveloped countries

7

live only in their own delusions" (15). Gibson goes on to say that according to Kissinger's hubris,

American intervention in the Third World not only brings technology and consumer goods into play but also brings *reality* to the Third World. In claiming the West's radical monopoly on knowing reality, the Third World becomes *unreal*. Those who live there and have retained "the essentially pre-Newtonian view that the real world is almost entirely internal to the observer" [actually, this is a *post*-Newtonian, postmodernist view] are therefore totally unlike the West and its leading country. Those who are totally unlike us and live in their own delusions are conceptualized as foreign Others. The foreign Other can be known only within the conceptual framework of technological development and production systems. For instance, the Other may have bicycles. Bicycles can be readily comprehended by the West as a form of "underdeveloped" transportation, as opposed to the trucks and automobiles found in the "developed" West. Bicycles are "less" than cars by definition. . . . Who defeated the most powerful nation in world history?. . . . Who defeated a war budget of more than one trillion dollars? For the most part, peasants of underdeveloped agricultural economies defeated the United States. . . . By Kissinger's theory such a defeat is *unthinkable*. Kissinger's claim to a monopoly of true knowledge for the West turns into its opposite. (16–17)

In other words, paralyzed by our own Newtonian paradigm, we defeated ourselves by persistently viewing the Vietcong as being different from us in degree (bicycle vs. automobile), when in fact they were different in kind. Underestimating them as being different only in degree, the U.S. military often contemptuously referred to them as "those raggedy-assed little bastards" (Sheehan, 205). To Americans, the Vietcong simply had less technology to fight with; but the Vietcong knew they had a different kind of technology—the land, and they used it to great advantage against U.S. technology. In his *A Bright Shining Lie* (1988), Sheehan relates a story that perfectly expresses how the Vietcong used nature in concert with their kind of technology. A Captain James Drummond is told by a prisoner that "the most important VietCong training camp in the northern Delta" is located in "clumps of woods" above a hamlet. When he gets there, Drummond finds ". . . four thatched-hut classrooms furnished with blackboards under the trees . . ." (88). The very idea that "blackboards under the trees"—a virtual oxymoron in American thinking—could be used to defeat the United States, is, once again, "unthinkable." It represents what psychiatrist Charles J. Levy calls "inverted warfare," which Gibson explains as "the sense in which American common sense on how the world operates was reversed or inverted in Vietnam" (122). (In *Dispatches*, Michael Herr sounds the same note with his "inversion of the expected order.") Gibson adds, "The foreign Other repeatedly took the 'bait' while the traps backfired" (123). Quoting Levy, Gibson summarizes this inversion: "The rationale for much of American technology had been the conquest of nature. But in Vietnam the VC/NVA used nature for the conquest of technology" (122). Similarly, they used the strength of our technology the way Eastern martial arts adsorb and redirect an opponent's aggression, strength, and momentum.

The Vietcong reversed or inverted other paradigms that Americans stubbornly clung to. Training the Vietcong in the early 1960s, Le Duan often gave the following paradigm-bashing catechism in guerrilla tactics: "When the enemy masses we disperse. When the enemy passes we harass. When the enemy withdraws we advance. When the enemy disperses, we mass" (Olson, 71). Le Duan understood something that was unthinkable to Americans at war, namely, that one can transform conventionally viewed weakness into a tactic of great power. Conversely, conventional military strength can be rendered ineffectual. In *Backfire* (1985), Loren Baritz says, "The fundamental weakness revealed in Vietnam was our strength" (324). Thus it is not surprising that a few years later, Vo Nguyen Giap, the North Vietnamese commander, boldly and correctly predicted "America will lose the war on the day when their military might is at its maximum and the great machine they've put together can't move anymore. . . . We'll beat them at the moment when they have the most men, the most arms, and the greatest hope of winning" (Olson, 175–76). As the war became more and more mad and brutal, even Kissinger, in one of his non-Newtonian moments, came to the realization that a conventional army loses if it does not win, whereas a guerrilla army wins if it does not lose.

My final example of paradigm paralysis (there are many others) resulted in an almost maniacal obsession for the Military Assistance

9

Command, Vietnam, and even the officers in the field. In turn, this obsession produced disastrous consequences for Vietnamese, Cambodians, and Americans. I speak of the futile, frenzied search for the Communist party headquarters in South Vietnam. Known acronymically as COSVN, this elusive, and perhaps non-existent, headquarters became an inverted El Dorado of the American imagination. And it was replicated like a sequence of Russian dolls down the chain of command, from the two-star general's certainty that there was an NVA regiment bivouacked "out there," to the battalion colonel's sure knowledge that there was an NVA reinforced company "out there." Exemplary literary representations can be found in *Meditations in Green* (1983): "The 5th NVA regiment. Where from? Where to? How big? How good? Find it!" (44) and *Dispatches*: "Somewhere out there . . . is the *entire First NVA Division* . . . Somewhere . . . Somewhere . . . Somewhere . . . Somewhere . . ." (102).

Having imposed Rockwell on the Vietnamese Dali, Westmoreland and his successor, Creighton Abrams, solipsistically just knew COSVN had to be "out there" some place. After all, we had our own headquarters, MACV; so there had to be a similar, very large brain center for the enemy too (Nixon called it the "nerve center"). Billions of dollars were spent killing millions of trees in the effort to destroy this phantom brain center. It never was found. But in 1969, General Abrams excitedly declared that COSVN had moved—to Cambodia. Thus began the massive and secret bombing of Cambodia, which initiated a series of events stretching from the Kent State killings in 1971, to the Cambodian "killing fields" in 1975, to the crazed world of realpolitik in that nation in the 1980s and 90s.

It's clear that COSVN was mistakenly viewed as the counterpart to MACV. But what lay behind this mistake? In literary terms, it was the insistence that all the world behave according to Western-conceived linear, causal plots. It was the assumption that the Vietcong couldn't be so successful in their widespread military engagements unless they were directed from above—top-down—by their own staff generals with maps, pins, and pointers in a large, above-ground structure that stayed put. In short, the paradigm we carried with us to Vietnam was that of the "omnisciently narrated" corporation, which functions with hierarchical, vertical management. The model is Newton's machine, the brain of which runs subservient parts.

By contrast, the Vietcong were organized more in terms of post-modern literature, or of what the physicist Fritjof Capra (*The Turning Point*, 1982) calls "living systems," which "exhibit multilevel patterns of organization characterized by many intricate and nonlinear pathways [tunnels? Borgesian labyrinths?] along which signals of information and transaction propagate between all levels, ascending as well as descending" (282). In other words, the Vietcong cadres were not dependent parts of the whole, they were inextricable, interdependent manifestations of the whole. The organizational principle, more lateral than vertical, was based more on patterns of surprise and unpredictability than on structures of power and domination. In a sense, then, COSVN was everywhere and nowhere. As it turns out, there actually was a mobile COSVN, but as Truong Nhu Tang says in his *A Vietcong Memoir* (1985), it was (like the VC training camp in the northern Delta) "a simple peasant hut" (128). Tang goes on to explain something that was lost on our military: "COSVN was, and had always been, people rather than a place" (128).

The greatest example of "inverted warfare" is the phenomenon of the Ho Chi Minh Trail. The United States dropped more bombs on this primitive trail stretching from northern Laos and North Vietnam to South Vietnam than were dropped in all of World War II in Europe. The strategy was utterly simple: destroy the Trail and cut off the influx of war materiel to the South. Unbeknownst to the U.S. military, they were getting themselves involved in a nonlinear equation, or better yet, an "inverse linear equation": the greater the bombing, the more bombproof the Trail became. Each time it was bombed, a new secondary or tertiary trail was added. Neil Sheehan reminds us that, "An American thinks of a road or trail as a line going from Point A to Point B, curving only as necessary to accommodate terrain. The Vietnamese [their hand forced] wanted a 'chokeproof' road system, so they built six or eight or ten different routes from A to B. . . ." (678). Sheehan points out that one crow-flying stretch of 250 miles actually comprised the better part of 9,600 miles. In reverse effect, the bombing "built" a labyrinth, a kind of topographical postmodern text that would outperform America's Newtonian arsenal. "To punish," Sheehan writes, "was not to prevail. Each double loop and triple bypass in this ever enlarging whirligig of roads" (679) became symbolic of American strength equalling weakness.

11

Imposing Rockwell on Dali backfired. Baritz's excellent book *Backfire* is aptly named, for, like an improperly "timed" engine, America's paradigms "combusted" because of their own internal solipsistic excess. Eventually, in April of 1975, ten years after the "triumphal" landing of the Marines near Danang, those paradigms started running backward. In describing the U.S. evacuation of Saigon, Gibson says, "It was as if an imaginary Western had turned into a horror show—the cavalry was shooting its horses after being chased by the Indians back to the fort" (3). But because Americans are not very good at defeat, more often than not, "inverted warfare" ends up right side up in our nation's postwar memories. Speaking at the 1984 Vietnam Writers Conference in New York City, John Clark Pratt, author of the metafictional *Laotian Fragments* (1974), called attention to this problem. He said the war "was being conducted and reported and understood the way people used to [and still do] write traditional novels." I would simply invert this: traditional novels of "top-down management" are still being written the way the war was conducted and understood. The canon imitates the cannon. In their structure, scope, and epistemological assumptions, the war's narratives emulate the narrow conventional preoccupations and presumptions of America's military endeavors in Vietnam. They refuse to relinquish the traditional "firepower" of authorial, "managerial" control. We can apply Sir Robert Thompson's objection to America's military policy to its literary memories: "It doubles the firepower and squares the error" (Olson, 167). According to Malcolm Browne, this results in the futility of using a sledgehammer to attack a floating cork (Olson, 158).

If I may extrapolate from his novel *Hocus-Pocus* (1990), Kurt Vonnegut might well respond to these war stories by saying that they—and America itself—suffer from a collective case of "dyslexia," so right side up looks inverted, and inverted looks right side up. Many Americans simply did not know how to "read" themselves or the enemy beyond the most simplistic frontier myth of the contest between good and evil. This pathological misreading continues to foster pathological miswritings. However, as will be demonstrated below, the handful of Vietnam novels, plays, and poems that do succeed as imaginative artifacts and as faithful expressions of the nightmare are those that eschew the dyslexic methods and the rationale of the U.S.

military operations. Instead they emulate the ways in which the Vietcong fought.

Written by Prospero, most Vietnam novels mirror the military operations in four ways. They are enamored of the sense-making "power" of maps (literal and figurative), they limit themselves to linear time, they overestimate the capabilities of technology, and finally, they are mired in cultural narcissism that results in racism and a shocking ignorance of Vietnam and its people. By reflecting the military's cultural assumptions, these novels "lose" for the same reason the United States lost the war: because of how they try to win.

In Stephen Wright's *Meditations in Green* (a novel that doesn't "lose") a character named Claypool tries to eat the mess hall food. Wright observes, "Everything moved toward the stability of mush. Claypool tried his fork. The food dripped through the tines" (103). A bit later he adds, "There is growth everywhere. Plants have taken the compound. Elephant grass in the motor pool. Plantain in the mess hall. Lotus in the latrine. Shapes are losing outline, character. Wooden frames turning spongy. The attrition of squares and rectangles. The loss of geometry" (135). It is these squares and rectangles—this geometry—that many of the war's writers, like the military before them, have tried to maintain through strategical and tactical devices. While in Vietnam, the United States spent more than a trillion dollars trying to keep that country from dripping through its technological tines. It was a futile undertaking, considering that the landscape of Vietnam was perceived as a never-ending cycle of growth and decay set on fast forward, a green monster of rioting vegetation, a botanist's madhouse, a florist's nightmare, a perpetual chlorophyll overdose. We discovered, as the psychologist Ken Wilber might say, that "Nature is not only smarter than we think, Nature is smarter than we can think" (17). Until Vietnam, we never had been forced to this sobering conclusion.

Yet the military—and often the U.S. news media—never gave up the effort to map and outthink that inferno and its indigenous residents. Onto the mythic, cyclical, seamless Tao of Vietnam we superimposed a geometrician's game plan. From a "carpentered" America of straight lines and right angles, we imported the maps and grids—I Corps, II Corps, III Corps, IV Corps, numbers and more numbers, codes, longitudes, latitudes, sectors, charts, graphs, coordinates. And let us not forget that we imposed a carpentered reality on a country (South Vietnam) that wasn't a country at all, but merely a recent, diplomatically created abstraction run by a series of corrupt puppets. Oblivious, Americans became "cartomaniacs" in Vietnam. Bungling alchemists, we thought we could transform symbols into reality. We were like Graham Greene's prototypical American protagonist, Alden Pyle, about whom the cynical Fowler says, "He gets hold of an idea and then alters every situation to fit the idea" (167–68). As Alan Watts once said, people often become so enamoured of the menu that they eat it instead of the food. As is the case with Joseph Heller's Doc Daneeka, if your name is on the flight manifest of a plane that crashed—you're dead, no matter that you weren't on the plane. A paper reality easily achieves dominion.

Paper maps have always provided the military with a reassuring ersatz reality, a caricature traced from the imagination of the American cultural landscape. In *Apocalypse Now* (1979), Francis Ford Coppola hilariously satirizes the imposition of this landscape onto Vietnam. Although the film's Colonel Kilgore scene strikes many vets as an outrageous falsification of the war, it is actually one of the most truthful metaphorical expressions to come out of the war. With mortars, flares, and machine gun fire going off all around him, the invulnerable Kilgore acts as if he were on his own ordered, private Malibu Beach, surfing, barbecuing T-bones, playing the guitar, shooting his latest John Wayne cavalry movie (now with Hueys instead of horses), and killing America's most recent Indians. His clothes say it all: despite the suffocating heat and humidity, they are impeccably starched and clean. Except physically, he's not even in Vietnam! As Loren Baritz says in the opening sentence of his book, "I write about the Vietnam War to clarify American culture" (vii). No character is more emblematic of the need for this approach than Colonel Kilgore.

Like Kilgore's surfing, barbecuing, and movie party, maps gave (and give) the illusion of doing battle against the amorphous. They are imbued with purpose, direction, shape, design. Unlike Maya Lin's memorial, they furnish one with a superimposed mental geography through which one can journey purposefully from a beginning to a middle to an end. They make destination possible. They seem to ori-

14

ent us—in both senses. But, in fact, whether it be war maps or the maps of cartographic writing, they disorient and delude us. As Ken Wilber says, "Boundaries are illusions, products not of reality but of the way we map and edit reality. And while it is fine to map out the territory, it is fatal to confuse the two" (31). Because the American experience in Vietnam had little to do with beginnings, middles, and ends, these maps, whether hanging on walls or within the pages of America's rememberings, dangerously distract us and disconnect us from what really happened in the primeval swamps and jungles.

David Halberstam recognized the disjunction in Vietnam between symbol and reality in his novel *One Very Hot Day* (1967), a book written early in the war and set even earlier, when America's presence in Vietnam was still merely advisory. His main character, Captain Beaupre, a veteran of two relatively "straight" wars (WW II and Korea), tells his straight-out-of-West Point lieutenant: "We didn't know how simple it was, and how good we had it. Sure we walked, but in a straight line. Boom, Normandy beaches, and then you set off for Paris and Berlin. Just like that. No retracing, no goddam circles, just straight ahead. All you needed was a compass and good sense. But here you walk in a goddam circle, and then you go home, and then you go out the next day and wade through a circle, and then you go home and the next day you go out and reverse the circle you did the day before, erasing it. Every day the circles get bigger and emptier. Walk them one day, erase them the next" (119).

No writer has had as much to say about America's collective delusion on this subject as Michael Herr. On the very first page of *Dispatches* (1977), he calls attention to the incongruity of maps in Vietnam: "There was a map of Vietnam on the wall of my apartment in Saigon. . . . That map was a marvel, especially now that it wasn't real anymore. . . . Even the most detailed maps didn't reveal much anymore; reading them was like trying to read the faces of the Vietnamese, and that was like trying to read the wind" (1).

Later, Herr says, "The terrain above II Corps, where it ran along the Laotian border and into the DMZ, was seldom referred to as the Highlands by Americans. It had been a matter of military expediency to impose a new set of references over Vietnam's older, truer being, an imposition that began most simply with the division of one country into two and continued—it had its logic—with the further division of South Vietnam into four clearly defined tactical corps. . . . And if it effectively obliterated even some of the most obvious geographical distinctions, it made for clear communication" (97).

Unfortunately, the military's obsession with geometrical clarity and maps is figuratively mirrored in most Vietnam War novels. They are written the way America fought, with a conventional symbology that doesn't apply. They are attempted maps, and perhaps as obsolete as the one on Herr's wall in Saigon. Nevertheless, they are maps that the writer hopes will chart and give shape and order to their experiences that seemed to dissolve even as they were forming. These novels are searches for ontological stability based on epistemological wishful thinking. The strategy of most of them is to make sense of Vietnam. The tactics? Often the conventions of the realist novel. But, again, to clothe the Vietnam experience in this kind of structure is like trying to "read the wind."

John Del Vecchio's well-received novel, *The 13th Valley* (1982), is an extreme—even literal—example of the book-as-map. At the 1984 Vietnam Writers Conference, Del Vecchio said, "I had the actual maps, and for that reason my story is so real." Throughout his mammoth novel he scatters maps, charts, lists, reports, and even a glossary and a list of historical dates going back to 2879 B.C. It's as if he felt that if he could amass enough "facts" they would add up to something significant. But the result is more a case of writing by the pound, by a writer who couldn't make up his mind if he wanted to create a novel or recite "straight" history. To offer up a hallucinatory experience as straight history, as an accumulation of facts and information, is to mediate that experience out of existence—a point that Michael Herr makes throughout his "crooked" history in *Dispatches*. Because of his continued popularity, Del Vecchio perpetuates, perhaps more than any other Vietnam novelist, those very attitudes and practices that marked our military's presence in Vietnam. The result is a book of literary, linguistic imperialism, of literary Agent Orange. Its military analogue is the destructive search for COSVN. It's what the narrator of James Park Sloan's *War Games* (1971) would call the "language of pure egotism" (74). A language disconnected from the reality it purports to express, a victim of epistemological inertia.

16

This disconnection is also the result of the second parallel between fighting in and writing about Vietnam—being hooked on the straight line of linear, continuous, irreversible Time of perpetual progress—the conventional time of realism. Meaning well, General Westmoreland did the worst thing he possibly could have by introducing the one-year tour of duty in Vietnam. This is without precedent in U.S. military history. He charged an already linearly oriented people with what resulted in an obsession with time that surpasses the one with maps. Many grunts became metaphysicians of time. Pages and pages of almost any Vietnam novel are filled with detailed descriptions of the grunt's two chief measuring devices of time in Vietnam—the short-timer's stick, whittled down each day until it is finally gone on the soldier's last day in country, and short-timer's calendars—often outrageous, obscene collages on which each day the soldier would ritualistically ink out one more fragment of his arch friend/enemy, time. And notice that the GI didn't number from one to 365; he numbered backwards. It was a process of erasure, not filling. It was a process of trying to erase a totally alien reality. So the experience in Vietnam was one of ever-decreasing length, not volume, chronology, not duration. It was a nerve-wracking battle of time against an ominous space. Metaphorically speaking, the grunts were convicts counting down the days left on their sentences, or worse, praying for a stay of execution.

Despite the fact that time didn't "add up" in Vietnam, but rather wound down, entropically, most of the war's novels are written as if this were not the case. Most of them are World War II novels with new content—new "facts." In the typical Vietnam linear narrative the author selects a group of recruits from the affirmative action stockpile (ranging from a street-wise black to a naive Iowa farmboy, a Yankee to a Southerner), puts them through basic training, where they become somewhat robotized, gives most of them nicknames, sends them to Nam, where they become disillusioned and brutalized, has them curse a lot and speak in the authentic argot, kills some of them, and sends the hero/narrator back home where Jane Fonda spits on him and calls him a baby killer. Like John Rambo, he usually hates the bureaucrats and brass who misran the war—maybe even the war itself, but he honors the "warrior" (who managed to be gullible enough to be suckered by Hollywood's testosterone, cinematic myths).

Perhaps this kind of linear narrative can expose individual courage, fear, frustration, and anger; perhaps it can tell us about fighting a "dirty" war—a war of blind brutality and senseless attrition fought for elusive reasons. But it remains very restrictive in its scope, limited to what little the coarse mesh of the "realistic" male initiation story net can gather. As the narrator says in Jack Fuller's *Fragments*, "The army counted corpses, but we counted days. And if both measures seem to have left out something important, well, maybe that was part of the problem" (57). At the Asian Society Conference, in 1985, called "The Vietnam Experience in American Literature," Tim O'Brien commented on this something that often is left out: "At times, it seems to me, it is as if the writers are being held prisoner by the facts of their own Vietnam experiences. The result is a closure of the imagination, predictability and melodrama, a narrowness of theme, and an unwillingness to stretch the imagination."

The third analogy between fighting the war and writing about it concerns America's awesome technology, its foolproof assurance that it could make Vietnam behave—or else. In Vietnam we talked a lot about our own guerrilla counterinsurgency, but we largely fought it in a manner inappropriate in a truly formidable frontier, conventionally. Despite the fact that Vietnam was used as a gigantic proving ground for the latest in technological wizardry, and despite our military's awesome firepower, much of our "genius" was deployed ineffectively. And despite the amazing mobility afforded us by the omnipresent UH-1 Huey helicopter, both the aircraft and its occupants were vulnerable and awkward as they hovered above clearings, giving the enemy a clear field of fire from the treeline. Landscapes bombed or defoliated by U.S. technology gave the enemy additional fields of fire, making the grunts humping across them easy targets. So we have another example of "inverted warfare": in a martial arts fashion, our firepower gave a tactical advantage to the enemy. In general, Americans made trips to the jungle and made attempts to fight Charlie in guerrilla fashion; but they were more tourists than travelers, eager for the chopper ride back.

America spent its time in Vietnam not only with an excess of cultural baggage, but relatedly, literal baggage as well. Tim O'Brien minutely details this in the title story of *The Things They Carried* (1990). Typically, the grunt, who had enough problems maneuvering his own body through impenetrable jungles and knee-deep mud in temperatures above one hundred degrees, carried a field pack weighing sixty to eighty pounds stuffed with technological goodies, plus his own weapon, and sometimes extra belts of M60 machine gun ammunition draped over his shoulders. Contrast this with the VC and NVA Regulars who slipped silently through the jungle with little more than their weapons (in the case of the VC, often World War II relic carbines or whatever else they could scrounge) and a few days' worth of rice and *nuoc mam*. We were Gulliver in Lilliput. Ironically, we were the ostentatious, easy-target Redcoats in Vietnam. Former VC and NVA have said that they not only could see and hear us coming, they could smell us. For one thing, as the war wore on, the grunts' clothing came more and more to reek of marijuana. And because we didn't eat the indigenous food of Vietnam, and because we used perfumed soaps and lotions (the preeminent weapons against the dirt of the organic inferno)—in short, because we in every conceivable way tried to superimpose America on Vietnam—even our very odor gave us away.

Therefore, to a great extent it is because of, not just in spite of, the products of our civilized technology and the resulting attitudes towards the dirty, ungeometrical jungle and its inhabitants, that we got into trouble in Vietnam. The baggage of realism both parallels and perpetuates this trouble. The realist novel maintains the illusion that absurdity and ambiguity can be defeated and the impure ore refined by exposure to the industrialized, enlightened can-doism of American ingenuity. Realism may be a fascinating artifice, but it is not necessarily a very realistic one. In itself, this is no problem; there is nothing inherently wrong with realism. But as it is practiced in the literature of war, it invariably turns war into a simplified and seductive PG-13 or R-rated affair. Ultimately, it's an artifice that is incongruous with what we did or what happened to people—Americans and Vietnamese—in Vietnam.

I say, "and Vietnamese," because it has only been recently that I've heard much at all about how the Vietnamese fit into the war's picture.

Thus, my fourth parallel concerns how most Vietnam War novels perpetuate the egregious racism that marked the American presence in Vietnam. It's common knowledge that when GIs weren't calling the Vietnamese gooks, dinks, slants, and slopes, they could be heard calling them Indians, and their habitat, Indian country. The purpose was clear: perceive the Vietnamese as subhuman (Erick Erickson called this "pseudo-speciation"), then righteously exterminate them. It was the same policy that enabled the Puritans to massacre the Pequots in 1637—in good conscience, of course. Neither the atrocities at My Lai 4 nor the good conscience of the high-ranking officials following it was new or anomalous. This good conscience persists in most Vietnam novels and films. We rarely find a fully realized sympathetic Vietnamese character. Often they exist merely as malign abstractions who are dirty and smelly. They're often presented as mere stick figures that place no value on life. (In the documentary *Hearts and Minds* [1974], General Westmoreland uttered his infamous "Life is cheap in the Orient.") The narrative voice of the realist novel is usually expressed exclusively from a narrow, combat-oriented, American point of view. That voice turns Vietnam into a Satanic wilderness and its people into fauna that look like monkeys who babble and yammer an infantile sing-song language that sounds like barking lap dogs (Groom, 138). At best, a Vietnamese character tells us in Robert Olen Butler's *A Good Scent From a Strange Mountain* (1992), Americans continue to view her people as being "fascinating and long-suffering and unreal"; at worst, "sly and dangerous and unreal" (174).

What is infantile, actually, is this caricature of the language and those who speak it. Very few Americans, past or present, have ever transcended this caricature. One who has, Lady Borton (*Sensing the Enemy*, 1984), reminds us that "Vietnamese is a difficult language for a Westerner because it's not spoken, but sung" (40). Furthermore, "Any sequence of letters may have six possible tones; *each* of these tones signals a completely different word" (41). While she was learning the language, Borton constantly feared using the wrong tone. It's a well-founded fear, for as she points out, asking a vendor for chalk in the wrong tone could very well be heard as a request for a box of feces (41). Imagine, if you will, the countless ill-toned interrogations of VC suspects conducted by Americans. How does a suspect respond to, say, "Where is your pants in the fishes mouth?" Worse yet, to sheer nonsensical noise? But in a typical ugly American distortion, we translated our ignorance into Vietnamese stupidity. Another character in Butler's collection of stories reminds us that even when Americans really try to be respectful toward the Vietnamese, they still can err outrageously: speaking to a Saigon crowd, an American diplomat ". . . wanted to say in my language, 'May Vietnam live for ten thousand years.' What he said, very clear, was 'The sunburnt duck is lying down' " (46).

Most novels and films also display racism in the way they focus exclusively on America's tragedy. For example, lost in the pathos with which Oliver Stone imbues American tragedy in *Platoon* (1986) is the fact that our losses were minuscule compared to those of millions of Southeast Asians, their landscape, ecosystem, and economy. Lost in the pathos are the generations of Vietnamese babies being born with three and four arms, or their faces where their navels should be—thanks to the sinister ravages of Agent Orange. Agent Orange has had sinister effects in the United States too, but they pale by comparison to those in Vietnam, where people have been exposed to contaminated water and soil for over twenty years. So far, there has been lots of crying, but it's almost exclusively over America's spilled milk, its black eye, its pulled hamstring, and its impacted wisdom tooth. This spilled-milk narcissism is captured in the very title of a huge, twenty-seven page, 20,000-word retrospective in the December 14, 1981 issue of *Newsweek*: "What Vietnam Did to Us." American writers have routinely failed to redress this tragic and narcissistic oversight. Until this happens, any talk about the "Great Vietnam War Novel" is absurd.

I have said that most Vietnam novels fail as imaginative artifacts and as faithful expressions of the nightmare because they're written the way Americans fought. But why this emulation of maps, linearity, technology, and racism? What characteristics deeply embedded in American culture made this emulation inevitable? Risking entry into the chicken-egg dilemma, I believe there are two closely related answers: the absence of self-irony, and the fear of chaos.

By "self-irony," I mean an irony directed inward, to the author himself, to his own book, his own language, and his own participation in the American myths of righteousness and innocence. For the three hundred years prior to the Vietnam War, America had celebrated its unique identity as a "City on a Hill," whose mission in part was to save the rest of the world—usually violently—from itself. Contrary to much popular "wisdom," this myth has survived the war largely intact. If we look just below the angry, disenchanted surface of most of our Vietnam War literature, it is not the myth itself that is under fire; instead, it's the bad war that prevented the myth from being reinscribed in history. One way to detect the superficiality of the disenchantment is to note how closely it is linked to the fact that we lost the war, or, as the cliché has it, we weren't allowed to win it. The phrases "never again" and "no more Vietnams" do not issue from a desire to deconstruct the myth, but from a determination, should we go to war again, to reinstate it with greater resolve.

With the myth itself left unscrutinized, what we read just beneath the disenchanted surface (and often on it) is "What was done to me?" Rarely do we read, "What have I done to perpetuate the dangerous myths of American culture?" So, instead of the fundamental interrogation of self-irony, we get mythic and literary Agent Orange. This lack of self-irony explains why the dominant literary mode of choice is realism. It reflects a belief that one can make the private nightmare public and bring it under control with that fictive rein, that one can linearize and cause-and-effect it into some kind of submission. The all-time best-selling novel of the Vietnam War, namely, Robin Moore's *The Green Berets* (1968), possesses absolutely no sense of irony: we were the good guys, they were the bad guys, and therefore, we'll win. (Fittingly, the John Wayne movie version—with all its pretenses of being realistic—has its hero at the end walking off toward the sunset—facing east.)

But even those novels that do engage irony almost always deflect it outward, which doesn't really enable the writer to reveal much of the Vietnam experience or compel the reader to go to a whole new track of thinking about America and the reasons it behaves on the frontier the way it does. The luxury of irony directed outward—satire—is based on the false assumption that there is an inviolable set of American standards—a norm—from which we can measure the temporary deviation of the Vietnam War. This is a not-so-subtle pat on the reader's back. It doesn't compel the reader to reorganize and rethink himself or herself at "a higher level of complexity" (Hayles, 20). The narrator of Charles Durden's *No Bugles, No Drums* (1976) notes the inappropriateness of this externalized irony: "The goddam military mind is a mockery in itself. And . . . it's impossible to mock what is already mocked any more than a hole can be punched in a hole. . . . I remember reading a book called *Catch-22* and I said this dude's gotta be crazy. He was, but he wasn't crazy enough" (199, 207).

Yet many novels try to punch holes in holes. Their targets include all officers, rear-echelon personnel, the military in general, all civilians, politicians, war protesters, the allegedly inept South Vietnamese army, all Vietnamese, and so on. For example, in his devastatingly angry book *Born on the Fourth of July,* Ron Kovic, a paraplegic because of the war, delivers some knockout blows to the apathetic, ignorant American public and to the malign neglect of a grossly inefficient, underfunded Veterans Administration. But at no point does Kovic direct that irony inward, to himself, his own gullibility, and his book. His book is an important one, and I like it. In fact, for varying reasons I value all of the dozens of Vietnam novels and memoirs I've read, and that includes even John Del Vecchio's overstuffed novel of baggage, *The 13th Valley*, a novel unsurpassed in its descriptions of jungle combat. Even at their worst, these books force people to remember that painful era, if ever so simplistically. But, as Peter Marin says of America in his article "Coming to Terms with Vietnam," so Kovic "failed to push [himself] far enough, failed to raise the crucial questions about [himself] that [he] ought to confront" (42). Because Kovic doesn't ask the questions behind the questions, his book remains within the penumbra of the American control myth. It is an angry attempt to restore a sullied map. A failure fully to engage self-irony.

That failure was ridiculed already in Graham Greene's novel *The Quiet American* (1955). Greene's American, Alden Pyle, is a descendant of a blindly assured Tom Sawyer, not a self-doubting Huckleberry Finn. The narrator, Fowler, says of Pyle, "He never saw anything he hadn't heard in a lecture hall" (32). Unfortunately, it is Tom

Sawyer, alias Alden Pyle, alias Graves' "He," who has written most of the Vietnam novels—"by the book," no matter how absurdly disconnected that book is from reality. Vietnam simply must adapt itself to the book, not the other way around. These novels are tacit contentions that "the book" was only tarnished, that Vietnam changed us only in degree, not in kind, and that it did not force us to rethink what we think and how we think. In retrospect, Vietnam wasn't really new wine, so the old bottles, with occasional minor modifications, will do just fine. In his article Peter Marin goes much further than saying that these old-bottle novels are disconnected from, retreats from, and falsifications of reality; he says that most Vietnam novels and films are completely encapsulated in American myths, and that as such they are morally inert and morally *stupid*.

This just might be the case with Del Vecchio, who at the 1984 Vietnam Writers Conference recollected Vietnam in tranquility. He told his audience that he wrote *The 13th Valley* "to set the record straight," as a corrective to the blatant distortions of the allegedly nihilistic, often "unmapped," film *Apocalypse Now*. Del Vecchio contends that America did know what it was doing in Vietnam and that it was doing the right and necessary thing. Ho Chi Minh was a bloodthirsty, despotic assassin. Americans did not—with few exceptions—commit atrocities. And so on. Several writers, among them the poet W. D. Ehrhart and novelists Stephen Wright and Larry Heinemann, responded angrily to Del Vecchio's set-the-record-straight comments. In fact, Heinemann impulsively erupted in his inimitable strident voice, shocking even himself when he realized what he had just said: "The war was evil and mean, and there was no redeeming . . . nothing redeeming about it, and don't let anyone tell you there was! We went there for *evil* reasons and we performed *evil*, and *millions* of people are fucked up because of it!" The most important word in Heinemann's explosion is "we." Humbled to the point of reading American history honestly, he clearly has no patience with third-person deflections.

The second reason why most Vietnam War literature fails to render faithfully and utilize the nightmare is the most fundamental: it is unconsciously immersed in America's fear of chaos. It abdicates from the messiness of history for the "technology" of realism. In *Walking*

Point (1988), Thomas Myers correctly argues that novels such as *The 13th Valley* and James Webb's *Fields of Fire* (1978) unconsciously "use the realistic mode much like a neutral camera," and "they often seem to abdicate the tasks of larger historical vision and cultural connection . . ." (39). It needs to be added that these two extremely popular novels unconsciously *masquerade* as neutral cameras. Because the reader is so habituated to mimetic conventions, he too is unconscious of how these texts violently impose the order of linearity, causality, and closure upon disorder and randomness. Peter Stoicheff says that the mimetic text is "a neutral window" (see Northrop Frye's department store window in the chapter on drama), which ". . . must maintain the reader's [and the author's?] happy ignorance of the illusion in which he is enmeshed, and not disrupt his intuitive belief that it is permitting a linear transmission of reality to him" (86). As a result, the very "strength" of the imperial mimetic text sustains a state of ignorance regarding the "larger historical vision and cultural connections."

In other words, rather than being truly mimetic, the mimesis of realism actually is a sleight-of-hand strategy that falsely reassures the reader that he lives in a world untouched by Wright's "attrition of squares and rectangles." As Stoicheff further observes, this illusion isolates the reader from "reality's contours": "A Euclidean narrative produces a Euclidean understanding of a Euclidean world" (95) Myers views this abdicated tautological world as a failure of the imagination: There is in such works "a kind of despairing faithfulness to facts and an unverbalized, collective denial of both the power and the responsibility of imagination" (40). Instead of problematical vision, therefore, we get itemized mimesis.

The writer's abdication is not merely a metaphorical parallel of the U.S. government's lack of historical vision, both regarding itself and the Vietnamese, and its tendency to do battle with complexity with sheer technological firepower; it actually issues from the same common denominator: the fear of disorder and complexity, and the addiction to the righteous power over that disorder and complexity. Thus, the numerous intensifications of bombing over North Vietnam and the Ho Chi Minh Trail were almost hard-wired responses to the very same cultural imperative against disorder that led Del Vecchio to saturate, or "carpet bomb," *The 13th Valley* with a "despairing faith-fulness to facts." He substituted literary firepower for complex under-standing. The connection between this firepower and simplifying a disorderly landscape with agent orange is more than metaphorical: it stems from the same culturally induced urge: to render chaos into simplified order.

James Webb does establish a historical context for his stand-in per-sona, Lt. Robert E. Lee Hodges, Jr., but not without first giving it a mythic scrub. Both writer and character are apparently in a state of irresponsible, unimaginative denial as to how that history should complicate their lives: it yokes them to a tradition of self-righteous atrocity, which runs through Mystic River, The Trail of Tears, Sand Creek, Wounded Knee, Samar, and My Lai. Webb's public statements make it clear he agrees with Hodges, who says "Man's noblest mo-ment is the one spent on the fields of fire. I believe that" (25). Before he leaves for Vietnam, Hodges' grandmother recites a litany of their family's frontier-mythologized military history. She calls it their "in-herited right to violence," and it stretches all the way back to the Revolutionary War. Throughout her sanitized ecstatic itemization, she finds nothing but "glory in them fields!" (30) Although she mentions Indian fighting, "them fields" gloss over the fields where the Chero-kee were exploited, dispossessed, slaughtered, starved, and forced onto the Trail of Tears. If Webb had allowed her to complete the total litany with any degree of honesty, no doubt "them fields" would also include the Philippine island of Samar, where General Jacob Smith ordered everyone over the age of ten to be killed. This is real military history, not myth, and as such it is usually suppressed or ignored. We see President Roosevelt's contribution to the grandmother's mythic litany when he merely scolds General Smith for his unprofessional swearing in public.

Expressing a self-congratulatory, condescending slipperiness, Hodges' grandmother professes awareness of "propagandized knowl-edge," yet neither she nor Webb realizes the degree to which their heads are stuffed full of just that. Thus, when he writes about "*serv-ing . . . on the altar of his culture,*" (33) he intends irony—not be-cause the "altar" might well be called a lynching tree or the site of massacres, but because it was sullied only in America's more recent field of fire: Vietnam. This irony doesn't responsibly twist back on the writer himself and his mythic hunger for order.

Many of the warrior-realist novels try to have it both ways—they too are slippery: despise the war, but honor the soldier; experience the war's confusion, but render it with understanding. For example, Webb refers to Vietnam as "amorphous folly" (162), yet his itemized realism artificially illuminates the folly like a "basketball," which he further itemizes in his chaos-fighting glossary: "An illumination-dropping aircraft mission, capable of lighting approximately a square mile of terrain." Webb's novel tries to do just that. Turning night into day by dropping gigantic flares, and turning night into day by writing the novel of mythic "narrativitis" issue from and replenish the identical American refusal to articulate confusion, or as Robert Jewett puts it, "to get the message of defeat straight" (189). As Loren Baritz says in *Backfire*, Americans—whether its military planners or its soldier writers—were and are self-victimized by a reversal of Big Brother's dictum "Ignorance Is Strength" (322). It doesn't seem to occur to fighters and writers insistent upon using "basketballs" that strength can be a weakness, and weakness a strength. It doesn't seem to occur to them that we should really *see* the darkness of military and literary undertakings rather than artificially illuminate them. To do the latter is to preserve ignorance.

Webb also calls the war a "black-humored theater of the absurd" (119), yet he never applies this to himself and his carpentered way of remembering the war. In his novel patriarchal myths of war's valorization come through the war without a scratch. Only the improperly scripted fields of fire in Vietnam come through worse for the wear. That same "amorphous folly" that could have happily deconstructed the long-preserved warrior myths was instead reviled as America's lack of will to fight and win. In war, the messenger with the bad news always seems to get shot.

Another way Webb tries to have it both ways is that, on the one hand, he complicates his script by playing the PC game to the hilt: militant blacks are given a sympathetic hearing; all the soldiers involved admit to the war's insanity; an Okinawan woman is sympathetically drawn, as is a Vietnamese "Kit Carson Scout"; Goodrich, Webb's Harvard dropout, is anti-war throughout the novel. Neverthe-

27

less, in his ignorance through strength, Webb still insists on a white-horsed honor and glory, an attitude that later found expression in his calling Maya Lin's black Vietnam Veterans Memorial a "wailing wall for antidraft demonstrators." After returning home, Goodrich partici-pates in a Harvard anti-war rally. Webb paints these students like stick figures: they're self-righteous, protected spoiled brats who never will understand honor, glory, and sacrifice on culture's altar. Goodrich accuses them of playing "GODDAMN *GAMES*," forgetting, as does Webb, that Dan, the Kit Carson Scout in his own novel, also refers to the war as an insane game.

Webb's own game consists of thinking about the war in the simple-minded terms of not being allowed to win it. Like so many novelists and journalists of all political persuasions, neither Webb nor his char-acters takes issue with why the war was being fought, only with why we we're not winning it. Perhaps Goodrich rightly condemns the innocence of the deferment-safe students, but he and Webb seem oblivious to a far more dangerous propagandized innocence that masquerades as experiential toughness: an ignorance of America's history of racist violence and violent regeneration that perpetually revives the Frontier myth of the noble warrior. In *The Invasion of America* (1975), Francis Jennings asserts that "the conquerors of America glorified the devastation they wrought in visions of righ-teousness, and their descendants have been reluctant to peer through the aura" (6). This reluctance results in what Noam Chomsky would no doubt call the "hypocrisy and moral cowardice" (292) of Amer-ica's post-Vietnam memory.

When we work up the much-maligned courage (denigrated as lib-eral, America-bashing) to peer through the aura, we see a country that from its European beginning used preindustrialized forms of Agent Orange to organize the wilderness, and body counts to give arithmetic stature to its errand in that wilderness. I don't mean to suggest that America's fear of and battle against chaos is unique to this country. Perhaps the only two things unique are that as a "new world" country, its battle is recent and fresh, and therefore raw and obsessive; second, it seems peculiarly and blindly righteous about its culturally mandated "defoliation" policy. But the battle itself is as old as the "let-there-be-light" bias of "civilized" Western society.

In her introduction to *Chaos and Order* (1991), N. Katherine Hayles says, "Creation myths in the West, from the Babylonian epic *Enuma Elish* to Milton's *Paradise Lost*, depict chaos as a negative state, a disordered void which must be conquered for creation to occur" (2). What she no doubt had in mind regarding Milton is the image of the preincarnate Logos spreading the perfect metonymy of order over chaos, namely, a compass (VII, 225). It's an apt symbol for America's Vietnam War fighters and writers, for whom chaos is viewed—in Hayles' language—as the "absence of order" rather than as "extremely complex information" (1). Conversely, the East has always had a much different understanding of chaos. No doubt, the East would agree with a growing handful of chaos scientists in the West that a better name for it is the science of complexity. Paraphrasing a Taoist creation myth recounted by Eugene Eoyang in "Chaos Misread," Hayles tells of "Shu (Brief) and Hu (Sudden) go[ing] to visit Hun-dun (Chaos), who graciously offers them his hospitality" (2-3). But they are very concerned that his head lacks the seven openings for seeing, hearing, breathing, and eating, so for each of seven days, they bore a new hole to make him properly human. In a reversal of the seven-day Judeo-Christian creation story, here on the seventh day he dies. Hayles comments, "Here the destruction of chaos, far from marking the beginning of civilization, bespeaks a provinciality unable to accept an other different from the self. In contrast to the triumphal climax of the Western epic, the Taoist story ends with an ironic twist" (3).

Even as America was engaged in disassociating itself from the perceived decadence of European culture, Euroamerica nevertheless adopted the Western bias against chaos with a feverish intensity. Having no penchant for ironic twists regarding its behavior, it recklessly and self-assuredly pursued a policy of eliminating a metonymy of chaos, namely, what Andrew Jackson called the "useless" forest. It was a very short step in Vietnam for Jackson's useless forest to become the defoliated forest. Clearly, the American obsession with triumphing over chaos and the "other" led to the Vietnam War and to the literary, imperialistic reifications of our rememberings. In both cases, the cultural mandate was to bore the proper holes. In both cases, everyone loses.

29

What Americans "saw" when they were in Vietnam often was nothing more than their order-entranced representations of it. They saw the map clearly, but not the territory. Neil Sheehan sounds this as a leitmotif in *A Bright Shining Lie*. In talking about the battle of Ap Bac, Sheehan notes, "From the air . . . these hamlets [and the tree-lined dike] gave no indication that they were the twin bastions of a fortress. . . . Even from a low-flying L-19 spotter or a helicopter, all appeared natural" (210). Of the actual battle, Sheehan says that after receiving fire, the combined Vietnamese-American fighter-bombers leveled the hamlets.

> Having never been on the ground to learn how the guerrillas fought, they had no sense that they were engaged in a futile exercise. A man in an airplane does not easily grasp the logic of a landscape beneath him. [Nor does the writer, as it were.] He does not naturally deduce that if the guerrillas are in the houses inside the hamlet, they will not be able to shoot at the infantry out in the rice field: the foliage around the hamlet will block their view. The optical relationship between a man in a diving plane and the profusion of a rural landscape also seems to focus a pilot on the largest man-made structures he can see. (242)

The Vietnam War's scapegoat, Army Lieutenant William L. Calley, has spoken about the same failure to "grasp the logic of a landscape." In John Sack's book, *Lieutenant Calley: His Own Story* (1974), Calley says "Our colonel would look for VC suspects from—oh, ten thousand feet, and play platoon leader with us. 'oh, Charlie One? I spotted a VC suspect. A few minutes from you.' Of course, the colonel could go a kilometer in thirty seconds and I was in the damn foliage: It might take me a lifetime. 'Go where the purple smoke is, Charlie One.' Of course, there was a fifty-meter hill in between us" (46). That far up, the vision of the strength-is-ignorance colonel bore little more relationship to the actual landscape than a crude map. In a nutshell, this colonel's "vision" describes America's misreading of Vietnam then and now, in both its fighting and in its writing about that fighting.

Even when that fifty-meter hill was seen, and the hedgerows and dikes did look ominous, both literally and symbolically, when the soldiers returned from and remembered Vietnam, they often fell victim to the distortions and simplifications of the child's game, "Telephone." Figuratively, the fifty-meter hill gets edited out. In his research on memory, the psychologist F. C. Bartlett discovered that ". . . people have a tendency to change 'odd' or unfamiliar figures into conventional or familiar ones" (Ornstein and Ehrlich, 174). In one instance he told a student an American Indian story. As he told it to this first student, the story was mysterious and ghostly. But very quickly, as the story was passed along from student to student, it became conventionally rational. Bartlett notes that the story becomes "more coherent, as well as much shorter. No trace of any odd or supernatural element is left: we have a perfectly straight-forward story of a fight and a death" (175). Robert Graves' "He" has the final say. Extrapolating from this research, the biologists Robert Ornstein and Paul Ehrlich say, "Memories are transformed to suit our attitudes" (175), and they keep us in a "blinkered" state.

The results of this "Telephone" experiment parallel what our military leaders "saw" in Vietnam. In a "blinkered" state, they saw only the "largest [American]-made structures." The United States did not restrict itself to the immaculate conception of maps; it literally tried to re-create Vietnam as a kind of macro-map of the American imagination. It tried to do this by replacing many hundreds of thousands of acres with an American industrial park. It took what O'Brien calls the "twisting, covert, chopped and mangled" (*Cacciato*, 300) landscape and turned it into billions of dollars worth of roads, airstrips, buildings, and bases. As Michael Herr says in *Dispatches*, "Nobody builds bases like Americans." In *The Perfect War*, James William Gibson points out that " . . . war-managers and their hired researchers became mesmerized by the spectacle of American construction" (237). They were probably also mesmerized—Westmoreland certainly was—by the spectacle of gigantic bulldozers, known as "Rome plows," turning huge tracts of "useless" forests into wastelands ready to receive American squares and rectangles—literally, according to Gibson: "War-managers . . . tried to create a physical terrain equivalent to the abstract mathematical space of 1,000 meter by 1,000 meter grid squares necessary for jets and artillery to find orientation" (123). Lester Maddox wasn't all that far from the consensus of American culture in calling for Vietnam to be turned into a parking lot.

Mesmerized by the clean, paved roads, the officials couldn't see that they were destroying the lives of the very "Indians" they were supposed to help. Like Graham Greene's Pyle, they literally could not see the war's blood they were responsible for. Greene's metaphor for this destructive blindness is a leper innocently walking among the people he wants to save for democracy. The roads were actually more like modern Trails of Tears for the Vietnamese who trudged down them toward concentration camps euphemistically and mythically scrubbed into "strategic hamlets." According to Gibson, "That refugees walked away from poisoned fields and burned homes on roads capable of sustaining thousands of two-and-one-half-ton troop trucks did not make their losses any less severe, nor did hard-surfaced roads and new bridges cause Vietnamese refugees to love the men who destroyed their traditional lives" (237). In seeing only the roads, not the poisoned fields and burned homes, the U.S. military tried to maintain the same mythically sealed, self-referential world as the grandmother in *Fields of Fire*. In both cases there is a narrativistic operation at work that ". . . selects, appropriates, and banishes in a process that aims to smooth over problems and straighten out contradictions" (Martin, xx).

Sheehan's book chronicles Colonel John Paul Vann's long-term agonizing recognition that no one was really seeing Vietnam in all its complex topographical, military, and political contours. He repeatedly offered to those who could hear, but not listen, his favorite observation, namely, that the best tactical weapon in Vietnam was a knife, and the worst, anything that flew. So in their version of "Telephone," even as the military leaders "heard the story" for the first time, they edited out the strangeness, and heard it conventionally and coherently; they insisted on it. On a microlevel, that hedgerow was not allowed to be ominous. On a macrolevel the Vietcong infrastructure was declared all but done for. Over and over, Westmoreland insisted on this.

But the grunts *did* "hear the story" correctly, over and over; they did see how unconventional and incoherent this war was. They had no choice but to live or die in the territory, not the map. On a microlevel, that hedgerow almost certainly looks like an ambush awaiting. On a macrolevel, the whole war made a mockery of the reassuring Newtonian worlds in the air-conditioned Quonset huts up and down

32

the chain of command. However, as the story was "passed along" from Vietnam to America, it somehow got conventionalized. The hedgerows were suburbanized. While still in Vietnam, the grunts instinctively despised the geometric, ersatz reality our leaders tried to impose on Vietnam. They repeatedly concluded that "it don't mean nothin'." They laughed sardonically at the generals with their maps and pins and flowcharts. Yet when they returned and wrote about the experience, they too did it with maps and pins, thereby imposing a good deal of ersatz somethin' on the nothin'.

Both the generals and the grunt writers are like the guy who loses his wallet in the dark but looks for it up the street because the light is better there. "Losing" because it tries to "win" with unexamined, conventionalized means, much of the war's writing is a deluding effort to package a morass in a box. Thus we are faced with a largely unnoticed paradox: even though the vets are obsessed with accuracy and authenticity in their rememberings, their conventional packaging of those memories actually does more to conceal than to reveal the war. As the penultimate lines of Graves' poem make clear, understanding, as it is normally perceived, actually can preclude understanding. Thus, as Lynne Hanley states in *Writing War* (1991), Vietnam narratives are acts ". . . not of remembering but of forgetting war" (118). They are cosmetic shields between consciousness and what Conrad's Kurtz calls "The Horror."

Guerrilla Texts

Conventional journalism could no more reveal
this war than conventional fire power could win it.

—Michael Herr

The best Vietnam writers eschew Del Vecchio's straight record and the entire inheritance of literary realism. To name a few, this includes the poets Bruce Weigl, John Balaban, Marilyn McMahon, Yusef Komunyakaa, D. F. Brown, and Walter McDonald; the playwrights David Rabe, Emily Mann, Amlin Gray, and Steve Tesich; and the novelists William Eastlake, James Clark Pratt, Michael Herr, Tim O'Brien, Ward Just, James Park Sloan, Larry Heinemann, Peter Straub, Gustav Hasford, and Stephen Wright. Many of these writers—whether in their works themselves or in public statements—have pointed to the absurdity of trying to reveal the Vietnam experience with conventional means. Nothing in Vietnam corresponded to those means. In military operations there was no front, no rear, no sense of progression; poof—there goes the structure of the conventional narrative. GIs rarely even dared to become close to another highly expendable person, and the enemy was indistinguishable from the ally; there goes the matrix of character. The days numbered down, not up; there goes the linearly conceived plot. Events did not move inexorably toward a necessary and meaningful collision; there goes the conventional climax (but one is usually forced in anyway). As the lyrics of Paul Hardcastle's rock-jazz "19" (referring to the average age of the soldier in Vietnam) repeat over and over, "Nobody knew what was going on"; there goes the omniscient narrator (but he stubbornly remains in many Vietnam novels). And as many writers have said, you didn't learn anything from the Vietnam experience—you either survived or you didn't; there goes the machinery of the novel of initiation.

So what makes these writers responsible tellers of the Vietnam story? Their novels, poems, and plays are conceived and written the way the VC fought—in the jungle, off the main, well-traveled roads. I certainly don't claim to have originated this idea; in fact, already in 1969 the poet Robert Duncan told James F. Mersmann, "The poet is and always has been, by necessity, a kind of Viet Cong" (225). Novels, plays, and books of poetry such as Stephen Wright's *Meditations in Green*, Emily Mann's *Still Life*, and Bruce Weigl's *Song of Napalm* (1988) are guerrilla night operations that necessarily and courageously probe the unsubdued forest of the psyche where, as Henry James Sr. told his sons William and Henry as they were leaving for Europe, "the wolf howls and the obscene bird of night chatters." They avoid what Eastlake calls the classic American blunder—of giving the Indians the cover (22). They are not written from the artificially cleared landing zones of convention; they are hot landing zones in ten-foot elephant grass. In short, they most certainly are not literature that tries to make sense of the war; they are, instead, literature that tries to make sense of the sense-making process. They are postmodern recon probes into unsettling fundamental questions concerning who we are and how we know what we think we know. They face up to Michael Herr's cardinal point, that "A lot had to be unlearned before you could learn anything at all" (224). The best Vietnam books are journeys of unlearning. They are ontological and epistemological meditations, not narrative histories and documents that pretend to "get it right." They are the avant-garde books of experimentation and improvization gone blue collar. And finally, they're all quite deranged, necessarily and fittingly so.

The best rememberings do not try to win aesthetically what we lost militarily. Rather, they try to reveal the Vietnam experience and how it did, or at least should, revolutionize the way we think about ourselves and our mythos. Tim O'Brien seems to have realized this, for, after completing his rather straightforward autobiographical *If I Die in a Combat Zone* (1973), he almost immediately began work on his guerrilla novel, *Going After Cacciato*. It, too, is deranged, but again, in a necessary way. Unlike the previous work, this one explores the dark, mysterious archetypal foundations of Paul Berlin's conscious and subconscious minds as he spends an anxious night up in a guard tower. There are no reassuring clocks or maps in this story. Instead, the reader must hang on as Berlin's mind abruptly and unpredictably shoots across the boundaries of conventional space and time, and memory and imagination. When we read these books we feel as if traditional structure has metamorphosed from a solid to a liquid to a gas. O'Brien's book is clearly off any recognizable main roads, far removed even from the relative comforts of a base camp. The only road in *Cacciato* is the patently fantastical 12,000-mile "Road to Paris," on which the equally fantastical, elusive, AWOL title character is fleeing. That journey is both a spatial and a temporal one. In effect, O'Brien takes us through the underground histories, geographies, and cultures of the half-world that lies between Vietnam and Paris. From the mud of Vietnam to the mahogany peace table in Paris— never on the main roads. And, as we will see in my discussion of O'Brien's next book, *The Things They Carried*, even the conventional "highway" separating fiction and essay is blurred.

Once off those roads, there are many ways in which these books parallel the way the VC fought (I will discuss the last two at some length). First, an often-repeated maxim already found in that most prophetic of novels, Graham Greene's *The Quiet American*, about which, Michael Herr says, "If you want to travel light, you don't need any other books about Vietnam" (Schroeder, 49), is that the day belonged to the Americans (to the French, in Greene's novel), the night to the VC. The guerrilla writers I've mentioned belong to the night. They take us on nightmarish, postmodern journeys into regions where everything is so dark and indistinct that we often don't know where we are. In Bruce Weigl's words, these journeys lead us into a "black understanding" (*Napalm*, 70), which makes us feel less guided than threatened by imminent "ambush." The light that we do experience is, according to Yusef Komunyakaa, from a spooky moon that ". . . cuts through / night trees like a circular saw / white hot" (7). Flares reveal, rather than explicate, chaos. Readers, so to speak, can either quit reading or become guerrillas themselves in the profusion of the landscape.

Second, as Herr says in *Dispatches*, the underground belonged to the VC, above ground to us. But clearly, the writings of people like Herr, O'Brien, Rabe, Mann, Wright, Straub, and Weigl are "underground." Their novels, plays, and poems lift up rocks and climb under them. "Tunnel rats," they low-crawl into the dark, subterranean texts of the American love affair with violence and the imperialistic mapping of reality. As Hayles would say of these guerrilla works, they tear "the constructed fabric of the world (or the text-as-world) . . . to reveal the void underneath" (14).

Third, like the "postmodern" VC, these texts often lull us into the illusion of safety, then suddenly ambush us in a kind of rock 'n' roll frenzy of mad, hallucinatory language, and just as suddenly quiet down again, and dissipate themselves into the utterly prosaic. Subverting traditional notions of sequence and closure, those who refuse to remember Vietnam simplistically engage—as did the VC—in what Foucault calls the "insurrection of subjugated knowledges." Kissinger's denigrated Third-World "delusions" end up turning the tables by subverting readers' Newtonian certainties. The "low-budget," illegitimate action is hit-and-run, unpredictable, discontinuous, and seemingly without design to those who are accustomed to paved roads and industrial parks.

Fourth, like the VC, characters suddenly appear, then disappear without a trace, leaving no "blood trails." At best, they frequently remain maddeningly out of focus. We rarely get to know them. In part, no doubt, this is a reflection of Westmoreland's 365-day tour, which resulted in a constant flux of GIs in and out of units. More importantly, it reflects the authors' conviction that this war was not about characters or individuals as heroes or even antiheroes. It was about characters trapped in "inverted warfare," which made any sense of identity as precarious as the Borgesian dreamer who dreams a man into existence only to discover that he too has been dreamed by another.

Fifth, like the VC and the American LURPs, these texts travel light. No cumbersome field pack, so incongruous in the jungle. They travel with very little of the presumptuous Occidental baggage of rationalist, causal thinking. Very few of the comfortable household furnishings of the traditional narrative appears in these novels. That's because, with *The Quiet American* in their "field packs," they have a healthy distrust both of messianic scripts (*The Green Berets*) and of those that rage at the war for not allowing warrior myths to bear fruit (*Born on the Fourth of July, Fields of Fire,* ad infinitum). Either way, solipsism "wins."

Sixth, both break the rules. Who *was* the VC guerrilla? A barber, PX worker, sniper, rice farmer, launderer, prostitute, booby-trap expert, hootch maid, drug dealer, politician, sapper, "Kit Carson" scout, husband, wife, son, daughter? Usually, he or she was many of these, which outraged U.S. soldiers. The most successful writers similarly transcend narrow specialization. Literarily, they refuse to be pinned down to what the army calls one's MOS (military occupational specialty). They especially refuse to be penned in by the conventional boundaries of genre. Thus Wallace Terry refers to his oral history, *Bloods* (1984), as an oral novella. Michael Herr refers to the journalistic *Dispatches* as a novel. In *The Things They Carried*, O'Brien treats fiction as fact, and essays as stories. John Clark Pratt's *The Laotian Fragments* is in part a fictional biography. David Rabe's play *Sticks and Bones* (1973) is an absurdist fictional account of a real family made famous by the *Ozzie and Harriet Show*. Leslie Marmon Silko's *Ceremony* (1977) blends poetry and fiction. Norman Mailer's book *The Armies of the Night* (1968) is subtitled *History as a Novel, The Novel as History*. And his "article-sounding" *Why Are We in Vietnam?* (1967) is a scatalogical allegory that doesn't even mention Vietnam until the final page. Lynne Hanley's *Writing War* (1991) juxtaposes her own expository prose with poetry. And so on. Herr sums up the attitude of all these writers in this chapter's epigraph: "Conventional journalism could no more reveal this war than conventional fire power could win it" (232).

There is another way in which the writers under consideration here won't stick to their MOS. Kit Carson scouts by day, they're double agents by night. For example, by day, in *The Things They Carried*, Tim O'Brien tells us alluring war stories; by night, he deconstructs those same stories by exposing the artificiality of their conventions. Like the Third-World VC denigrated by Kissinger, O'Brien does this because he recognizes reality as a social construction, which means that "the real world is almost entirely internal to the observer" (Kissinger, 49).

The seventh parallel (we'll need to take our time here) concerns the ingenuity of the VC, particularly in how they were adept at scrounging American junk and waste and putting it back together in new combinations for new purposes to make crude but effective weapons and other essentials for survival: rubber tires became sandals, Coke cans became grenades, scrap metal became shrapnel, exhaust pipes were refashioned into mortar tubes, and so on. Even today, water-filled bomb craters are profit-making fish ponds, and the notorious Cu Chi tunnels have become a low-tech amusement park. Something similar happens in the best literature of the war. It is poetic junk. The most compelling books are composed of the leftovers, the fragments and debris of technology and the frontier myth. They are black pop art, and Picasso's "sum of destructions." In a word, they are collages, but not the mischievous collages of Tristan Tzara designed to shock people out of their philistine lethargy. No, they simply are the only form available to these writers. In a fundamental way, they *make do* with the collage. In fact, within these literary collages we often find literal collages that function as artistic analogues for the books themselves.

In both the literature and the analogues, we see that these collages are attempts to create something from "nothing." That is, the raw material for their tenuous collages consists of dislocated fragments and the toxic waste products of the war. (In *Dispatches*, Herr uses this very language. Speaking of Hue, the Imperial City, he says it was "composed of destruction" [259]). These "structures" are often at best barely controlled chaos; at their most extreme they are thoroughly macabre. As we will see later, literal examples of the former occur both in Wright's *Meditations in Green* and in Herr's *Dispatches*. In *Meditations*, the colonel of the 1069th Intelligence Group calls their "Big

Board" "subversive junk"; unwittingly, he's absolutely right—about it, and Wright's novel. Both subvert the West's bias against chaos. Through Griffin, his narrator, Wright refuses to impose order on the disorder of war; instead, Griffin scrounges for coherence in his life by looking for patterns within the disorder, like the field of bomb craters so arranged as to resemble a "species of farm crop." Rather than negate disorder and destruction, he choreographs the reciprocity and dialectic of negation and creation (Hayles, 14). In Emily Mann's *Still Life*, Mark's collage captures this reciprocity, containing as it does not only fresh bread, grapefruit, and an orange, but also a fly, broken egg, and a grenade.

Perhaps the supreme example of the macabre collage is the one in Gustav Hasford's *The Short-Timers*. For propaganda reasons, the narrator, Joker, is ordered to take atrocity photographs at a mass grave site. Despite the crippling stench of bodies decaying in the Vietnam oven, Joker says, "So I borrow some demolition wire from the Arvin snuffies and, crushing the stiff bodies with my knee until dry bones crack, I bind up a family, assembled at random from the multitude—a man, his wife, a little boy, a little girl, and of course their dog. As a final touch I wire the dog's feet together" (127). No doubt, Hasford is laying on gallows humor pretty thick, but he's doing more than that. Like Wright, Mann, Herr and others, he's saying that if we're going to make something real from the Vietnam War, we're going to do so from the real nothings produced by that war. The war deconstructed our cherished myths and our confident epistemology. We must start right there, with that fact. Thus we will utilize disorder, not flee from it into the falsely consoling order of "realism." The fragments and "broken images," and nothing else, must be our raw material. We will use what we're left with, not ask for a new epistemological inventory.

Paul Bäumer, narrator of Remarque's *All Quiet on the Western Front*, announces the war writer's starting point when he says, "the first bombardment showed us our mistake, and under it the world as they [teachers, parents, and other figures of authority] had taught us broke in pieces" (13). The raison d'etre for this book is my concern over what America does with the pieces of its myths shattered by the Vietnam War: its writers and critics too often order Humpty Dumpty back together. As a result of their obsession with coming to a new understanding, they actually come to a "new confusion of [their] understanding," rather than a "new understanding of [their] confusion." And readers gladly climb aboard. It never seems to occur to these writers that our nation can survive and be a lot less dangerous to itself and the rest of the planet if it respects the pieces as pieces. It is especially necessary to respect them as pieces once we see how myth works. In America, at any rate, the most pernicious myth is the belief that we have no myth. Euroamericans have long been confident that they are in command of the truth, not mere victims of belief. Perhaps no people on this earth are more attached to the belief in the empirical reality of belief. That is why so few of them are willing to really stare at Vietnam, for to do so is to risk seeing the status of truth lowered all the way to false belief in American goodness, uniqueness, and power.

The great fear in this country is that nothing can be done with beliefs that are shattered. It seldom seems to strike people that disillusionment can be experienced as the relief of being relieved of an onerous illusion. Or, as Paul Fussell says, we can gain *power* from "facing unpleasant facts." However, according to Peter Marin ("Living in Moral Pain"), "We seem as a society to have few useful ways to approach moral pain or guilt; it remains for us a form of neurosis or a pathological symptom, something to escape rather than something to learn from, a disease rather than—as it may well be for the vets—an appropriate if painful response to the past" (43). As Camus once put it, Sisyphus learns precisely at that moment he turns to descend the hill to retrieve his rock.

But to America as a whole, scrounging and rock retrieval are not highly regarded activities; so a blown B.F. Goodrich tire is, as it were, just that. An empty Coke can is an empty Coke can. A spent shell casing is a spent shall casing. A bomb crater is a bomb crater. A broken egg is a broken egg. A lost war is a lost war. I suspect that many of the war's writers unconsciously replace the pieces with wholes by subjecting the chaos and degradation of war to the compensatory illusions of conventional narrative. We can extrapolate what is wrong with this kind of writing by listening to Anne, a character in Tesich's play, *The Speed of Darkness* (1989). She puts her finger precisely on

41

the problem. Talking to her Vietnam vet husband, Joe, she says "We were so happy to learn that our broken parts could mend, that we didn't care how they mended. . . . We mended crooked. . . . [We need] to get all broken up again and try to mend right" (66–68).

Even the war's most recognized literary-cultural critics could learn something from Anne's diagnosis and orthopedic recommendation. Important as their voices are, they sometimes overtly and explicitly will Humpty Dumpty back together—crookedly. Philip Beidler uses the two-word phrase "sense making" innumerable times in his book, *American Literature and the Experience of Vietnam* (1982). What is wrong with accepting as our starting point that we engaged in a sense*less* slaughter in Vietnam, and that we ourselves are terribly susceptible to senseless delusions of national grandeur? Wouldn't it be a good idea to curb our voracious appetite for sense? Isn't that what gets us in trouble so often? Can't we be satisfied with a new understanding of our confusion? As Daniel Swain, a veteran, asks: why can't we accept that ". . . what we *should* feel [is] mind-torturing guilt for the rest of our lives? Can't anyone see that we *deserve* to feel guilty?" (108).

In Beidler's second Vietnam book, *Re-Writing America* (1991), his agenda is even more obvious: he wants to remythologize America. Seemingly on every page, we read such phrases as "redemptory myth," "major reconstruction" of myth, "mythic recovery," "mythic transport," and "mythic reinscription." But John Hellmann (*American Myth and the Legacy of Vietnam*, 1986) is even more insistent upon mythic recovery and the restoration of the American frontier narrative. He uses George Lucas's *Star Wars* trilogy to discuss America before, during, and after the Vietnam War. Hellmann says that the original *Star Wars* (1977) "follows the mythic traces of the ideal pre-Vietnam American self-concept," offering us a "beautifully" compressed "mythic memory of its pre-Vietnam time" (215). Of course, this memory is terribly self-serving. It conveniently ignores the memories of despoiling a continent, practicing imperialistic, land-grabbing genocide on Native Americans, enslaving the black race, and fomenting misery and death in multiple Third-World countries out of economic greed and political paranoia.

According to Hellmann, *The Empire Strikes Back* (1980) parallels the trauma of Vietnam by bringing us face to face with the devastating knowledge of our complicity with evil, which leaves Luke Skywalker with "terrible doubt" (217). It would seem that Hellmann does not concur with Loren Baritz, who says, "Freed of doubt, we are freed of thought" (347), which is what happened to America in the Reagan era. Finally, in *Return of the Jedi* (1983), Hellmann says, Luke is "chastened" but no longer in doubt. Instead of being permanently humbled by newly realized epistemological limits, he now possesses the "power of self-knowledge" (217). He picks up the pieces and reassembles the American narrative—with a few nicks and scratches, but otherwise intact. Which leaves us where? According to Hellmann, with the sure knowledge that "No nation can survive without a myth" (222) (Can any nation today survive *with* one?); and "Surely America should not give up its sense of uniqueness and see itself as an ordinary country" (223). In this single sentence, Hellmann's immaculately restored myth takes us all the way back to the early seventeenth century, when John Winthrop boldly proclaimed that America was a "City upon a Hill." And woe be unto any "savages" who hampered his construction project!

I do not wish to mislead the reader regarding the critical thought of scholars such as Beidler, Hellmann, Thomas Myers (*Walking Point*), and Susan Jeffords (*The Remasculinization of America*, 1989). I am indebted to all of them. Beidler's comprehensive studies are must reads for anyone trying to get a handle on the massive literary output of the Vietnam War. Hellmann's myth criticism, even his application of Lucas's trilogy to the Vietnam War era, often is ingenious. As a critic "walking point," Myers is unsurpassed in detecting the American enemy lurking in the jungles of mythic assumptions. He, especially, is worth paying attention to. And Jeffords' feminist deconstruction of the war's literature and film is a sorely needed alternative to the male preoccupations and assumptions of the war's literature and criticsm. All four critics offer valuable insights into the impact of the war on our literature and culture. As I state in my preface, however, these critics remind me of the man who realizes he simply has to clear out his cluttered, firetrap attic. Several hours later, the curb is covered by mounds of junk. Early the next morning, however, we see him returning with a lot of the stuff to the attic. He just can't part with it.

Similarly, on the one hand, these critics are "hip" to the paradigm-clearing missions of postmodernism; they readily admit to America's guilt, shame, evil, self-righteousness, hubris, patriarchal hegemony, proclivity to atrocity, and so on. But, if we watch them carefully, we see them returning mythic junk to the attic, where they seem to eat their cake and still have a lot left. Their "closet" passion is to *rewrite*, not unwrite. They are excellent writers, but I wish they were as good at recognizing the attic junk as merely that. I wish, then, that they were as good at scrounging junk in order to change its taxonomy as they are at saving it (like Kissinger saving Newton, or Jeffords saving the rationalist Descartes, whatever the situation), thereby maintaining the dangerous clutter of the American mind.

The final parallel also concerns the ingenuity of the VC. At night when the Americans were asleep, they would sometimes oil their bodies, infiltrate the impenetrable concertina wire, turn our claymore mines around so they faced us, slip back through the wire, and wake us up by whatever means. Whereupon, if everything went according to VC plans, the American soldiers would detonate their claymores and take the blast themselves. This is one of the classic examples of how the VC used our technology against us. Similarly, recognizing the limitations of our acculturated language, the aforementioned writers turn that language against itself. That is, their sense of irony is directed less outward than inward—to our language and to their very novels using that language. As a result, the well-groomed language of the traditional narrative becomes more like what Michael Herr calls "word salad," and the truth-telling illusion of realism ironically turns back on itself, destroying its own momentum and biting off its own head. Instead of "traced" war stories, the reader gets stories about stories. His claymore is turned around. Eastlake sets this ironic tone in the very first paragraph of *The Bamboo Bed* (1969), a novel in which a suspenseful momentum lasts for one sentence: "Madame Dieudonné arose, stark and stripped, in her underground villa at 0600 as was her wont, turned on the short-wave radio and heard the report from Laos that Captain Clancy was dead, then she walked, still naked, to her jewel box, removed a small, black, heavy object, raised it to her head and blew her pretty French brains out. Pas Vrai. Not true" (1).

44

Throughout the novel, Eastlake seduces the reader with such narrative momentum, then he abruptly denies the veracity of what he has just said. He knows how easy it is to lure adventure-hungry readers out onto the main "trails" of narrative; so, like the VC, he "booby-traps" them with metafictional fragmentation. The opening sentence of his novel serves as Eastlake's announcement that what one will read in the remaining pages is built on the principles of narrative cancellation and epistemological doubt. The components of his story look back and forth at each other, interrogatively, with suspicion.

Thus the most authentic Vietnam novels rise from the ashes of the traditional novel. As we will see, this happens almost literally in *Meditations in Green*, where a character scatters the pages of *Atlas Shrugged* across the length and breadth of Vietnam. But Wright's irony is not merely directed at Ayn Rand's Western, technological hubris; his novel, too, will be a "sum of destructions" or nothing at all. In the last paragraph of the novel he says "Everywhere the green fuses are burning and look now, snipping rapidly ahead of your leaping eye, the forged blades cutting through the page, the transformation of this printed sheet. . ." (322). Recognizing the defensive madness of trying to trace a reality into existence, and recognizing the defensive madness of believing we can package the morass of Vietnam in the geometry of realism, these writers respond with offensive madness: they sabotage their own language and mimetic conventions, and then they try to observe the nothings of war until they start appearing as fictive potential, inchoate form, or "fractals," as chaos scientists refer to disordered order and ordered disorder.

I have already stated that the most pernicious myth in America is that it has no myth. To paraphrase the psychologist Arthur Egendorf (*Healing From the War*, 1985), we convince ourselves that our fictions are reality. We accomplish this by playing our theatrical parts earnestly and for such a long time that we forget who wrote the play, or even that it is a play (159). What is dangerous about this myth is that it allows for no editing, revising, deleting, or self-directed laughter. Tim O'Brien's character Doc Peret recognizes the danger of confusing myth with reality: "What you remember is determined by what you see, and what you see depends on what you remember. A cycle, Doc Peret had said. A cycle that has to be broken. And this requires a fierce concentration on the process itself" (248). In a word, what Doc Peret is calling for here is metafiction, something which all the critics above find dissatisfying. Myers suggests that it is "entropic" and "de-historicized" (111). At least that is what he says of James Park Sloan's metafictional *War Games*. Beidler says the same book suffers from "arty oppressiveness" (89). Jeffords claims metafiction "leads the reader to a point of paralysis" (23). It would seem that most people don't mind *knowing* that they are reading fiction; they don't want to be *told* they're reading fiction. Likely, this is because they find "the process itself" with which one imbues fiction with the authority of reality to be boring. But Peret believes that the degree to which we don't do this is the degree to which we remain trapped within an unbroken, solipsistic cycle. Peter Stoicheff agrees. He says that in order to get beyond a closed, self-referential Euclidean understanding, we need a "metafictional 'narrative of chaos,' " because only in the latter is "the process of self-interrogation . . . built into the narrative, freeing it from the tautological determinism that inhabits earlier narratives" (95). Cognizant that it is the tautology and not the metafiction that paralyzes us, Peret is O'Brien's radical epistemologist: "Doc was right . . . that observation requires inward-looking, a study of the very machinery of observation—the mirrors and filters and wiring and circuits of the observing instrument" (247–48).

Sharing Peret's concerns, Robert Ornstein and Paul Ehrlich state that an "area left largely empty in our culture [is] training in knowledge of the mind" (*New World New Mind*, 144). To many people, such training likely smacks of ivory tower, philosophic doodling. But, as Howard Zinn points out in *Declarations of Independence*, "We can reasonably conclude that how we *think* is not just mildly interesting, not just a subject for intellectual debate, but a matter of life and death" (1–2). If we recall how the Dick-and-Jane domino theory enslaved our "brightest" minds from places like Harvard and M.I.T. during the entire course of the Cold War, and if we dwell for a moment on how the religious belief in that theory resulted in the deaths of millions of people, and in the economic and ecological ruination of countries around the globe, perhaps we will concede Zinn's point.

For Ornstein and Ehrlich, as well, watching the mind at work as it caricatures complexities into crude but mythically satisfying, simplistic narratives is a matter of planetary survival. They use a computer analogy to express how the mind is conditioned not to look at the filters and wiring: "When you 'boot up,' or start a computer, it begins with a set of what are clumsily called default positions, procedures it will follow unless someone deliberately replaces them with different instructions. So it seems with the human mind. . . . [T]he human mind's 'defaults' take over if other routines are not consciously 'called up.' . . . Humanity is suffering from a serious case of dangerous defaults" (91–92). In IBM language, when Doc calls for metafictional introspection, he's urging us to get into "Format" (Shift F-8) or "Reveal Codes" (Alt F-3). Only in so doing can we check out and rethink, so to speak, how the hyphenation, margins, justification, base fonts, and tabs of our minds have been preset in ways that prohibit us from redesigning and rereading our mythic narratives with greater honesty and complexity. To one degree or another, the novelists, playwrights, and poets in which I'm interested in this book spend a lot of time in "Format" and "Reveal Codes." That's because they are willing to work within the Vietnam War's most valuable, but ignored, legacies: epistemological doubt, and the courage to turn our claymores around.

Yet, as the reader will have noticed, I have "bookended" even these guerrilla deconstructionists (in the internal six chapters) between the two opening and two closing chapters. My rationale for this organization is fear—fear of the "war souvenirs" that even the deconstructionists may have left in the attic (see chapter 8). Because the Vietnam War remains a powerful attractor to this day, we all run the risk of being fixated by it, like Lot's wife staring backward at the burning Sodom and Gomorrah. When this happens, nostalgia obliterates metafiction. Therefore, wary of the seduction, in the opening and closing chapters I often take us "off camera" and off location in order to examine the sobering revelations of texts that are more peripheral (even parenthetical) to the war itself.

In a beautiful passage from his book, *Out of the Vietnam Vortex* (1974), James F. Mersmann gave me the inspiration for doing *Fighting and*

Writing. The passage's opening "It" refers to Vietnam War poetry, but I've taken the liberty of extending it to all guerrilla texts: "It finds in our desire for certainty, stability, security; in our desire to remain in control, to possess, to manipulate, to dominate; in our desire for order, system, sameness, and permanence; in our desire to retain the past and determine the future—in these desires it sees a longing for death; in these it sees a fear of life, a fear of perpetual change, fluidity, mystery, magic, sensation, vulnerability, sacrifice, beatitude" (254–55). In the chapters that follow, Mersmann's worries and celebrations will also be mine.

Stephen Wright's Chlorophyll Overdose

"A new motto: If you can't trans-cend, you might
as well des-cend. I'm scoping out the bottom here."
—*Meditations in Green*

In David Rabe's supremely black comedy *Sticks and Bones*, a contemporary David Nelson (son of TV's Harriet and Ozzie, brother of Rick) returns from the Vietnam War blinded and no longer able to share in his family's own blindness—their unexamined fudge-and-cookie, comic-book sweetness and light. Midway through the play, David shows the family his Vietnam War "home" movie. All they (not to mention the audience) can see is a screen filled with flickering shades of green. We then hear the following exchange:

> HARRIET. Ohhh, what's the matter? It didn't come out, there's nothing
>   there.
> DAVID. Of course there is.
> HARRIET. Noooo. . . . It's all funny.
> DAVID. Look.
> OZZIE. It's underexposed, Dave.

After this goes on a bit longer, David howls

NOOOOOO! LOOK! (161).

He proceeds to describe scenes of horror and atrocity that none of us can see.

＊ This scene is paradigmatic of the Vietnam War's best literature in two ways: the movie is allegedly about nothing, and that nothing is colored green. First, because David's movie is composed of the war's "scrounged junk," it is utterly alien to his family. It's not that they don't understand what they see in his movie; they see nothing to understand or interpret. The Vietnam War—from a grunt's point of view—did not, and perhaps could not, appear on the American screen. But Ozzie is wrong; the reason he, Harriet, and Rick can't see anything is that David's movie is *over*exposed to the Vietnam fallout of America's mythic ordnance. Rabe gradually exposes this ordnance concealed beneath the formica—particularly in the form of deep-seated xenophobia and racism, two "strategic weapons" we un-leashed in Vietnam. As Sergeant Colby tells Philip Caputo in *A Rumor of War* (1977), "Before you leave here, sir, you're going to learn that one of the most brutal things in the world is your average nineteen-year-old American boy" (129). In the same vein, after a character in Tim O'Brien's *The Things They Carried* (Azar) straps a claymore mine to a platoon member's puppy and blows it up, he says "What's every-body so upset about? I mean, Christ, I'm just a *boy*" (40). Much too often, when this same "average nineteen-year-old American boy"—whether Rabe's David Nelson or Stephen Wright's James Griffin—returned home to the "supply depot" of the mythic ordnance, he was no longer recognizable in his overexposed state. Blinkered by the "Telephone" game clean-up process, Americans didn't recognize themselves in him either. With his blinkers off, David Nelson is so foreign to Ozzie that the latter wants him fingerprinted and his teeth checked against dental X-rays.

The second reason I find this scene especially interesting is that it calls attention to the color of the Vietnam War—green. It's the color of the cosmic Southeast Asian jungle, the unmappable life-giving and life-taking jungle that is a cycle of growth and decay set on fast for-ward. For many Vietnam veterans, the word "Vietnam" is virtually synonymous with the jungle and the color green—a green Vietnam

50

that was at once sublimely beautiful and terrifyingly menacing. In his poem, "Memory Bomb," R. Joseph Ellis writes: "I expect to remember other things. / But it is always the color that comes first. / The incredible greens, almost sinister / in their growing . . ." (14). In a pastoral reversal, Jan Barry entitles one of his poems "Green Hell, Green Death." Repeating the word "green" more than thirty times, he ends this rather short lyric with "Green ghosts: flitting through green / trees— / green fire: from green fingers / on green guns— / green jungle: green hellfire: green death" (29).

Similarly, in just about every Vietnam War novel one picks up, the author underscores America's adversarial relationship with the jungle. I should add that this adversarial relationship is one of long standing. As William Eastlake says in *The Bamboo Bed*, "Americans love the open. Americans do not trust the jungle. The first thing the Americans did in America was clear a forest and plant the cities" (22). It certainly was no different in Vietnam, where we came to detest the color green, and defoliation became a primary tactic in the war—almost a rite, accompanied by such ironic litanies as "We Eat Forests" and "Only You Can Prevent Forests." Agent Orange was the medium. Agent Orange enabled us to see what we wanted to see. Because it chemically induces accelerated growth, it literally made the enemy—greenness—grow itself to death. It was the perfect chemical for a war that merely seemed to flip America's mythology upside down. Agent Orange demystified the jungle by erasing it, by turning presence into absence. However, as we will see in *Meditations in Green*, Agent Orange never could erase enough of the jungle.

As I said in chapter 1, there is a parallel between this military-botanical phenomenon and the practice of writing novels about that war. I have further suggested that the most successful novels are those that are not literary Agent Orange; that is, they neither defoliate the horror and absurdity of Vietnam by "making sense" of the experience, nor nihilistically wallow in it. Principal (and possibly the finest) among those novels that avoid both extremes is Wright's *Meditations in Green*. Green is the great god-devil in this novel. It's the medium of therapy for the main character, Griffin, and the reason he needs therapy: as an American, Griffin overdoses on the rioting vegetation of Vietnam, not to mention marijuana.

51

Green in Vietnam is like the all-consuming whiteness of Moby Dick. It comes to symbolize everything that was inscrutable and thus hateful. But neither Wright nor his main character feels compelled to destroy the green. Rather, each wishes to be "destroyed" by it. As the title intimates, Wright's book has affinities with the practice of Eastern thought. When Griffin isn't flashing back to scenes in Vietnam and his tour of duty with the 1069th Military Intelligence Group, he's back home trying to recover from acute drug addiction and from post-traumatic stress disorder (PTSD). His psychologist, Arden (Shakespeare's pastoral forest), prescribes Eastern meditation. It is by means of these Buddhist exercises that Griffin hopes to meditate his way down the evolutionary ladder to the level of plant life, thereby purging his human consciousness of the nightmare visions and of Western man's antipathy toward nature and its eternal cycle of birth and death.

Americans tried to stop this cycle in Vietnam; it didn't work, and thousands of GIs and millions of Vietnamese were victims of the failed experiment. This includes Griffin, who, as Wright's Prospero during the war, directly participates in the U.S. defoliation stategy in his second assignment with the 1069th. Griffin's new experiment is to reflect his way back East, to a way of thinking characterized by interplay and interpenetration of man and nature, rather than aloofness and subjugation. He must work his way to being a participant with nature (and all the agony and ecstasy that entails), not the baton wielder. He must meditate his way to the crooked, wavering flow of the Buddhist "Tao" rather than the Euclidian geometry of his commanding officer, Major Holly, a man obsessed with cleanliness, straight lines, and symmetry. Brandishing the compass of Milton's Logos, the major tries to turn his little nook in Vietnam into a tidy Monopoly board.[1] "From the air," Griffin notes, "the compound of

---

1. In his novel *The 13th Valley*, John M. Del Vecchio ridicules this geometrist obsession and points out how it could even cost lives. A Lieutenant Brooks notices a trench that had been dug to protect the company from rocket attack. "The L-T's eyes fixed on the trench. They never do it right, he thought. . . . This trench is so straight . . . he saw an image . . . it should zig-zag . . . an image of a rocket exploding, erupting at one end of the trench . . . dominoing the soldiers within, falling in order to the other end" (35).

the 1069th Intelligence Group was a triumph of military design. Living quarters for both officers and enlisted men consisted of fifty-five identical hootches arranged in five ranks of eight hootches, then three ranks of five. . . . [T]he unit's basic geometric design possessed a pleasing sense of natural logic and finality that seemed somehow magical to the mind" (37).

Wright does not attempt to restore destroyed geometry. He doesn't try to make sense of Vietnam (he's acutely aware that it *didn't* make sense). The novel does not try to fill our minds with clarification or after-the-fact encomia. It neither condemns nor justifies America's presence in Vietnam (most novels do one or the other). Instead, the vortex of *Meditations* pulls Griffin and the reader down to the point of what Buddhists call "empty mind." This novel doesn't "add up" in the traditional sense. It adds *down*, and as such, Harriet and Ozzie would see nothing in it either. The reason they would see nothing is that they have been raised on a steady diet of Western rationalism, of which one of the kingpins is *ex nihilo nihil fit*. Wright would counter this with *solo ex nihilo aliquid fit*—something can come only from nothing.

We can more fully appreciate Wright's warp or inversion if we take note of Griffin's first assignment with the 1069th: he was an "aerial reconnaissance image interpreter." His job is to study aerial photographs and detect somethings in the formless jungles so that the B-52s could make them nothings. His task is that of a geometrician amid the amorphous. But Griffin soon comes to realize that the task is hopeless: "Shapes are losing outline, character. Wooden frames turning spongy. The attrition of squares and rectangles. The loss of geometry. Form is emptiness, emptiness is form. Mind is a magpie" (136). Griffin knows that superimposing his grids on the jungle is like trying to force the square peg into the round hole. He knows that the focus he brings to the murk is a lie. He recognizes that "a wish became a guess, a guess an estimate, an estimate the reality" (206). He recognizes the something for what it is, fraudulence—not a something or a nothing but a vacuum.

My students have frequently remarked that Griffin, our "genial storyteller," is stoned and that this accounts both for the chaotic nature of the novel and for the fact that they therefore shouldn't have to take the book seriously as art. Indeed, he is stoned—often! I submit, however, that what really makes this a "stoned" novel is that by tapping into nonordinary states of consciousness, Griffin also finds a channel into the energy sources and paradoxes ("koans") of Eastern mysticism and modern physics. The drugs do not alter his consciousness so much as they increase it. In his book *Walking Point*, Thomas Myers writes that the drugs are only *apparently* a "historical escape mechanism." Actually, they are a "guarantee of deeper confrontations with the war. . . ." His heroin habit " . . . heightens [memory's] colors and sharpens its contours" (201). This complicates Griffin's world, but that very fact enables him to make the simple recognition (which is almost impossible to recognize) that the geometry we impose on reality is in fact an imposition—an illusory, cultural wish fulfillment. In *The Tao of Physics*, the physicist Fritjof Capra says of the Hindu god Shiva that he "reminds us that the manifold forms in the world are "maya"—not fundamental, but illusory and ever-changing—as he keeps creating and dissolving them in the ceaseless flow of his dance" (243). As already stated, Americans (Westerners, in general) try to stop this process. They try to improve nature by arresting, framing, and mapping it. One time, while flying with Lieutenant Mueller over the Ho Chi Minh Trail, Griffin is amazed at the discrepancy between the map and the reality. We read of him that he was "astonished at the difference between the insignificant tracing on a map and the broad avenue of actuality. 'It looks like an eight-lane freeway,' he exclaimed" (203).

Of course, it's easy to say that we must stop confusing the map with the actuality, that we must stop separating the rocks of Vietnam that Major Holly orders painted, from the general cultural imperative against the "botanist's madhouse" of the void. "The General," for example, is a reasonably intelligent man; but having grown up in a "carpentered" society, he simply cannot get it into his head that the fabled 5th NVA Regiment is just that: a fable, a scaled-down version of COSVN. Like so many of his compatriots, "The General" has fallen in love with cartography.

Griffin soon figures out that America's "geometry" in Vietnam was nothing more than "outlines of a consensus formed in the murk" (206). The actual reality was the photosynthetic green riot of tropical nature. So one can turn the 1069th into a Monopoly board and paint everything that doesn't move (Major Holly). One can repeatedly play with tidy numbers and stick sharp pins into tidy maps ("The General"). One can kill all the mongrels and remove all the dog shit from the compound (Sergeant Anstin). One can destroy thousands of acres of forest with Agent Orange (the "WE EAT FORESTS" C-123 pilot). One can make tidy circles around suspicious shadows on aerial recon film so those shadows will be cleaned up the next day by aerial assault (Spec 4 Griffin); but sooner, rather than later, nature will defeat geometry, and energy will defeat mass—even massive technology. As Griffin says, with "collapse and regeneration occurr[ing] at the same moment" (261), ". . . the adhesive [will come] loose in the humidity, the edges [will begin] to curl . . . [the] boundaries [will burst] like ribbon" (223).

Griffin knows all of this, but that doesn't change the fact that this attrition of geometry is accompanied by, and largely causes, the attrition of his own psychic geometry. In one of the many times he comments on this, Griffin speaks of himself in the third person:

> Once he had been so backward as to think thoughts such as these: if mind was an engine requiring maintenance and tune-ups for dependable performance down reality road, what happened when you mislaid the tools and your feeler gauge came apart, blades of metal falling into the big oil drum, lost. (273)

As in the climate of Vietnam, so it is in Griffin's mind: "everything moved toward the stability of mush." As we've seen, Wright finds an apt metaphor for this loss of solidity. Sitting down to eat GI chow, Claypool, one of the novel's characters (who ironically is from New Harmony, Indiana), "tried his fork. The food dripped between the tines" (103). Another Claypool scene is a masterful description of the loss of form:

> [Claypool] seemed to have awakened from a nightmare and found himself trapped in completely unrecognizable surroundings. . . . He watched and wrote in dirt upon the wall notes for his superiors of what he saw. Through wire mesh that sparkled like a theater screen he could see outside bands of the green people walking to and fro with buckets of liquid. When they applied this liquid buildings would vanish. Of course he knew the liquid

55

was white paint but it wasn't. He couldn't be fooled again. The paint was a chemical like typewriter correcting fluid and soon all the mistakes would be erased. As they worked, the crews of green people drank the liquid from smaller cans. He knew this was beer but of course it wasn't. Like the walls and the hootches these people would disappear too, as surely and completely as mistyped letters in an interrogation report. Day after day, as he watched, the crews of green people continued their work and the light got brighter and brighter. It wouldn't be long until the screen was as clean and white as a page upon which nothing had ever been written. (220)

Claypool's characterization thus runs parallel to Griffin's: he too is an interpreter, but of the Vietnamese language. He too despairs of his task and ultimately throws his dictionary away—into the green jungle.

The "screen" concept is especially important, for to a great extent what Wright (like Rabe) concerns himself with in his novel is the tension between blank screens and filled screens, erasure and writing, the void and plenitude, entropy and vitality. Throughout the novel, both in Vietnam and back in the United States, where Griffin continues his therapy for geometry attrition, we encounter this image of the form-seeking screen. These screens are the loci of Wright's and Griffin's search for something. For example, at one point Griffin dreams about his mother washing windows, ". . . a stone mansion of a hundred windows, gray and brown streaks across the glass. The water in the bucket turning ink black and even when all the windows had been washed no one could see in or out" (237). Stateside, Griffin experiences another example. The walls of his apartment are covered with inscrutable graffiti, which he whitewashes so that his girlfriend Huey can paint strange, vast abstractions she calls "soulographs." But the originals bleed through, like a palimpsest. In the middle of his room we see sculptural collages of "trash" that remind one of the works of the sculptor Jean Tinguely. In Vietnam, Wright self-consciously projects the flares, flashes, and tracer rounds of night fighting on a gigantic black screen. And just after the apocalyptic scene near the end of the novel, where the North Vietnamese regulars have all but overrun the 1069th, Griffin sees a light in the chapel where the troops had been watching a horror movie as the fire fight broke out. The movie is long over, and now "the reel spun round and round, the last foot of celluloid slapping repeatedly against the projector. The screen was blank [like David Nelson's movie], a rectangle of burning light" (318).

And then, finally, there is the most conspicuous "screen" in Griffin's outfit in Vietnam: the 1069th unit collage. I've noted that the collage phenomenon occurs in almost all Vietnam novels, whether the collages be deliberate and literal or implicit in their structures, as is the case with the most complexly remembered texts. Invariably, these collages are wildly absurd and obscene; they are desperate, lonely attempts to create a black but reassuring structure. And in Wright's case we again see the tension between erasure and filling: "The cutting and pasting had been in progress for years now and though rain and humidity had managed to bleach out most of the earlier contributions or caused them to peel off limp and faded as dead skin, fresh clippings went up often enough so that the board continued to renew itself like some exotic snake" (112). Like the VC, the collage achieves its viable identity by working in concert with nature. It is the antithesis of Holly's painted rocks.

The more recent contributions to the degenerating/regenerating collage range

> . . . from the ancient mamasan in conical hat and black latex to last year's Playmate of the Year from whose glossy pink ass a stick of five-hundred-pound bombs dropped onto a football field mined with pizzas where one team marked AFL [American Football League] rushed another team marked NLF [the Vietnamese National Liberation Front] for possession of the oversized head of Mickey Mouse decapitated by the blades of a Cobra helicopter streaming rockets into the U.S. Capitol dome that was a beanie on the head of Ho Chi Minh. In the upper right where pigs grazed on the White House lawn under a rain of pubic bushes cut into the shape of hydrogen bombs and Jesus with golden halo and folded hands lay on his side in a pile of charred Asian dead from which rose the Statue of Liberty who was taking it stoically in the rear from Pham Van Dong's dong. (112–13)

It's important to note that Wright's form-seeking screen is not a meaningless assemblage of unrelated images. To Major Holly, of course, they are obscenely unrelated. But the difference between his Monopoly game and the unit's collage is that the former imposes patterns, while the latter discovers it lurking beneath Harriet Nelson's formica. The former merely brings America to Vietnam, while the latter also brings Vietnam home to America. Finally, where Holly would see only chaotic disjunction, Wright's black-humored GIs see disturbing connections between, on the one hand, fantasies, cartoons, and sacred or secular icons; and, on the other, the violence of the Vietnam War.

All of Wright's "screens" function as artistic analogues to the task that he and his main character try to execute—namely, the creation of a real something from "the stability of mush." But the analogues that are the most intriguing and revealing belong to a character who here and there weaves in and out of the narrative like an elusive VC—Wendell Payne. Payne is an entrepreneur, unit eccentric, and self-made guru of the avant-garde. He's Werner Herzog, John Cage, and Jimi Hendrix rolled into one very deranged person. (I include Jimi Hendrix because before the war, so the novel tells us, Payne had been the sound mixer for the grunt's national anthem, namely, Hendrix's "Are You Experienced?" That experience just may have mixed Wendell as well.) Throughout the novel Payne constructs and fills his screens. He engages in four projects, all of which mirror the novel thematically and structurally.

Wright says that Payne's projects "had, to the displeasure of several superiors, diverted [his] energies so thoroughly he could rarely be found on the set of the real war." Note that here Wright sees the whole war in Vietnam as a movie, an observation that occurs throughout Vietnam War fiction. And in Wright's novel one of the characters remarks that the war is "all a grotesque hoax . . . concocted for economic purposes. There is no war, there is no Vietnam. We're sitting inside a secret sound stage somewhere in southern Arizona. Yeah, [says another character] right next to the studio where they faked the moon landing" (27). "In fact, the war and Wendell's duties pertaining to it seemed to be at best props" (150).

His first project, "begun only days after his arrival, had been the creation of the famous all-star rodent circus, a warren of cages constructed from pilfered wire and ammunition crates and stocked with dozens of unsavory-looking black rats he trained to fight for sport and gambling or to run through mazes equipped with no-no panels of flattened C-ration cans connected to jeep batteries" (150–51). This rodent maze is analogous to Wright's labyrinthine guerrilla novel of "nonlinear pathways." Like the Unit's collage, it works with juxtapositions, not linear, top-down progression. Characters are lost in a tangled military bureaucracy. As his interchangeable name suggests, one character, Lewis Simon, is especially unstable ontologically, wavering in and out of focus. In fact, our certainty of his identity is inversely proportionate to the number of his appearances on Wright's set. The letters he sends home are a microcosm of Wright's "disappearing" novel. Five of his letters are evenly spaced throughout the novel, and at the same time that his salutations shrink from "Mom and Dad" to "Mom and Pop" to "Ma and Pa to "M and P" and finally to "Folks," his signatures shrink from "Lewis" to "Lew" to "L" to "me." Finally, Simon essentially disappears from the novel, not that he was ever very much present. I should add that several other rather prominent characters—Claypool, Kraft, and Franklin—similarly fade in and out of the novel. Griffin himself tells Arden to call him "G," because he's "down to the initial" (226).

Also paralleling Wendell's first project, the moods of the characters abruptly shift from intense boredom to orgasmic fear and back again. Many of the characters also are "wired" into the plentiful marijuana, the metallic paroxysms of Jimi Hendrix and the Doors, and the nightly mortar-rocket-artillery attacks and counterattacks that achieve little more than the attrition of human bodies.

The purpose and form of Payne's second project is so indefinite that it is labeled "Wendell's Thing" by his comrades: "Cages, rat ring, and maze were soon replaced by colored wire, tubes, transistors, circuit boards, instrument panels all soldered together until the crammed room resembled a cockpit to the moon. At night people gathered on the floor while Wendell plugged in some plugs, switched on some switches, and tubes glowed, lights blinked, as a series of unearthly sounds escaped from huge stereo speakers placed at intervals about the walls—mercury dripping from a faucet, galactic winds, ball bearings rolling across the floor of a vacuum—a sort of sonic doodling" (151).

"Wendell's Thing" is a clear analogue to the war, a war in which many of the military operations lacked any apparent purpose. This is one of the themes dealt with most frequently in Vietnam fiction, and Wright's book is no exception. In his novel, at any rate, "military intelligence" is a gross misnomer. The "Thing" is also a miniature version of night combat, complete with the view of flares, tracer rounds, and arc light from B-52 strikes: "The distant fire fight proceeded in eerie silence. It was like watching the electronic display of a fancy pinball machine on which all the bells and buzzers had been disconnected" (176).

Wendell's "sonic doodling" also applies to Wright's method of constructing his novel. His novel is a literary happening, a graffiti event, an assemblage of ionized fragments. And it parallels Griffin's meditative attempts to recover from the trauma of Vietnam and from drug addiction: "Destination was unimportant. What mattered was rapid movement between points, traversing vast distances, intersecting possibilities" (172). "Wendell's Thing," Griffin's meditations, Wright's novel—they're all experiments in search of connections and intersections that had disappeared, like David Nelson's flickering images, from the screen.

The third project, Wendell's most extravagant, is his movie about the war. Wright's novel has already portrayed the war as a movie, so we now have a movie within a movie. It is cinema verité carried to outrageous (and at times very funny) lengths. Wendell views Vietnam itself as a gigantic movie set with stunning special effects and thousands of low-paid stunt men; and there is no way he is going to miss out on making the great American movie—a movie of a movie of huge proportions, with a budget of twenty-five million a day. In fact, one could say that Wendell is merely editing his movie of The Vietnam Movie. Wendell's movie, again like Wright's novel, is a pastiche of seemingly unrelated fragments with the volume set on high and the tempo frenzied. What the narrator says of the movie and of its maker, Wright is saying of his fiction: "Wendell's camera began to stray. Quite often the colonel, midway through a pulse-quickening address to the troops, would look up expecting to see the familiar eye of the lens staring blankly back and instead, with dismay, discover it inspecting some rotting telephone pole, meaningless puddles in the road, the undistinguished profile of some private's face. . . . For a couple of days he even followed Thai [the unit's pet mongrel] on his hands and knees for a short section entitled *The War in Vietnam: A Dog's Point of View*" (152–53). After Wendell has been shooting his movie for months, Griffin has the "treat" of viewing some of the footage—four-and-a-half hours' worth. Again, his comments about the film are those of the self-ironic Wright about his novel: "when the wall finally went blank he wasn't sure what he had seen. . . . There's no beginning, no middle, no end. There's no coherence" (250–51). But in fact there is, fragile though it may be. The mirrored images of the breakdown of structure are what gives the novel structure and makes it much more than what Griffin describes as "asteroids speeding along at different rates, burning up at different temperatures" (282).

Payne's final project is one he works on, as far as we can tell, for the entire time he is in Vietnam: reading Ayn Rand's *Atlas Shrugged*, the 1,200-page melodramatic paean to capitalism, high technology, and distorted Nietzscheanism—all of which blew up in America's face in Vietnam. This fourth project of Payne functions both as a parallel and an ironic artistic analogue to Wright's novel, and to the war in general. Rand's novel is everything that Wright's is not; yet, strangely, it is also much that the latter is. Rand's main character, railroad tycoon Dagny Taggert, certainly reminds one of Wendell Payne with her extravagance and crazed apocalyptic vision. Also, like Wendell's projects and the nature of warfare in Vietnam, *Atlas Shrugged* is marked by excess and extremism. Moreover, Rand's rabid anti-Communism is consonant with America's ostensible reason for fighting in Vietnam.

It is as an ironic analogue, however, that *Atlas Shrugged* works best. Whereas Rand's novel celebrates the heroic in man and his power to control his destiny, Wright's novel portrays the fears and vulnerability of the U.S. military forces—enlisted men and officers. They felt confused, frustrated, and powerless fighting the unseen enemy in the green labyrinth. And they were treated as heroes neither there nor here when they returned. Furthermore, Rand's novel prophesies that high technology will take over the world. While driving through Michigan, like the president of the United States touring a disaster area, Dagny Taggert sees a farmer pushing a plow. This angers her and reaffirms her belief that America has let itself become ripe for the

61

plucking. This sort of technological hubris, we now know, took it on the chin in Vietnam. The United States was defeated by a people whose technology did not extend much beyond the water buffalo. Millions of tons of bombs and billions of dollars worth of materiel often were beaten by punji sticks and homemade booby traps. One character in *Meditations* is killed by a medieval weapon put to "modern" use—a crossbow booby trap. The narrator says, "There was a sense that that arrow had been set some millennia ago, and had waited patiently through the centuries for its victim" (266).

We reach the greatest level of irony when we compare Rand's and Wright's novels. Implausible though *Atlas* often is, it is nevertheless structured purely in a traditional linear and causal manner. By contrast, Wright's novel often appears to have been written by someone having an out-of-body experience. But there is something more important to say in this context. It's not just that Wendell reads Rand's novel; it is *how* he reads it. Midway through Wright's novel we find:

> From the thigh pocket of his fatigues, [Wendell] extracted a well-worn copy of Ayn Rand's *Atlas Shrugged*, front and back covers both gone. The book itself only two-thirds its original size. When Wendell read he tore off each page as he finished, dropping it wherever he happened to be. The densest concentrations, modest piles on the floor beside his chair, his bunk, were swept up daily by the hootch maid, but page after page had been found throughout the unit, I Corps, all of South Vietnam: in the latrine, the mess hall, the EM club, the chapel, the hangar, the detention cells, the supply room, in the bunkers, on the floors of cockpits, in air terminals up and down the coast, on helicopters, C-130s, Cobras, Beavers, Bird Dogs, the whole zoo of military aircraft, page one hundred and eighty seven was even rolled up and smoked one desperate night. Once a couple loose pages got sucked up into the right engine of one-nine. . . . (154)

Meditations is the only novel I know of that destroys, page by page, a conventional novel. Wright carries this one step further. He links the gradual destruction of Rand's novel with the gradual "creation" of Wendell's movie and therefore with the making of *Meditations*. Wendell's movie and Wright's novel "grow" at the same rate that Rand's novel shrinks. Wright would certainly seem to be suggesting that there is a relationship between the two processes. In the final rocket attack and fire fight Wendell lies on the ground, mortally wounded, and therefore unable to shoot his greatest footage yet—what he calls "The War in Vietnam: The Final Hours" (314). So he takes on the role of director, and in the final moment of his life, after shouting out instructions to his "honorary cinematographer," namely Griffin, he says,

> "I'm never going to know how it comes out."
> "How what?"
> Wendell's hand was pawing at the side pocket of his fatigue pants. "My book."
> Griffin reached over and pulled out the dog-eared paper brick of *Atlas Shrugged*.
> "It's okay," he said. "Money saves the world." (314)

Initially, "it" and "my" seem to refer to Wendell's movie, which Griffin will now have to finish. (Even if we immediately realize that "my" does refer to *Atlas Shrugged*, what Wendell is saying here is that Rand's novel becomes his as he is destroying it.) Wright wants us to see that "it" refers to Rand's novel and Wendell's movie and *Meditations* and the war itself. This momentary confusion over how "it comes out" establishes Wright's linkup of erasure and filling.

The main point to be made about this novel is that Wright's creation will grow out of destruction or not at all. This paradox is difficult for Western minds to grasp. Robert Ornstein and Paul Ehrlich explain this difficulty: "The world that made us is now gone, and the world we made is a new world, one that we have developed little capacity to comprehend" (8). Thus, it is just as difficult for Western people to understand the physicist's statement that life is a "dance of creation and destruction" (Capra, 240) as it is to understand that Wright's novel is "the sum of destructions," which is what Picasso said of his own paintings. *Meditations* never strays from this antiphonal interplay of Shiva's dance; it is one of the dominant motifs in the novel. Like Jack Fuller's Neumann, who tries to build a village dispensary from the blasted rubble left from an earlier B-52 strike, Griffin searches throughout the novel for the something that will rise from the destruction. Even though Neumann's mission fails, Fuller, like Wright, points us in the right, and perhaps distinctively un-American direction: rather than cover up our past with pre-fabbed distractions, we must use it, learn from it, and build with it.

Griffin looks for the seed that will sprout from the bomb crater. For example, while studying the effects of B-52 "carpet bombing" (there's a Vietnam oxymoron!), he becomes intrigued with the weave of the craters (the structure of absence), and "the not uncommon crater within a crater. Chinese boxes of destruction; the lone un-touched tree at the center of a field of matchsticks; the bomb distri-bution games of connect-the-dots and see a smiling fish, a happy flower" (53). While on an aerial recon mission he again is intrigued with "a remarkable field of craters arranged in such neat nearly sym-metrical rows as to resemble a bizarre species of farm crops" (202). Actually, Wright begins this harvesting-destroying motif on the first page of the novel, in Griffin's first meditation: "Colorless sky, luster-less sun, sooty field of rusted television antennas, the unharvested crop of the city." In one of Griffin's Vietnam nightmares, Wright pushes the motif even further, this time viewing the human body as future crop. Griffin sees arms and legs and various bits and pieces of human bodies scattered over the landscape. "The General drove up in a huge bulldozer. It's okay, he said, scooping cinders, cover 'em up, water daily, and next year you've got a fresh crop good as new" (15). In other examples, after one of the novel's characters detonates a booby trap, the narrator says his bloody chest resembles a plowed field (72). When Sergeant Anstin orders all the compound dogs killed, their howling is compared to "a nursery of unhappy babies" (268). Finding a severed head in Major Holly's tulip beds, the flight surgeon suggests that "Maybe it just growed" (284). During the apocalyptic scene when the 1069th is being overrun, and absolutely everything is in flames, we read: "A flaming plane drifted across the flight ramp into a line of parked helicopters. Huge metal blades spun like windmills through the billowing explosions" (310). Finally, Grif-fin describes a burning hangar as an "egg of flame" (316). Like a chaos scientist, Griffin looks for patterns within the disorder of his life. As James Gleick would say, he ". . . analyz[es] irregularity as a building block of life" (300), "dissipation [as] an agent of order" (314). Of course, it is not at all the kind of order that Major Holly could possibly recognize.

What Wright seems to be saying here is that structure and destruction are not opposites; they're merely the yin and yang of Shiva's dance, if I may mix cultures. Each side needs the other in order to exist. In fact they are sometimes indistinguishable, as Griffin observes one morning after his unit has been mortared the night before. Surveying the partially destroyed compound, he says that it resembles a construction site (189). I do not think there is any doubt that Wright, in part, means these observations of Griffin to be ironic, even grimly so. But it is not an irony that gnaws on itself until consummated in nihilism—the nihilism that is embodied in two refrains that echo throughout Vietnam War fiction: "There it is" and "Don't mean nothin'." Moreover, I believe, again in part, that Wright sometimes intends no irony at all with this construction-from-destruction motif. Despite (and because of) man's clumsy, ignorant attempts to perpetuate himself and his maps of reality by going to war, Griffin embraces both the drum of life and the tongues of fire in two of Shiva's four hands. This is Griffin's (and Wright's) tactic for survival and for recovery from the nightmare. So Wright does attempt to connect the dots of destruction; but it's a risky tactic, because his search for potential life takes him to the very void of destruction. Wright leaves us uncertain as to whether the tactic works for Griffin. What we *do* know is that this tactic is the one he uses.

On Griffin's new meditative track of being, he is to become a humble plant. Instead of overdosing on drugs, he is now to overdose on chlorophyll, so to speak. He is to become the locus of photosynthesis, to convert the waste of Vietnam into new forms of energy. Wright's novel does not build up; it unravels. In the last paragraph of the novel we read: "Everywhere the green fuses are burning and look now, snipping rapidly ahead of your leaping eye, the forged blades cutting through the page, the transformation of this printed sheet . . ." (322). Like his main character, Wright's novel "meditates" its way down the evolutionary ladder. In his very different version of the "Telephone" game, the ultimate content of *Meditations* is no thing but waiting energy. And it remains that after we finish it, for, as I've said, we really have very little idea what will become of Griffin. Like Claypool's green people, Wright's green Griffin becomes invisible. He disappears as conventional protagonist, reappearing only as a possibility within Wright's choreography of fictive strategies.

Significant among these strategies is what Wright does with the narrative mode. Why does he switch back and forth from self-conscious first-person storytelling (Griffin calls himself "your genial storyteller"), straight third-person narration, and a combination of the two in which Griffin is spoken of in the third person—sometimes, one senses, by another, unnamed narrator, and sometimes, one gets the clear feeling, by Griffin himself? And then why does Wright repeatedly and abruptly interrupt the narrative momentum with Griffin's fifteen Janus-faced meditations, which, like the novel as a whole, are antiphonal interplays between growth and destruction, life and death, fertility and barrenness, poetic flights and the utterly prosaic? What is Wright's purpose in this staccatoed narration? One feasible answer would seem to be that, like Wendell's "edges," Griffin's "edges" "remained perpetually, maddeningly out of focus" (152). There is something eerie about Griffin's referring to himself in the third person, but this is one of the keys to the novel. Griffin is not Griffin anymore: "each time he witnessed another raw incident [in Vietnam] his past took on more and more of the insubstantial characteristics of fantasy. The war was real; he was not" (180). He realizes that his prewar self is now rubble: "His eyes and the world shattered simultaneously. It was like staring into a cracked kaleidoscope at bright pieces of color that no longer resolved themselves into any unified pattern" (275).

Composer Karlheinz Stockhausen once said that the distinction between the traditional and the modern composer is that the former showed the same object in many different lights (think of the famous four-note motif of Beethoven's Fifth Symphony), whereas the latter shows many different objects in the same light. This distinction is analogous to the one that sets the traditional Vietnam narrative apart from Wright's novel. Very early in *Meditations*, for example, we see four "screenplays" operating in the same light: (1) the ubiquitous Vietnam collage ("The white walls dissolved and through my room moved a parade of silent disconnected objects: a bolt, a door handle, a brass eyehole, the black letter U, a steel grill, a pane of glass, a row of wooden struts, disks of yellow light, spinning tires, parts of a truck, of several trucks, a battalion of trucks, a convoy in a fog. A quick skinny dog ran up barking" [14]); (2) a Vietnam nightmare of grotesque proportions; (3) a crazy Vietnam War video game with Griffin

66

at the controls (first of the game, and then of a helicopter with which he reduces Vietnamese to "miscellaneous parts"); (4) finally, throughout, Griffin's hallucinatory state of mind that adds to and is precipitated by the other three "screenplays." Wright repeatedly calls attention to the parallel between the addictive and the identity-altering power of drugs, and the addictive power of the 3-D movie known as Vietnam. Griffin is the dominant character in his collage, his nightmare, his video game, and, of course, in his drug-induced hallucinations; but, as he says, "I was being played by someone else" (14).

With Griffin's identity so elusive, Wright had to come up with an equally elusive narrative strategy and structural principle. He organizes his novel in interesting, overlapping, spiraling circles, which often echo, duplicate, and bleed through each other like the whitewashed graffiti on Griffin's palimpsest walls. Unlike the superficial tracings of names on the VVM, *Green* taps into the literal meaning of "palimpsest," namely, "to rub again." To put it another way, this novel, like Peter Straub's *Koko*, consists of texts within and behind the texts-within-texts, or movies within and behind the movies-within-movies.

But there's another reason for Wright's elusive narrative strategy and structural principle: survival and recovery. We can understand this if we contrast the postwar tactics of Griffin and his army buddy, Trips. They both suffer from extreme cases of PTSD. In their psychoses, neuroses, paranoias, hallucinations, and bad trips, they're veritable textbooks on the subject. But Trips is especially sick. Befitting his name, he's what's been called a "tripwire veteran"—a tortured recluse locked up in a space-time capsule marked "Vietnam." Having only a hammer for a tool, Trips views the world as his personal nail. Totally unable to transcend Doc Peret's "cycle," he focusses all his rage on a narrow, laser beam of hate leading directly to Sergeant Anstin, the bureaucratized lifer who had his pet dog, Thai, killed in Vietnam. He allows nothing peripheral to compromise his rage. He will spend the rest of his life frantically spinning off to nowhere, accelerator pedal to the floor, on a sheet of ice. Instead of utilizing Vietnam, he is used up by it.

Having worked with troubled Vietnam veterans for many years, Arthur Egendorf clearly understands this confusion. He describes the no-win situation that entraps Trips (and likely *all* of us, to one degree or another): "In war we fight to defend our rigidly defined selves and battle our enemies firmly believing they alone threaten our security. What rips into people's self-assurance in moments of horror is the nothingness that wars and crusades try to conceal" (166). Whereas Trips blames everything on Vietnam, and has distilled that everything to one man, one act, and one motive, Griffin has the double-edged gift of recognizing a much more complicated world, one in which the concealed is revealed. It's scary, but it's also potentially liberating. Egendorf says "The more amply we reach out to grasp our past, the more we can look on old pain gratefully [like bomb craters in the landscape and the psyche], recognizing it as the instigator that provoked us into growing to encompass it" (74).

Unlike Trips, Griffin knows that he and the world are suffering from an illness, not a disease. Trips' greater illness consists of his failure to diagnose his disease *as* illness. In *The Turning Point*, Capra says, "Disease is viewed as an [external] enemy to be conquered" (145), whereas illness is systemic, and it is both externally and internally caused. We can apply what Capra says about individual patients to civilization itself, a whole world where insanity and dehumanization have reached a state of critical mass: "In the process of reducing illness to disease, the attention of physicians has moved away from the patient as a whole person. Whereas illness is a condition of the total human being, disease is a condition of a particular part of the body, and rather than treating patients who are ill, doctors have concentrated on treating their diseases" (152).

Wright draws attention to the illness, and he does so in a number of ways: looking out on Griffin's Boschean, urban wasteland, we see every bit as much insanity, violence, boredom, paranoia, and delusion as we do in the Vietnam passages. Thomas Myers refers to Griffin's urban existence as "postgraduate work in booby traps and defense perimeters" (199). The name of his stateside girlfriend—Huey—is a continuous reminder of what Michael Herr calls Vietnam's "provider-waster" "meta-chopper" (7). Huey's drug-dealing, gang-member brother, Rafer, skulks the back alleys of this urban jungle like a Vietcong. The heroin that Griffin is hooked on perpetuates an East-West interface, with Ho Chi Minh's head replacing the Capitol dome. His stateside nightmares and drug-induced hallucinations are eerie amalgamations of Vietnam and America. Finally, we must not forget that after just one trip into the jungle, the now green-meditating Griffin had a frantic desire to turn Vietnam into an Agent-Oranged parking lot. Experiencing a "chlorophyll freakout" in the "claustrophobic botany," he says "The whole stinking forest should have been sprayed long ago, hosed down, drenched in Orange . . ." (262). Part of his double-edged gift, though, is that he no longer can fool himself into believing that Vietnam was special, that it was some kind of aberrant visitation upon the American psyche. As Thomas Myers puts it, Vietnam was simply America's "most visible promontory" (198).

Trips never figures this out. His problem is that he views Anstin the same way doctors and patients alike view bacteria—as a foreign invader that needs to be zapped and "wasted" rather than be treated as a vital part of Shiva's dance. Thus Griffin literally identifies the fragments that keep coming to the surface of his leg with his therapy: "my fragments, my therapy" (322). This is yet another example of using detritus—bacteria, as it were—as the raw material of construction. Literally and figuratively, respectively, the body and the psyche need bacteria to remain vital; they need disease to be immune from disease. For some reason, this is difficult to accept, even in a nation that receives millions of doses of flu every year to prevent the flu.

Even though Griffin is also very sick, his tactics at least give him a chance of healing. Wright enables him to transcend "The Trips Syndrome." He does this by giving him a much larger canvas to work on and a greater sense of context—the element missing in the lives and narratives of so many fighters-turned-writers. Structurally, Griffin's/Wright's approach to healing is multiple-minded. The hallucinogenic horrors of Vietnam have their dizzying momentum repeatedly interrupted by the series of fifteen meditations on plant life and back-home narrative passages. Griffin is a composite character—the "I" of the back-home passages, the "he" of the Vietnam passages. Furthermore, as the "I" reminds us, Griffin is our "genial story teller." Addicted to drugs though he be, he's a descendant of Melville's Ishmael and Conrad's Marlow. Like them, his job is to create from the destruction he witnessed. Trips, on the other hand, is a kind of pop-culture version of the obsessive Ahab and Kurtz, each of whom insists on

69

"reading" the universe intensely but simplistically. Misdiagnosing his problem, Trips reminds me of a story told about Magellan in David Rabe's play, *The Basic Training of Pavlo Hummel* (1973). Trips thinks that because his piece of rope does not touch the bottom of the ocean, he is over the deepest part.

Griffin knows better; he knows about the void between the rope's end and the ocean floor. He knows there is something below the damaged ego that Trips desperately tries to hold on to. So his therapy consists of erasing what's left of his naive prewar ego until he reaches "the void at the heart of fertility" (16). Only here will the "plowed field" of his traumatized memory be receptive to seed. His therapy and this novel's movement is a process that has shifted "the structure of . . . awareness from a solid to a liquid to a gas. In accordance with the laws of evaporation" (30). His task is to "transform himself simultaneously into both wave and a corpuscle" (222)—energy and incipient form. Character as aril. Novel as seed. Reader as sunlight. Denouement as potential beginning. As Griffin says in his eleventh meditation, even a *dead* tree lives on as pencils and baseball bats.

Michael Herr's Spectral Journalism

No one wanted to waste time on a line of work that was going awry, producing no stability. . . . Why go to all that trouble just to see chaos?

The new geometry mirrors a universe that is rough, not rounded, scabrous, not smooth. It is a geometry of the pitted, pocked, and broken up, the twisted, tangled, and intertwined. . . . The pits and tangles are more than blemishes distorting the classic shapes of Euclidean geometry. They are often the keys to the essence of a thing.

—James Gleick, *Chaos*

In a much-quoted passage from *Heart of Darkness*, the external narrator, just as he is about "To hear about one of Marlow's inconclusive experiences," explains the difference between the way Marlow and other men of the sea tell stories:

The yarns of seamen have a direct simplicity, the whole meaning of which lies within the shell of a cracked nut. But Marlow was not typical (if his propensity to spin yarns be excepted), and to him the meaning of an episode was not inside like a kernel but outside, enveloping the tale which brought it out only as a glow brings out a haze, in the likeness of one of these misty halos that sometimes are made visible by the spectral illumination of moonshine. (68)

This description sheds a great deal of "moonlight" on the story Marlow is about to tell; but it also sheds light on *Dispatches*, written by Michael Herr, another 1970s heir of Conrad's early-day literary journalist. Herr's reportage is as different from conventional journalism as Marlow's is different from conventional sea tales. The link between the two men became secure in 1979 when Herr did the voice-over for Francis Ford Coppola's version of Marlow—Captain Willard—in *Apocalypse Now*. More important, both men realized that what they had witnessed in the heart of darkness was simply beyond any kind of conventional storytelling, and perhaps beyond even *un*conventional storytelling. Their experiences had been altogether too dark or, because of what they revealed about Western behavior in Third-World countries, altogether too light. All "straight history" and straight anything became seriously compromised. In one of Herr's great lines for Willard, we hear "Charging a man with murder here is like handing out speeding tickets at the Indy 500." The only illumination Marlow and Herr did experience was the illumination of the disintegration of their confidently straight Western consciousnesses, like tracer rounds illuminating objects targeted for destruction. Herr suggests an analogue for this disintegration as he observes "the phosphorescence that gathered around rotting tree trunks and sent pulsing light over the ground from one damp spot to another" (269).

Instead of structuring episodes on a continuum, Herr moves pulsatingly from one "damp" critical mass to another. The episodes that Conrad's external narrator speaks of are like a tier of new cement blocks: coherent, self-contained parts of the larger structure. But for Marlow and Herr, all is *a*-part. Meaning is as elusive as the muddy serpentine Congo River or the ominous, unmappable Central Highlands of Vietnam. Instead of kernels, both stories are swirling strobes eerily illuminating the spooky shadows. Herr will have nothing to do with James Webb's "basketball" flares that impose day on night.

Thinking back on his experiences, some of which were "a trans-

72

lucent blur" (95), Herr says that everything stood in "a strange light; the light told the story, and it didn't end like any war story I'd ever imagined" (277). He says the experience of horror leaves one "changed, enlarged and . . . incomplete" (260)—like a glow bringing out a haze. And as the participle "enveloping" suggests, this glowing haze is a process in which experience past and experience present are interwoven. Neither storyteller relates a story that already exists—no more than Neumann's dispensary already exists. It comes into being as it is being told. To a great extent the process is the content. Their past experiences are less things in themselves than they are catalysts for a future act. As Paul Fussell says in *The Great War and Modern Memory* (1975), "it is only the ex post facto view of an action that generates coherence or makes irony possible" (310). *Heart of Darkness* and *Dispatches* are ex post facto collages that provide Marlow and Herr their only way of knowing their horrifying experiences. As Herr expresses it, "Plant you now, dig you later: information printed on the eye, stored in the brain" (268). Or, "The problem was that you didn't always know what you were seeing until later, maybe years later, that a lot of it never made it in at all, it just stayed stored there in your eyes. Time and information, rock and roll, life itself, the information isn't frozen, you are" (20).

Herr needed to immerse himself in time, memory, and the creative act in order to thaw himself out. "Immersion" would seem to be one of the primary earmarks of literary journalism. And both Marlow and Herr were immersed beyond their wildest imaginations. (Herr was so immersed that, as he ends his book, he says, "one last chopper revved it up, lifted off and flew out of my chest" [277].) But the crucial kind of immersion is the secondary one, after the fact, when the writer does not recollect, nor even recreate, so much as he or she correlates, creates, and images the fragmentary raw material of the first immersion. So Herr is not really speaking hyperbolically when he says of this first immersion in Vietnam, "I hadn't been anywhere, I'd performed half an act" (268). This brings up two paradoxes of Herr's and Marlow's literary journalism. First, the storyteller achieves immersion with distance—in both space and time. Herr wrote the greater share of *Dispatches* 12,000 miles from Hue and Khe Sahn—years after the fact. Marlow created his story aboard the *Nellie* more than 4,000 miles from the Congo—again, so one can infer, a number of years after the fact. Conrad himself was thirty-two when he went to the Congo, forty-one when he wrote *Heart of Darkness*.

The second paradox is that both Marlow and Herr scooped their stories by delaying the telling. By abjuring deadlines and wire services (literally, in the case of Herr), they assured an exclusive for themselves. A voice within them repeated the words that the *Commercial Advertiser's* Lincoln Steffens said to his reporters: "Go on now, take your time" (317). To emphasize just how slow Herr was being in getting the "news" out, he calls his only in-country dispatch to *Esquire* "a lost dispatch from the Crimea" (226). Thus, it is paradoxically appropriate for Ward Just, Vietnam novelist and a former reporter for the *Washington Post*, to call Herr the premier war correspondent from Vietnam, even though Herr rarely corresponded with anyone back in the States. He waited and struggled almost ten years before he did.

What do we call his belated response? Even if we label it "literary journalism," which I think we can, there are some nagging questions associated with that label. First of all, literally speaking, Herr's book is not any kind of "journalism," if we go by the root meaning of the word, "daily." But there is a greater labeling problem: because of the fact-fiction tension that exists both in literary and journalistic circles, we've seen an awkwardness in deciding how to categorize certain books. This awkwardness is especially acute in the field of Vietnam War writing. Thus, memoirs such as Ron Kovic's *Born on the Fourth of July* and Tim O'Brien's *If I Die in a Combat Zone* are often referred to as novels. This is not surprising; as Paul Fussell says, it is sometimes impossible to distinguish between a memoir and a first-person novel (310). And when it comes to *Dispatches* the lines separating fact, fiction, journalism, memoir, history, and autobiography become extremely blurred. Herr is the first to admit that his assignment in Vietnam was "vague" (227). The way he "wanders" (as in "vagabond") between categories is a clear manifestation of the word's literal meaning. And because "literary journalism" wanders between two perceived worlds, each of which is itself always evolving, it is a problematical appellation. It's impossible to pin an "MOS" on either Herr or his book.

One of the most profound problems in studies of the Vietnam War is the stubborn Euclidean assurance that fact and fiction are easily recognized opposites from two different worlds. Were it so neat. War has a way of blurring such tidy categories, but only when one stops hovering over the "landscape" at 10,000 feet, like Lieutenant Calley's brigade commander. If writers and readers would only accede to Colonel Vann's wishes and get out of the aircraft, as it were, they would then see that at 10,000 feet fact and fiction can easily trade places. Once on the ground, they will see the chaotic epistemological terrain for what it is—especially during the sanity-crushing experience of combat. Thus, in *The Things They Carried*, Tim O'Brien finds himself forced to speak oxymoronically: "In a true war story nothing much is ever absolutely true." "A thing may happen and be a total lie; another thing may not happen and be truer than the truth"(88). O'Brien simply is echoing the thoughts of another fighter-writer— Robert Graves: "The memoirs of a man who went through some of the worst experiences of trench warfare [in World War I] are not truthful if they do not contain a high proportion of falsities" (32–33).

In a similar recognition of the slipperiness of the words "fact" and "fiction," William Eastlake has said that, for the Vietnam War, history is the fiction and fiction is the history. Paul Fussell quotes a World War II RAF flyer who expresses this same paradox. Having kept an accurate, detailed, truthful diary during the war, he now finds that "from all the quite detailed evidence of these diary entries I can't add up a very coherent picture of how it really was to be on a bomber squadron in those days. . . . No wonder the stuff slips away mercurywise from proper historians. No wonder they have to erect rather artificial structures [like Major Holly's Monopoly board] of one sort or another in its place. No wonder it is those artists who re-create life rather than try to recapture it [or trace it] who, in one way, prove the good historians in the end" (311).

There is something almost explicit in the language of this flyer, O'Brien, Eastlake, and Graves—and most Vietnam War scholars and writers of all kinds seem afraid of going in after it. To get at the source of this fear, we need to return to the analogy from Joseph Heller's *Catch 22*. Yossarian would seem to be a model paramedic, as he cleans, packs, and wraps Snowden's hip wound. The hip wound is not all that serious, so Yossarian can't figure out the relationship between such a minor wound and Snowden's deathly paleness. Finally he removes Snowden's flakjacket and his viscera comes sliding out. Similarly, the wound suffered by America in Vietnam is far more serious—far more radical—than we have admitted.

Michael Herr is one of very few writers to have removed the flak jacket. In his judgment, behind the sanitized columns of "factual" conventional print and the imperialistic sense-making stories on the six o'clock news was a "dripping, laughing death-face; it hid there in the newspapers and magazines and held to your television screens for hours after the set was turned off for the night, an after image that simply wanted to tell you at last what somehow had not been told" (233). To this day, conventional journalism and "kernelized" storytelling cover up a disemboweled epistemology. (The war in the Persian Gulf was an egregious example.) Herr realized that most people can't even see the wound because they are blinded by a habitual way of knowing.

On the other hand, everyone has taken note of the hip wound. For example, everyone has pointed out the wounds that truth was subjected to at the hands of Orwellian doublespeak, euphemisms, or what Herr calls "language fix" (43). But, as John Hellmann says of Herr,

> he sees a deeper gulf between the consciousness of Americans and the actuality of the war that from the beginning produced an artificial, fictive 'reality' conditioning the nature and course of the experience (143). . . . He experienced . . . an inability to comprehend the actuality before him as his consciousness seemed to protect him from the reality of the experience. Herr knows that if he is to capture the reality of the experience he must go beyond reporting, for the struggle is as much with his and the reader's consciousness as with the facts (144). Herr searches for a meaning, Hellmann goes on to say, not available in the fictive forms already imposed by one's culture upon the experiencing mind. (146)

Herr encountered the horror of a fictional world without an exit. Those obsolescent yet stubbornly kicking, fictive forms enable one to make assumptions no longer available to a writer of Herr's insight. Because the horror and the "hundred-channel panic" undermine everything—the ability to distinguish between fact and fantasy, reason,

76

logic, controlled linear time—it also renders inoperative those conventions that assume such controls, whether literary realism, formula journalism, or even literary journalism, as it is perceived by some. For, when the subject is war, especially one as insane and absurd as the Vietnam War, literary journalism too must give up more control than perhaps it is used to.

So, when Herr says, "I went to cover the war but the war covered me," he is admitting to the traumatic wound; he is admitting that his assumptions were disembowled, so the story he did get was that our linguistic certainties no longer obtain. The story he got was that Vietnam was a story. The term "nonfiction" lost its currency in a hurry. [1] Being "covered" by the war does not mean simply that Herr was overwhelmed by the war; it means he was *written* by it. The time-honored Western distinction between subject and object simply disintegrated. Herr says he was "debriefed by dreams" (277), and in Borgesian fashion he discovered that the dreamer (writer) dreaming a dreamed man (the story) is in turn being dreamed by another dreamer (the protean war itself and the myths that sent us there to fight it). This leaves him in a terrifying hall of mirrors where he must resort to gasping for ontological air and scrambling for an epistemological footing (the very predicament, as we will see, suffered by Amlin Gray's Reporter in the play *How I Got That Story*; 1979). In this hall of mirrors, there is no way Herr can maintain the ruse of using Webb's or Del Vecchio's "neutral camera." Finding himself in a situation where "a non-operation [is] devised to nonrelieve the non-siege of Khe Sanh" (166), what would he aim the camera at? What would he do for light?

1. In his novel *DelCorso's Gallery*, Philip Caputo explores this conflation of fiction and nonfiction in the fleld of photojournalism. Two photographers, DelCorso and Dunlop, have been at odds with each other for years, first in Vietnam, and later in the streets of Beirut. DelCorso accuses Dunlop of selling fraudulent photographs because he "doctors" them in all sorts of ways in the lab. Dunlop accuses DelCorso of being unartistic because he simply photographs the bald degradation of war. But Caputo would have us understand that both men change reality; it's just the means and timing that are different. Dunlop merely makes the changes later than DelCorso, who, on the scene, makes his modifications with shot selection, context, lighting, distance, lenses, and F-stops.

Thus, Herr carries literary journalism to new heights (or depths). After his many-year battle to write *Dispatches,* he came to understand that recognizing the conventions of hard journalism as just that is but one step. It is an important step to realize that the journalist needs to tap into the reservoirs of fiction and dream to get a truer story. Herr, however, takes two more steps, both of which will be elaborated on below: (1) he knows he is dreaming, and that "you could ask yourself whether you were sleeping even while you slept . . . cataloging the specifics . . . without ever waking" (148). That is, he does something far more radical than merely use dream structures as a rhetorical device to make "facts" meaningful—he experiences them; (2) he knows he is being dreamed in turn. In short, he knows that when the journalist's subject is the absurdity and bondage of an insane war, all linguistic structures are mere provisional conventions, as unlike reality as a menu is unlike the food it lists. Herr knows that trying to fine-tune our habitual epistemology to make it dovetail with the reality of Vietnam is like trying to modify a pick-ax for use in brain surgery. Finally, he knows that instead of a solid kernel within a nut, he has liquids changing into gases.

Taking the first step, Herr points to the direct correlation between conventional fighting and writing in the Vietnam War: neither works. Earlier he says that "it would be as impossible to know what Vietnam looked like from reading most newspaper stories as it would be to know how it smelled" (98). Between Command, the Administration, and the conventional press, Herr saw a "cross fertilization of ignorance." As a result,

> the spokesmen spoke in words that had no currency left as words, sentences with no hope of meaning in the sane world, and if much of it was sharply queried by the press, all of it got quoted. The press got all the facts (more or less), it got too many of them. But it never found a way to report meaningfully about death, which of course was really what it was all about. (229)

Herr thus radically separated himself from those who were so enamored of their conventional symbols and interpretations that they kept up the practice of eating the menu instead of the meal. As David Eason points out, not even New Journalism is exempt from the practice of menu-eating. The difference between Herr's mode of journalistic immersion and that of the menu-eaters lies at the center of Eason's illuminating article, "The New Journalism and the Image-World: Two Modes of Organizing Experience." Eason designates these two modes of New Journalism as "ethnographic realism" and "cultural phenomenology." Herr clearly operates in the second mode. Whereas the first mode assumes that the reporter can make sense of the world by putting new wine in old bottles, the second assumes a radical epistemological crisis. Whereas ethnographic realism is fine-tuning, cultural phenomenology is a total overhaul. According to Eason,

> Whereas ethnographic realism, like other forms of journalism, reveals the act of observing to be a means to get the story, cultural phenomenology reveals observing to be a vital part of the story. Observing is not merely a means to understand the world but an object of analysis. . . . Ethnographic realism represents style as a communicational technique whose function is to reveal a story that exists 'out there' [like a kernel] in real life. Cultural phenomenology represents style as an epistemological strategy that constructs as well as reveals reality. (57, 59)

Herr's immersion in the Vietnam War forced him into the overhaul mode of cultural phenomenology.[2] In Eason's language, it didn't take him long to experience "what it feels like to live in a world in which there is no consensus about a frame of reference to explain 'what it

2. Almost all other Vietnam writing partakes of the ethnographic mode. Irony in this writing remains selective, not radical. Snowden's hip remains the concern, not his abdomen. Literary devices, such as shifts in point of view and disruptions of linear time, seem more tactical than strategic. As we've seen, even in Ron Kovic's bitter memoir *Born on the Fourth of July* the irony is directed solely outward. Guilt is largely imputed, not confessed. Notice that whereas Herr says "you were as responsible for everything you saw as you were for everything you did" (20), Kovic maintains a mythic continuity of wronged innocence. It is only those who defiled and reneged on the myth that he targets. Kovic engages in an intra-familial quarrel, an act visually manifested when at an anti-war rally he displays the American flag upside down. As an ethnographic realist, Kovic is angry over his disillusionment; as cultural phenomenologist, Herr uses this disillusionment as a terrifying opportunity to radically interrogate all of his and America's inherited belongings. As Peter Marin puts it, "All men, like all nations, are tested twice in the moral realm: first by what they do, then by what they make of what they do" (51). The power of *Dispatches* issues from Herr's unflagging willingnesss to take—and perhaps pass by failing—this second moral test.

all means'" (52). After hearing the much-quoted, inscrutable Lurp story early in the book ("Patrol went up the mountain. One man came back. He died before he could tell us what happened" [4–5]), Herr comes to the conclusion that his epistemological training had ill-prepared him for the wacky reality of Vietnam. He arrived in Vietnam believing that if something was inscrutable it simply needed to be restated. He was used to a language of "defoliation" that had imperialistic control over the formless and the inconclusive, a language that insisted on order when there was none. Herr discovered that the way Americans engaged in "language fix" found its perfect analogy in the motto of an Air Force defoliation outfit: "Only we can prevent forests" (163), an American mantra that in its figurative sense was not at all limited to the military's "five o'clock follies." In fact, as both Philip Knightley (*The First Casualty*, 1975) and Daniel C. Hallin (*The "Uncensored War": The Media and Vietnam*, 1986) point out, the editors of America's dailies and weeklies routinely "prevented forests" by ignoring their Vietnam correspondents whenever they happened to blow the whistle on the brutal farce of the war. However, even when these correspondents did try to tell the truth, they restricted themselves to ethnographic realism. Knightley informs us that even very late in the war most journalists never got beyond the "subversive" news that the United States was losing the war: "the correspondents were not questioning the American intervention itself, but only its effectiveness" (380). Almost everyone who had the power either to make or print "news" engaged in language fix, whether by outright lying or by arguing over tactics instead of the strategy of intervention. Either they claimed there was a light at the end of the tunnel or that the military was incompetently retreating from it.

To borrow another metaphor from Alan Watts, it was as if by the convention of perspective, American generals, politicians, and the media painted a doorway on an impenetrable wall (125). The Lurp story is but one instance where Herr banged his head against this illusory opening in the labyrinthine landscape of Vietnam. Herr learned from his headache, though; he largely separated himself from those who insisted that the opening was real: "My ties with New York were as slight as my assignment was vague" (226–27). Rather than pledging allegiance to an illusory world of nonfiction, he plunges into a more promising world of self-conscious artifice—this is his second step. He calls *Dispatches* "My movie" (201). His many allusions to modern, existentialist writers such as Wallace Stevens, Stendhal, Proust, Graham Greene, Malraux, Camus, Conrad, and Heller are a tip-off that this book is indeed a new kind of journalism, one that ends up blurring all categories. *Dispatches* is a freewheeling collage of straightforward remembering, hallucination, irony, acid sarcasm, jump cuts, freeze frames, stream of consciousness, incongruous juxtaposition, realism, surrealism, Dadaism, and metafiction. It is a bulemic book that pigs out at the literary supermarket as it desperately tries to satisfy its appetite for a *real* opening in the wall. Finally, because Herr is acutely aware of "the fictive forms already imposed by one's culture upon the experiencing mind," his book is founded on a paradox: *self-conscious* artificiality engenders authenticity.

The discovery of the illusory door and the search for a real opening into his and America's consciousness form the foundation of Herr's counterepistemology. The "painted" door is much like the maps that Americans were obsessed with in Vietnam. Already noted is his cynical reaction to these maps hanging on the walls of military bureaucrats throughout Vietnam. As far as he was concerned, they were ignorance meticulously scripted so as to insure "clear communication" (98). And there we have it—thought and language used as a cosmetic (98); carefully treated hip wounds; Monopoly games played in swamps.

Herr's difficult time writing this book was caused by his search for a different kind of map, one that, instead of imposing order, truly followed the contours of Vietnam, the war, and America's complicity in the heart of darkness. *Dispatches* contains a number of analogies that serve as objective correlatives of Herr's recon mission. Late in the book Herr offers us the analogy of his book's "contour flying." He goes up in a Loach (a wasp-like, speedy, agile helicopter) with the First Cav's star flier:

> We flew fast and close to the ground, contour flying, a couple of feet between the treads and the ground, treetops, hootch roofs. Then we came to the river where it ran through a twisting ravine, the sides very steep, almost a canyon, and he flew the river, taking us through blind turns like a master. When we cleared the ravine he sped straight toward the jungle,

dipping where I'd been sure he would rise, and I felt the sharp freezing moment of certain death. Right in there under the canopy, a wild ship-shaking U turn in the jungle, I couldn't even smile when we broke clear, I couldn't move, everything looked like images caught in a flash with all the hard shadows left in. (274)

This is part of the counter map that *Dispatches* offers us, and it's not one you can pin on your wall. In the words of James Gleick, this is the kind of map that "mirrors a universe that is . . . scabrous, not smooth" (94). At times the "language" of the map almost is like the Soldier's Prayer, not the standard one "printed on a plastic-coated card by the Defense Department," but the "Standard Revised, impossible to convey because it got translated outside of language, into chaos . . ." (60).

Subjected to a Dali meltdown, conventional time also fails to survive Herr's contour flying. In his own words, "I was leaking time" (277). "It became possible to take a journey first and then make your departure" (68). In fact he arrives in Vietnam long after he got there—on page 177. Herr underscores a cyclical vortex on more than one occasion. "There was," he says, "the terrible possibility that a search for information there could become so exhausting that the exhaustion itself became the information" (68). And of fighting the VC, "it was us looking for him looking for us looking for him, war on a Cracker Jack box, repeated to diminishing returns" (64). Everywhere, Herr denies himself the comfort of fixed-wing, linear flight. Early in the book he says, "It started out sound and straight but it formed a cone as it progressed, because the more you moved the more you saw, the more you saw the more besides death and mutilation you risked, and the more you risked of that the more you would have to let go of one day as a 'survivor' " (7).

A second analogy has to do with where Herr spent his time in Vietnam. He eschewed the light of civilization in the official press clubs of the major cities; he stepped outside, way outside, into the tangled geography of Vietnam and his imagination. Herr was afraid of the dark, but he knew that if he was to "report" this war, that is where he had to spend his time. He knew that "hiding under the fact-figure crossfire there was a secret history, and not a lot of people felt like running in there to bring it out" (51). Herr didn't feel like it either, but he did it. And he did it by refusing to use what James William Gibson both figuratively and literally means by "the old trails" (11), which led only to the destruction of serious intellectual and artistic inquiry, just as the literal trails ominously ensured the likelihood of ambushes, Bouncing Betties, and assorted booby traps.

Like the Long Range Reconnaissance Patrols (known acronymically as LURPS) that spent many days at a time observing the enemy in the darkness of the far reaches of nowhere, so Herr's LURP book pushes itself and the reader off the old trails and away from the artificially cleared landing zones of convention. *Dispatches* avoids the blunder of giving cover to the guerrillas; instead, it explores the cover. The book is a deep-recon probe (without fire support) into murky questions about who we are and how we know. Herr replaces the language-fixing, laundered narrative of old-trail realism and conventional journalism with a camera dropped in the bush, where it catches the weird, secret subtext of the war (224) and its "smaller, darker pockets" (205).

Someone once said that in Vietnam a grunt learned to live in the bush; a LURP learned to *be* a bush, so thoroughly did he cut himself off and meld with his surroundings. Herr's book is a bush. No Vietnam book so completely follows the eight parallels between bush fighting and writing as Herr's. From being an "underground," "night-time," paradigm-breaking, "scrounging" operation to turning the reader's "claymores" around, *Dispatches* is different in kind, not degree, from most of the war's fighting and writing. It is not so much about the Vietnam War as, in frightening ways, it is about the war. In both form and content, *Dispatches* is serpentine, unpredictable, chaotic, and hot—as different from conventional war stories as the "purple haze" and tortured notes of Jimi Hendrix's "Star-Spangled Banner" are different from the surfboards and happy harmonies of the Beach Boys.

Both Herr and the LURPS realized that rather than throw the book at the enemy (which America did, with both its technological arsenal and its "language fix"), they needed to throw the book away. It was obsolete—"Pentagon" pegs in amorphous holes. Conventional writing was as inappropriate as conventional fighting. It makes no sense to set up ambushes, as it were, or to go out on sweeps and search and destroy missions when the enemy has in fact already tunneled beneath your base camp, shining your boots by day, satchel-charging you by night.

Late in *Dispatches* (which appropriately occurs earlier in his Vietnam sojourn than previous parts of the book), a grisly experience provides us with another analogy of Herr's search for a new map: "They were bulldozing a junction into Route 22 near Tay Ninh and the old Iron Triangle when the plows ran into some kind of VC cemetery. The bones started flying up out of the ground and forming piles beside the furrows, like one of those films from the concentration camps running backward" (267). Herr's "film" runs backward. Like Marlow, he travels back in time to the debris of his first immersion. Both men needed to make a decision regarding what portion of their former idealistic selves needed to be exhumed from the dark center of their consciousness. Appropriately, Herr uses the term "triage" frequently. Obviously he is fascinated by the concept. Like a doctor sifting through battlefield casualties, deciding who will have to be left to die and whom he will attempt to save, Herr sifts through language and epistemology, deciding which fictions of the American consciousness need to be saved by deconstruction. Like the city of Hue, which, according to what may be the most important sentence in *Dispatches*, "had been composed seemingly of destruction and debris" (259), Herr's book is composed of the fallout of a shattered epistemology.[3] And frankly, not much survives Herr's triage; what's left is

---

3. This idea of composition from decomposition is a motif that "crops" up in the books of several Vietnam War writers. Already noted is Stephen Wright's *Meditations in Green*. In *Del Corso's Gallery* Philip Caputo says of a journalist by the name of Harry Bolton that he "followed wars the way a migrant worker follows harvests" (37). But as with Stephen Wright, the motif is particularly insistent in the work of Herr and Tim O'Brien. We've already seen that Herr uses the word "furrows," which one can readily free-associate with farming, John Deere tractors, New Holland implements, fresh milk, and double-yolked eggs—all of which Herr puts in the context of mass slaughter. This same bizarre contextualization occurs in O'Brien's *Going After Cacciato*, where the title character earnestly fishes for walleyes in the putrid water of bomb craters. All of these composition/decomposition motifs point to one thing: the construction of new fictions often involves the self-conscious destructive revision of old fictions, just as the Vietnam War forced destructive revisions of conventional journalistic credos.

the same sobering, humbling truth discovered by Marlow—namely, that there is a horrible heart of darkness within the soul of all mankind. Herr expresses this in the famous concluding line of his literary journal: "Vietnam Vietnam Vietnam, we've all been there" (278). Just as Marlow realizes that all of Europe went into the making of Kurtz, so Herr discovered that all of America went into the making of the Vietnam quagmire.

In a sense, it was only by not corresponding in the conventional sense that Herr became a correspondent—the premier radical one of the war. Herr's book is an archaeological dig that seeks correspondences between the historical strata of American consciousness. Herr finds them, and the *all* of "we've all been there" serves to take out of isolation the most recent stratum, namely, the war itself and those who found themselves physically in it. By taking his time, Herr discovered time in a much broader, more meaningful sense. To paraphrase and ruin the end of Yeats' poem "The Second Coming," Herr was able to see that America was self-vexed to nightmare by a rocking "Captain America Complex" (Robert Jewett). In his slow time Herr has seen the almost imperceptible movements of the rough beast, its hour come round at last, as it slouches towards Vietnam to be born, once again.

In Herr's words, Vietnam was the place where America's "mythic tracks intersected" (19). Thus, when Herr dates the beginning of the war, he goes way back:

> Mission intellectuals like 1954 [when the Vietminh captured Dien Bien Phu] as the reference date; if you saw as far back as War II and the Japanese occupation you were practically a historical visionary. "Realists" said that it began for us in 1961, and the common run of Mission flack insisted on 1965, post-Tonkin Resolution, as though all the killing that had gone before wasn't really war. Anyway, you couldn't use standard methods to date the doom; might as well say that Vietnam was where the Trail of Tears was headed all along, the turnaround point where it would touch and come back to form a containing perimeter; might just as well lay it on the proto-Gringos who found the New England woods too raw and empty for their peace and filled them up with their own imported devils. (51)

Finally, as he nears the end of his book, Herr underscores the correspondences between the American mythos and the war: "there's been nothing happening there [Vietnam] that hadn't already existed here, coiled up and waiting, back in the World" (268).

The admission that "we've all been there" is Herr's third step, the most disturbing step of the book; for it asserts that Herr's irony is inclusive, not selective. His archaeological dig discovers an entrenched, coiled complicity much too democratically pervasive for comfort. Thus, when he says that you were responsible for what you saw (not just did) in Vietnam (20), he is acknowledging that Americans, including the reporters and photographers, were entangled in a script written long before the beast arrived in Vietnam.

Herr's confession of self and collective guilt may well have had its genesis in yet another analogy, the collage of Davies, a flipped-out door gunner "scrounger" that Herr met in Vietnam. As in *Meditations in Green*, the collage here[4] acts as an artistic analogue for *Dispatches* in that it sees around America's fictive consciousness and thereby also sees the incoherent coherence within the officially unrecognized chaos. Scrapping the Newtonian linear order that we brought with us to Vietnam, Davies' collage is a hip spatial emblem of cultural phenomenology, a nonlinear equation that lumps together grotesque "coefficients." Herr says "years of media glut had made certain connections difficult" (223). Davies' collage is a microcosm of Herr's book in that it does make these difficult connections, connections which all the Major Hollys and Henry Kissingers would no doubt consider junk. And, again, they'd be right. Nonetheless, this junk is often a courageous, self-deprecating expression of Herr's and America's complicity. Among the collage's startling juxtapositions: a created-in-Hollywood Ronald Reagan and the narcotic cannabis; the procreative genitalia of machismo and the destruction of bombs; Cardinal Spellman and a Huey gunship; patriotism and money; the myth of the warrior hero and hog butchering; the beautiful ugliness of "one large, long figure that began at the bottom with shiny leather boots and rouged knees and ascended in a microskirt, bare breasts, graceful shoulders and a long neck, topped by the burned, blackened face of a dead Vietnamese woman" (187).

4. For additional discussion of the role of collages as artistic analogues in Vietnam War literature, see John Clark Pratt, quoted in Timothy Lomperis' book *Reading the Wind: The Literature of the Vietnam War*, 90f.

Obviously these seemingly disparate correlations are testimony that a whole lot more than containing Communism was going on in Vietnam. Herr engages in no self-righteous posturing; indeed, he admits more than one wishes to the alluring correlation of eroticism and violence, like being in a firefight and "undressing a girl for the first time" (144), or intensely hating and loving the war, almost simultaneously (66). One feels uncomfortable with Herr's oxymoronic connections. But that's the whole point: the mythic die that stamped America's Vietnam into existence is so deeply rooted in what man loves to loathe that it is very hard to part with.

If the content of Davies' collage reveals a great deal about the counterepistemology of Herr's cultural phenomenology, so too does its placement within *Dispatches*. First of all, as I've said, it appears in a book which itself is a collage of colliding memories and free associations as he crisscrosses Vietnam in the omnipresent oxymoronic "saver-destroyed, provider-waster, right hand-left hand" collective meta-chopper (7). Second, it appears in the middle of a frenzied collage-like section called "Illumination Rounds." In it, in the space of twenty-one pages, "dipping where [we're] sure he would rise," Herr rapidly fires off sixteen vignettes that seemingly do not correspond with each other. The reader feels as if he were caught in an L-shaped ambush. This section would likely make writers of straight history squirm, because it offers them no kernel, no hook, no linear progression, no angle—actually, far too many angles. But as Thomas Myers has said, these vignettes

> bring momentarily darkened history into view. As the fading suggestion of each image hangs in the textual air, he launches a new one to bring the reader closer to the historian's problem of focusing on and correlating within individual imagination the plenitude of suggestions, of dealing aesthetically with the nonstop accumulation of quick glimpses and possible correspondences. (163)

Myers' point is well taken. However, he does seem to position Herr in the ethnographic realist mode. That is, he implies that Herr's way of writing is a *means* or a tactic to remedy "the historian's problem." More likely, it is a strategy, not a tactic. Herr doesn't react to "contact," he initiates it. Like the hit-and-run operations of the VC, his vignettes are designed to harass the master narrative that America tried to inscribe on Vietnam. This is why Davies' collage is the heart of *Dispatches*. As a collage within a collage within a collage, it aggressively undermines the wishfulfilling linear power of narrative. Thus, for Herr, the historian's problem isn't a problem at all. Instead it is an asset that takes him to a more revelatory epistemological track. Relinquishing Webb's "basketballs," he learns to see in the dark. The only real problem, Herr believes, is the assumption that an understood confusion is unacceptable. Those who deluded themselves and the American public with the narrative consolations of a confused understanding drove him into "mad, helpless rages" (154).

These consolations were offered like placebos to the gullible throughout the war. But nothing enraged Herr more than the reassuring doubletalk that characterized the Khe Sanh fiasco. Rewriting a time-tested narrative, General Westmoreland declared that Khe Sanh was " 'a Dien Bien Phu in reverse' " (173). In so declaring, he not only inscribed a narrative, but also turned it into a victorious one. Running for more than eighty pages, the "Khe Sanh" chapter of *Dispatches* seems to have broken Herr's ethnographic realist back. Immediately following it he begins the cultural phenomenology of "Illumination Rounds." Responding to the military's narrativitis, he envelopes his "map," like "a glow bring[ing] out a haze," with the apparent chaos of Davies' collage. In doing so, he urges us to stop looking for easy exits from the war, and to stop banging our heads on the painted doors we forget we painted. The war is too metastasized in American culture to allow an "early out."

One final correlation in the collage needs to be looked at, for it not only brings us back to America's love of maps; it also goes a long way toward summing up what Herr discovered in his struggles as a cultural phenomenologist. In one part of the collage Davies has superimposed a reversed Vietnam over a map of California, the shape of which resembles a mirrored Vietnam. Rather than continuing the mistake of seeing Vietnam in our own image, this cartographical countergesture would have us see our image in our own Vietnam, an "East-West interface, a California corridor cut and bought and burned deep into Asia" (45). It would have us demystify the most recent progenitor of the mythic die: the fiction-making capital of the world—Hollywood—the repository of the male, frontier mythology, forever "facing west," as Richard Drinnon puts it, making "movies," defoliating and sanitizing whatever gets in the way.

To paraphrase David Eason, Davies' gesture would have us admit the disorienting truth that in America's trillion-dollar Vietnam movie, we all were actors, not audience. This is the spectral, hazy opening that Herr would have us develop the courage and humility to walk through.

Tim O'Brien's Understood Confusion

The old epistemology that equated human beliefs with cosmic reality is now a minority report. . . . We haven't yet quite figured out
how to live with what we know, and we don't know what a curious
piece of knowledge it is—part jewel, part bombshell.

—Walter Truett Anderson

Unlike Stephen Wright and Michael Herr, Tim O'Brien has made a
literary career of the Vietnam War. Whereas Wright and Herr each
wrote one brilliantly disturbing book about the experience, O'Brien
has written five, three of which place Vietnam at center stage. That
Vietnam is his permanent "haze" brought out by a "glow" is reflected
in the following series of statements stretching over a period of fourteen years. At the 1978 Vietnam Writers Conference at Macalester
College, in St. Paul, Minnesota, O'Brien, consistently the most inter-
rogating and epistemological of the war's writers, voiced two fears—
that America would forget the Vietnam War too quickly or remember
it too simplistically. In 1981, O'Brien did a special piece for A. D.
Horne's book, *The Wounded Generation* (1981), in which he says:

And here at home, weren't the shrinks and scriptwriters and politicians telling us, at least by implication, that we *ought* to be seeking social and psychological readjustment? Heal the wounds, pick up the pieces. Well, we've done it. By and large we've succeeded. And that's the problem. We've adjusted too well. . . . We've all adjusted. The whole country. And I fear that we are back where we started. I wish we were more troubled. (205, 207)

In 1991, in a seminar of mine called "Images of War in American Literature," he sobered my students—most of whom I suspect were secretly high on America's "success" in the Gulf War—by telling them that this latest war proved that we were back where we started. Vietnam never happened. History and memory had been airbrushed out of existence. The "He," not the "I," of Graves' poem was running the show again, and in charge of the public memory.

As Graves' "I," O'Brien has spent a great deal of his prime time in the last quarter of a century troubling over America's infinite capacity to chimerically adjust to, simplistically remember, and quickly forget a war that inconveniently challenged this country's righteous, positivistic paradigm. Likely, this is true for all wars—even "The Good War," which Studs Terkel wisely decorated with quotation marks. Speaking about that war, Paul Fussell says that because America knows so little about its real tragedies and ironies, "as experience . . . the suffering was wasted." "America has not yet understood what the Second World War was like and has thus been unable to use such understanding to re-interpret and redefine the national reality and to arrive at something like public maturity" (268).

It seems to me that part of public maturity would involve processing the messiness of war, which Fussell painfully details. I mean the real messiness of bodies scattered in minute fragments across cratered wastelands—like Curt Lemon in O'Brien's *The Things They Carried*, reduced to bits of hamburger in the jungle foliage, or Kiowa, mortally wounded, almost inextricably sinking into the sucking ooze of the shit field along the flooding banks of the Song Tra Bong River. Hollywood, the arbiter of American epistemology, has its own self-imposed law prohibiting the showing of this kind of battle scene, which leads Fussell to his claim that "the twentieth-century age of publicity and euphemism" (269) has created a "pap-fed mass public, [unable] to face unpleasant facts" (270). When the facts do become unpleasant, something less disturbing is "dubbed in"—sometimes literally. To cite but one example, this happens whenever the networks air *Good Morning Vietnam*. On a primary level the film is about how Armed Forces Radio censored unpleasant facts and bad news during the Vietnam War. Exemplary of extreme irony, the network showings dub an already "dubbed" film by rendering "goddamn" as "gow dern" or "gosh darn," "ass" as "rear," and "fucking" as "freaking." This is merely a tiny example of how the guardians of American culture sanitize war and encourage simplistic remembering: "Pick up the pieces"—quickly, before anyone identifies the hamburger with Curt Lemon.

Fussell is wrong about one thing, however: we can't just blame a sentimental society of nonwarriors or venal Hollywood for the lack of understanding. To a great extent the warriors themselves have often been the ones who've passed out the pap—the prechewed baby food. Many of us have eaten it, to be sure, but they are the ones who reassembled hamburger into tough, realist novels of survival and camaraderie. They "G-Ied" their Vietnam experiences by picking up everything that moves and painting everything that doesn't. Stephen Wright's Major Holly would be pleased, for they learned their boot camp lessons very well. Unfortunately, they applied them to their writing about the war, and this results in simplistic remembering.

Several times in *Going After Cacciato*, O'Brien juxtaposes the messiness of Vietnam with the tidy, geometrically sound houses that Paul Berlin's father builds back in Iowa. Berlin (the narrator) and O'Brien have nothing against well-built houses; they simply feel the profound disjunction between those carpentered houses (with floor plans replete with 45- and 90-degree angles, squares, rectangles, isosceles triangles, and reassuring perpendicular relationships) and what was happening to their eroding epistemology in "America's longest war." Somewhat less gently, I suspect, O'Brien juxtaposes the messiness with Berlin's Iowa neighbor, Mrs. Stone. Her obsession with order and control is analogous to the habit of hungering for facts, cleaning up the messes, raging for the destruction of the phantom COSVN, and, in general, denying the world we really live in. Berlin thinks about her while dialing home from Vietnam.

> She was nuts, that Mrs. Stone. Something to ask his father about: Was the old lady still out there in winter, using her broom to sweep away the snow, even in blizzards, sweeping and sweeping, and in the autumn was she still sweeping leaves from her yard, and in summer was she sweeping away the dandelion fuzz? Sure! He'd get his father to talk about her. Something fun and cheerful. The time old Mrs. Stone was out there in the rain, sweeping the water off her lawn as fast as it fell, all day long, sweeping it out to the gutter and then sweeping it up the street, but how the street was at a slight angle so that the rainwater kept flowing back down on her, and, Lord, how Mrs. Stone was out there until midnight, ankle-deep, trying to beat gravity with her broom. (192)

Principal among the writers who use a "compost" rather than a broom, who make things of the dirt and refuse rather than sweep it away, O'Brien permits the messy interlopers in the backyards of our Protestant, sanitized paradigms to do their jobs: coalesce, infect, and break down. In so doing he deters the irresistible tide that sweeps Americans back and forth from crude forgetting to crude remembering. From his memoir, *If I Die in a Combat Zone* (1969), to his *Going After Cacciato* (1975), to his *The Things They Carried* (1990), O'Brien has sought to make us a more imaginative nation. He has done this by manifesting in his fiction the sentiments of the novelist Carlos Fuentes, Mexico's great interrogator of the paralysis in the human-cultures paradigm: "Art will not reflect *more* reality unless it creates *another* reality" (68). In a letter written to me in 1989, O'Brien echoed Fuentes when he expressed his belief that the novelist must "create new *kinds* of knowledge, new *kinds* of reality," as opposed to rehashing the formulas of realism, which have been around long enough to be perceived as representations of a God-made prototype.

The problem with this prototype, as O'Brien has reminded me several times, both publicly and privately, is its addiction to facts. Emulating gravity-defying Mrs. Stone, many fighter-writers use facts to overcome or deny the eroding epistemology. In the face of a crisis of knowledge, they unconsciously try to achieve a veneer of authenticity with clean, hard-edged facts about their Vietnam experiences. But

93

instead of alleviating the crisis, this approach only exacerbates it; it reinforces the limited "reality" of the shadows cast on the wall of Plato's cave. Instead of discovering that the shadows are shadows and then reinterpreting human reality on the basis of the discovery, it confidently provides quantitative, factual descriptions of the shadows. This takes us back to John Del Vecchio's claim that his book is real because he "had the maps" to guide his writing. A happy citizen of Plato's cave, Del Vecchio doesn't see that by "scrounging" about in the limits of human knowledge, one can discover the possibility of another reality.

In Vietnam, soldiers discovered (or should have discovered) two sets of shadows. First, the myth of the righteous warrior making the world safe for democracy turned out to be a tautological reflection of a national lie. Second, the assumption that America could make sense of and impose its will on Vietnam with a Western Positivist strategy turned out to be a reflection of cultural arrogance. What does one do with these deconstructions of epistemological certitude? They often seem to be forgotten or overruled by "default positions" in the literature of the war. As the psychologist Arthur Egendorf says, there are two ways of not drowning in deep water: "You can refuse to go in, or you can learn how to swim." You can get wet, or you can "brag about staying dry" (70). One can see a lot of the latter in the literature of the Vietnam War.

Tim O'Brien, however, is one of the war's best swimmers. Not that he's unafraid of the water. Discovering all of a sudden that one's feet don't touch the bottom is always frightening. One senses a good deal of O'Brien's fright in chapter 39 of *Cacciato*, where he catalogs an epistemological collapse. Page after page, he writes an anxious litany of everything the soldiers no longer knew:

> Not knowing the language, they did not know the people. They did not know what the people loved or respected or feared or hated. . . . They did not know false smiles from true smiles. . . . Not knowing the people, they did not know friends from enemies. . . . He didn't know who was right, or what was right. . . . [H]e didn't know what speeches to believe. . . . [H]e did not know where truth lay. . . . He just didn't know if the war was right or wrong. And who did? Who really *knew*? . . . They did not know even the simple things. . . . They did not know good from evil. (309–21)

94

But, as Walter Truett Anderson said earlier, discovering that your feet don't touch bottom can be experienced as a "bombshell" and as a "jewel" that can turn "enormous uncertainties" into "vast possibilities" (xii). The responsible fighter-writer doesn't leave the enormous uncertainties at Saigon's Ton Son Nhut airport; both the bombshell and the jewel need to be taken home. If Remarque's Paul Bäumer begins his postwar memories of "The Great War" with the civilized world in pieces, then Stephen Wright begins his of the Vietnam War with the hallucinatory attrition of geometry, and Michael Herr, with "hundred channel panic" feeding back through his prose years later. In his turn, O'Brien begins with the awareness of Doc Peret's supreme piece of critical analysis of the military's pins and maps: "No fucking tail, no fucking donkey" (131). The problematical status of the donkey and its tail points to a world in which substance is so elusive and unreliable that there may be nothing to cast even a shadow.

In other words, the starting point for O'Brien, as well as Wright and Herr, is the admission that what they knew of reality before war was nothing more than a publicly-agreed-upon fiction—a communally embraced shadow. That communal shadow was quickly blasted by war. Language itself seemed to stop casting shadows. There seemed to be an entropic void between word and object. O'Brien relates this very experience in his memoir. Trying to imagine a girl's face back home, he can't get beyond the point of merely seeing the four letters "F.A.C.E." printed out before him. Hemingway's Frederick Henry (*A Farewell to Arms*) may have scornfully rejected abstract nouns like "honor" and "glory," but O'Brien was losing contact even with concrete nouns.

There are three kinds of reactions to the encounter with the public lies unmasked by war. For most Americans and most Vietnam writers, the reaction is that of Robinson Crusoe: you admit you're shipwrecked, but then you compulsively try to make your new home just like the old one, by putting up comforting calendars, walls, and fences to guard fences guarding fences—so that you can forget that you ever were shipwrecked. Egendorf says that in order to protect your identity from the crisis of knowledge, you ". . . convince yourself that your persona—the concoction of stratagems [Crusoe's fences], life stories, and lessons you've drawn from all that has happened—

is the real thing. You must ignore the fact that you put it all together or else the conviction will drain away. So you play the act, [and] forget who wrote the play . . ." (159). And with that forgetting (a devilish habit, as I have already called it), you're back to the solipsism of Baritz's "enabling ignorance," where Crusoe's fences keep out the vertiginous truth of the public game you're playing, and where Doc Peret's filters are nowhere to be seen. Once again, "A Euclidean narrative produces a Euclidean understanding of a Euclidean world" (Stoicheff, 95).

The second kind of reaction is marked by long-term disillusionment. Instead of being viewed as an onerous impediment to authenticity, illusion is unconsciously treated as a source of meaning and purpose that is now in pieces. Nihilistic apathy is the result; one is shipwrecked because one is shipwrecked; the bombshell is a bombshell—nothing more; enormous uncertainties are enormous uncertainties; "scrounging" is not viewed as an option.

The third kind of reaction is economically labeled in Keats' two words—"negative capability," which he describes as a state of mind ". . . when man is capable of being in uncertainties, Mysteries, doubts, without any irritable reaching after fact & reason." As we will see, no Vietnam War writer has more advantageously worked through the ramifications of negative capability or his shipwrecked status than O'Brien. No one is as adept as he at navigating between the bombshell and the jewel. Not that he is unaware of the Crusoe mentality among fighters and writers. Near the end of his tour, he served under a Crusoe. He writes about him in *If I Die*—a Major Callicles, his battalion executive officer. (Why is it that the worst "Crusoes" always seem to be majors?) Mrs. Stone to the bitter end, Callicles simply refuses to let the experience of Vietnam reveal the shipwrecked nature of the whole enterprise. Surrounded by degradation and wholesale death, he obsessively and maniacally tries to eradicate the four deadly sins: moustaches, prostitution, pot, and sideburns. He reminds me of a *New Yorker* cartoon from years back, in which a sardonic employee working the Complaint Department window tells an irate customer "The whole world's going to hell and you're upset because the light on your waffle iron doesn't go on!?"—or words to that effect.

The placement of this chapter—just before the book's final four pages where O'Brien leaves Vietnam—has the effect of pointing an ironic finger back on his own rather "Calliclesian" central project in the preceding pages: searching throughout history, literature, philosophy, and theology for anything that will validate him as a soldier, anything that will dovetail his Vietnam experience with the past. It's a broad search pattern; he seeks analogues in Homer, Socrates, Plato, Aristotle, Horace, Melville, Frost, Eliot, Pound, Auden, Hemingway, Heller, and Tillich, to name some.

But the search fails to pay off. This failure is summed up in O'Brien's reaction to Horace's famous "Dulce et decorum est pro patria mori." He calls it "an epitaph for the insane" (174). Like Wilfred Owen, he reveals the "old lie" "in this whole game." But as Thomas Myers says in one of his superb attic-cleaning moments, "O'Brien's historical victory lies in his defeat before the feet of myth" (82). The Callicles chapter, ironically named "Courage Is a Certain Kind of Preserving," is strategically placed to culminate O'Brien's defeat/victory, which would lead to the great negative/capability of *Cacciato* and *Carried*. The character of Callicles—supposedly the quintessence of a World-War-II kind of professional soldier—totally deflates the myth of the noble warrior. Like his namesake in Plato's dialogue *Gorgias*, Callicles is rendered ludicrous because of his epistemological certainty and his obsession with a paradigmatic, Crusoe myth he would preserve at all costs. It's easier to shave moustaches than to raise wrecked ships. The chapter also deflates the myth of just wars when the news is released about what was perhaps the greatest blow ever to the "Captain America Complex": the massacre at My Lai 4.

Actually, O'Brien doesn't just point an ironic finger back on his memoir; the very first chapter, "Days," points a finger forward. Thus, the book is bracketed by that rare self-directed irony. Stressing the purposelessness, literal aimlessness, and monotony of the grunt's experience, this chapter cuts off all access to the validation of an epic journey. Sampling some of O'Brien's observations, we read "No targets, nothing to aim at and kill. Aimlessly, just shooting to shoot. It had been going on like this for weeks" (16–17). "Things happened, things came to an end. There was no sense of developing drama" (17). "No reason to hurry, no reason to move. The day would be

97

yesterday. Village would lead to village, and our feet would hurt, and we would do the things we did, and the day would end" (19). Caught between his own bracketing fingers, O'Brien's quest for mythic validation results in the antiepiphany of the memoir's final sentence: "It's impossible to go home barefoot" (205). So much for the war's facts. But this failure to achieve epiphany—as Myers agrees—is a victory. Because from now on, rather than trying to find meaningful placement within the prescriptive, received myths of the past, he will, like Fuentes, aggressively seek to create alternative spaces in the evershifting nexus of memory and imagination.

In *Cacciato* we can learn a great deal about O'Brien the artist if we examine several of his characters, particularly Paul Berlin, Cacciato himself, and the medic, Doc Peret. Much has been written about the Berlin-O'Brien link, so I'll just reiterate that, like Berlin's mental journey to Paris while on guard duty, O'Brien's book is like an observation-post enterprise in which past, present, and future, idea and fact, flight and engagement, movement and stasis are all interwoven in a collage of memory and imagination.

It may seem demeaning to O'Brien to compare him to Cacciato, whom Doc Peret describes as a "guy who missed Mongolian idiocy by the breadth of a genetic hair" (21), and by Harold Murphy as being "dumb as a month-old oyster fart" (14). Obviously neither of these characterizations describes Tim O'Brien. But there's something about Cacciato's moral and epistemological audacity that aligns him with his creator. Just as Cacciato imagines and acts on an alternative to the slaughter and insanity of the war, so O'Brien imagines and acts on a wonderfully contrapuntal, polyphonic alternative to the traditional war novels of people like James Webb and John Del Vecchio, both of whom continue to believe in war as a crucible in which men are validated.

Furthermore, just as Cacciato is described as being "curiously unfinished" (21), so O'Brien is an ever-changing, dynamic writer as he moves from *If I Die* to *Cacciato* to *Carried*. Of course we laugh at Cacciato when he fishes for walleyes in the putrid water of bomb craters; we laugh at his "sophisticated" tackle—an aerosal deodorant can for a bobber and a safety pin for a hook. But this is simply Cacciato's symbolic insistence, shared by O'Brien, that there is life after empiricism and after the factual nomenclatures so obsessively and repeatedly recalled in most Vietnam books. There is the reality of the imagination. There is the truth of fiction—if it is recognized as fiction. This is a difficult idea to swallow, particularly in the West, where we can actually observe the paradigm shift to realism as we watch the meaning of "fiction" change from the purely neutral, medieval sense of kneading dough or clay to a highly charged contemporary sense of anything *feigned*.

In *Cacciato*, O'Brien creates a character caught up in the reality-versus-fiction paradigm. Even as Paul Berlin extends Cacciato's imaginative act of stepping out of the war and "actually" follows him to Paris, he and his pursuing squad are arrested in Tehran, Iran. Eventually they are interrogated by a positivist *Savak* colonel, who has no patience with the phrase "truth of fiction." He is willing to accept reality or fiction, but not Berlin's hybrid: in a pleading, yet demanding tone, one can infer, he says, "Now tell me that this . . . this mission, this so-called *mission* . . . tell me it is fiction. Tell me it is a made-up story" (276).

It is the Doc Peret-O'Brien link that best reveals O'Brien's philosophical and artistic concerns, as well as his development as an ever more radical writer. Doc reveals O'Brien's growing preoccupation not with what we saw in Vietnam, but, more radically, how we saw it and through which culturally implanted mediation. (O'Brien once stated in a letter: "The issue of 'how we know' is so central to my work that it would take a whole book to properly address it." In *Carried*, he says, "I want to tell you why this book is written the way it is" [203].) As I have stated, Peret is O'Brien's radical epistemologist. In perhaps the most significant passage in all of Vietnam War writing (and therefore worthy of reiteration), we read of Doc:

> He was right, too, that observation requires inward-looking, a study of the very machinery of observation—the mirrors and filters and wiring and circuits of the observing instrument. Insight, vision. What you remember is determined by what you see, and what you see depends on what you remember. A cycle, Doc had said. A cycle that has to be broken. (247–48)

He adds that we must make a "fierce concentration on the process itself" (248). Without that ferocity of attentiveness we're prone to mistaking unrecognized "defaults" for common sense. He learns this lesson—quite painfully, one imagines—as a boy. Intrigued by a large air conditioner his father has just purchased, he takes it completely apart, looking for the box that has all the stored cold air in it. Of course, he doesn't find it. Even though he says "And I still tell him . . . if he'd just let me alone I'd have found that damn—" (177), this strikes me as an ongoing family in-joke, the anger and disappointment dulled by the passage of time. Likely he now understands that in defiance of common sense, the air conditioner makes cold air with heat, just as O'Brien will tell us in "How to Tell a True War Story" that fiction makes truth, and just as Anderson insists that a bombshell can be a jewel. If we simply look for the box containing the Vietnam War ("just the facts, ma'm"), we end up with disassembled fragments of the war's surface.

Heeding Doc Peret's advice regarding looking at ourselves, Tim O'Brien is a tragicomic Hamlet cum Don Quixote cum Pirandello. Conscious of the fact that we unconsciously live in a defaulted literary world, he knows that he not only reads, but is *read*. He knows that he not only writes but is written. Arguably, the F.A.C.E. episode of *If I Die* first started leading O'Brien to this moral and aesthetic posture. Also arguably, the "They-did-not-know" chapter of *Cacciato* is the second step. We can infer, precisely because of the multitude of things they did not know, that there is one more thing that O'Brien himself doesn't know, and this is what happily sets him apart as a writer who understands his confusion. I speak of not knowing or accepting the hardened distinction between content and form, between events and the "concoction of stratagems" for perceiving those events, between object and subject, between object and lens, and, finally, between fact and fiction. The task O'Brien seems to have assigned himself in *Cacciato*, and even more so in *Carried*, is to see himself metafictionally seeing himself as writer, like Berlin seeing himself outside a labyrinthine tunnel while looking at himself—future to the past—through a periscope inside the tunnel. Berlin (and O'Brien himself) tries to step outside his boots, unlike Billy Boy Wadkins, who tries to put his foot-occupied boot back on his amputated leg.

I first delivered my thoughts on *The Things They Carried* in a paper at an academic conference. Because the book had not yet been published, and because most people had at best read only the essay-like "The Things They Carried" and "How to Tell a True War Story," both serialized in *Esquire*, my panel was designated "Nonfiction Representations of the Vietnam War." Even though I recognize that session titles often are somewhat arbitrary because of the scores of papers being delivered, this designation, at the very least, suggests that we try to put our foot-occupied boot back on; it implies that we're confident of the difference between nonfiction and fiction, that despite what Vietnam should have taught us, we steadfastly remain a genre-sure country. I maintain that this genre-sureness got us into Vietnam in the first place. Not recognizing the powerful influence of our positivistic paradigm, we simply didn't—and still don't—see our "essays" as fictions. In its righteous, anti-Communist paradigm, it wasn't just that America "forgot who wrote the play"; it forgot that it was acting.

This has resulted in a lot of wasted time and suffering and has prevented us from studying the machinery of observation itself. O'Brien is not at all sure of the strength of the walls erected by clear-cut genre distinctions. A number of the separately published chapters of *Carried* dissolve the wall separating essay and fiction. We often find ourselves in what O'Brien calls the "no-man's land between" the two, "between Cleveland Heights and deep jungle." We "come up on the edge of something" and "swirl back and forth across the border" (115).

In the chapter entitled "On the Rainy River," O'Brien provides a geographical analogue for his genre-straddling. After receiving his draft notice in Worthington, Minnesota, he flees north to the Rainy River, located on the U.S.–Canada border. While staying at the Tip Top Lodge, for six days he vacillates in anguish—cowardice or bravery, Canada or Vietnam? On one occasion he literally vacillates while fishing on the river. He says " . . . at some point we must've passed into Canadian waters, across that dotted line between two different worlds" (58). Because the "dotted line" at times is on the river itself, it's not that O'Brien is on a body of water that neatly separates two land masses; instead, carried by currents and eddies on a snaking river in the middle of a wilderness dominated by "great sweeps of pine and birch and sumac" (50), he can't tell which country he is in.

This geographical ambiguity directly corresponds to his liminal uncertainty. He understands that the old man running the boat has taken him to a wavering edge. But he says " . . . what embarrasses me . . . and always will, is the paralysis that took my heart. A moral freeze. I couldn't decide, I couldn't act . . ." (59). Even when he does decide on one shore or the other, he inverts what for many people would be a common-sense interpretation of fleeing to or not fleeing to Canada: "I would not swim away from my hometown and my country and my life. I would not be brave" (59). "I passed through towns with familiar names, through the pine forests and down to the prairie, and then to Vietnam. . . . I was a coward. I went to the war" (63).

It is precisely because of his liminal uncertainty that the author could not make *Carried* memoir or fiction, essay or story, autobiography or metafiction, no more than he knew while on the Rainy River if he was in the United States or Canada. The line separating genres is at most a dotted, wavering one. Like "Nuoc Vietnam," it's watery. Moving from *If I Die*, to *Cacciato*, to *Carried*, O'Brien seems to have developed an ever-finer appreciation of how fact and fiction interpenetrate one another, and how the ultimate fiction is the belief that fiction is one thing, reality quite another. In fact, I'm certain O'Brien would agree with me that because America was blinded to the fictionality of its "essay," it was, as I've suggested, self-lured into the Vietnam quagmire. In its genre cockiness, America was epistemologically crude and naive. O'Brien's genius is that in the face of his wonderment he has found a way to take advantage of "a new understanding of [his] confusion." More sophisticated epistemologically than most Vietnam writers, O'Brien is able to pilot the reader through the shifting contours, eddies, and currents of the imagination.

I once had the opportunity to witness O'Brien's piloting skills, and the reaction of people who are suddenly made aware that they're on the Rainy River, not terra firma. It's akin to lifting the mostly empty milk carton that you think is full. Shortly before *Carried* was released, O'Brien visited another one of my classes, this one solely on the Vietnam War. Also in attendance were the book editors from the *Saint Paul Pioneer Press* and the *Minneapolis Star Tribune*. O'Brien started out by saying that he would like to tell us something about himself back in 1968. He admitted that what he was about to tell us embarrassed him, and that he had never told it to anyone before. He told us he was from Worthington, Minnesota, and that he had graduated from Macalester College in St. Paul. He related that when he was drafted in the summer of 1968, he worked in the Armour meatpacking plant, where his job was to remove blood clots from the necks of dead pigs. He mentioned that it was impossible to get rid of the pig smell and that he therefore had trouble getting dates. He talked at length about his misgivings regarding the morality of the war. During this narration—and with increasing enthusiasm as it went on for some twenty minutes—one of the reviewers was writing down all this fantastically good copy. Eventually, O'Brien told us that because of his opposition to the war, in desperation he headed north—to the Tip Top Lodge on the Rainy River. He ended his "confession" by saying, "I passed through towns with familiar names, through the pine forests and down to the prairie, and then to Vietnam. . . . I was a coward. I went to war."

There was an electric silence in the classroom. Everyone was spellbound by the personal details O'Brien had shared with them and by his honesty. Whereupon he said, "There are two things you should know about what I just told you: all of it is made up, and all of it is absolutely true." When the reviewer from one of the papers heard "All of it is made up," he immediately began feverishly erasing everything he had written down. After all, he couldn't print lies. There's got to be more than a mere dotted line between fiction and reality. He simply could not allow "all made up" and "all absolutely true" to coexist. You have to be on one side of the border or the other. I think he left the classroom that day in "a new confusion of his understanding."

Moving chronologically through O'Brien's three Vietnam books, we can notice the metamorphosis of a solid line to a dotted line to one that sometimes disappears altogether. In part we witness these metamorphoses in the changing role of O'Brien himself in his three books. We first find him playing himself, in memoir fashion. Then he creates the artistic-minded O'Brien persona in Paul Berlin. Finally, in an act of aesthetic and epistemological audacity, he creates a character named Tim O'Brien who isn't Tim O'Brien. A "barber" by day, he's a "VC sapper" by night. In an interview with Michael Coffey, O'Brien states: "All along, I knew I wanted to have a book in which my name, Tim, appeared even though Tim would not be me; that's all I knew" (61). Why would O'Brien want to do this? And what are the implications of such a decision?

To answer the second question first, O'Brien seems to accept as his starting point the fictionality of *all* thought. Furthermore, the more conscious we are of fictionality, the greater the likelihood of grasping some small part of reality. Facts, by themselves, so he tells us in *Cacciato*, simply don't add up to anything much. In the Coffey interview, he says ". . . of the whole time I spent there [Vietnam] I remember maybe a week's worth of stuff" (60).

Regarding the first question, if all thought is fictional, that includes the way we think of ourselves. To think of the real self as a single, fixed, objective, finished entity is as inappropriate as stopping the motion of a mobile, then believing we haven't radically altered its essence. Bluntly, Tim is not Tim because as author he is not God. Not ever able to know his self directly and absolutely, he too must be mediated by a persona. Another plausible explanation for O'Brien's decision to make Tim not Tim is that, fortunately, he couldn't forget Doc Peret's fifteen-year-old advice. As a work of metafiction, *Carried* looks at the components of the "observing instrument" itself. Simply translated, the metaphor means we must study the way all reality is mediated by how, where, and when we look at it. O'Brien knows that reality is accessible *only* through mediation. That being the case, he spurns the Western paradigm of Manichaean dualism, which convinces most of the people most of the time that they can tell the difference between reality and fiction. *Carried*, on the other hand, seems to be written on the assumption that there is only conscious and unconscious fiction, conscious and unconscious paradigms. Thus, O'Brien has fictional status both as character and author. So, instead of pretending to be real, O'Brien really pretends. As such, his metafiction writes a contract between reader and fiction that is similar to the one between audience and the theatre that operates with the being of real pretense, as opposed to the pretense of being real (see drama chapter).

At the very least, O'Brien would agree with the "fictional" Father in Pirandello's *Six Characters in Search of an Author*. To the "real" people, the actors on the stage getting ready for a rehearsal of a different Pirandello play, he says that he and the rest of his fictional family, abandoned by their author before the book was finished, are "less real perhaps, but truer" (217). Eventually, the "real" Manager of the acting company sarcastically says to the Father, ". . . you'll be saying next that you, with this comedy of yours that you brought here to act, are truer and more real than I am." To which the Father replies, "But of course; without doubt!" (266). Along similar lines, Linda, a character in "The Lives of the Dead" (*Carried*), describes death as "being inside a book that nobody's reading" (273).

In his discussion of Pirandello's theatre, Robert Brustein distinguishes between "apparent realities and real appearances" (315). In conversations and interviews, O'Brien, in turn, has frequently distinguished between "happening truth" and "story truth." Clearly, both he and Pirandello see a greater power of veracity in the "real appearances," because in these moments the author is at least conscious of the mask he is wearing. As Stanley Fish says in *Self-Consuming Artifacts*, "I would rather have an acknowledged and controlled subjectivity than an objectivity which is finally an illusion" (407). On the other hand, the reason the artifice of realism reveals so little of import is that it is blind to its own mask and to the filters that ensure the continuation of that blindness.

O'Brien is part of a long tradition of healthful ontological and epistemological wonderment. This is the key to dovetailing his Vietnam experiences with the past that he hadn't yet discovered in his memoir. His failure ("bombshell") there created the opportunities ("jewel") in his next two works. There's nothing new about the tradition of wonderment. It's as old as Heraclitus, Socrates, Erasmus, Montaigne, and Cervantes. It's as new as Kosinski, Borges, Fuentes, and Morrison. The problem is that throughout Western civilization the new ground that these skeptics uncover keeps getting paved over by the dominant cultural paradigm, which is built on the denial that masks are being worn, except perhaps at masquerades. In fact, nothing is more pervasive in America's Western orientation than the belief that its masks are naked.

To write his ultimate Vietnam War fiction, O'Brien happily donned the mask, and made Tim not Tim. For only in so doing could he underscore the fictional nature of all human perception. But whereas

Pirandello saw this as a galling human limitation, a comic tragedy, O'Brien sees it as an opportunity to turn story viewed as reality (the very reason we got into and waged the Vietnam War) into a reality viewed as story—a tragicomedy. Only in so doing, O'Brien implies in his novel, can we save ourselves from the disjunction between an absurd, inscrutable flux of events, such as those of the war, and America's realist paradigm. Like David Eason's "cultural phenomenologist," and like the "I" of Graves' poem, O'Brien begins with a recognition of "broken images." But because he does so, and because he mistrusts and questions the relevance and factuality of these broken images, he's at an advantage: instead of being limited to naive "quick and dull" faith in public reality, he is skeptically "slow and sharp" as he investigates *alternative* realities.

Robert Scholes would call O'Brien a "fabulator." "Fabulation," he writes, ". . . means not a turning away from reality, but an attempt to find more subtle correspondences between the reality which is fiction and the fiction which is reality" (8). As a fabulator, O'Brien persistently undermines belief and the suspension of disbelief in order to reach for more complex truths. In "How to Tell" he writes, "In many cases a true war story cannot be believed" (79). Thus, he inverts the conventional author-reader contract, the whole goal of which is credulity. The problem with belief, says Scholes, is that "it is in a sense the enemy of truth, because it stifles inquiry" (7). There is no danger of O'Brien stifling inquiry. Confronting head-on the story-reading paradigm, which demands credibility, *Carried* blows fuses from beginning to end, where the novel's last word underscores O'Brien's real subject: not war, but "story." Any reader insistent upon the story-telling conventions that create the illusion of reality will stub his toe and bang his head a lot in this novel. Concerned that we believe the reality of story rather than, conventionally, the story of reality, O'Brien places the wiring and circuits front and center, which is reminiscent of the various means used by Brecht to ensure *Verfremdungseffekt* in the theatre. This literally enables O'Brien to incite reader inquiry in response to the way the author revises, edits, even contradicts fiction's conventions. He takes us into a polyvocal world in which we can finally see the limitations of our univocal reading paradigm, where we merely remember what we see and see what we remember.

Carried is an ongoing series of "correspondences between the reality which is fiction and the fiction which is reality." Part of O'Brien's polyvocal world consists of what might be called his *Roshomon* gambit. Just as we settle into believing a certain account of an event, O'Brien offers a different version. For example, in "Speaking of Courage," we find out that Norman Bowker is suffering from extreme guilt because he lost his nerve and failed to save his buddy, Kiowa. In "Notes" we learn that he even commits suicide. But in "In the Field" we discover that an unnamed soldier is responsible for Kiowa's death. He turned on his flashlight that night so he could show Kiowa a picture of his girlfriend. This enabled the enemy to bracket the platoon's position with mortars, one of which killed Kiowa. Then in the same story the commanding officer takes full responsibility because he had had the platoon set up camp in an indefensible shit field. Another character, Azar, confesses that if he had kept his mouth shut Kiowa would probably still be alive. In "Field Trip," the O'Brien character returns to Vietnam twenty years later, and in a ritual of expiation for his guilt he walks back into that same shit field where Kiowa was killed. There is not even a hint in any of these other versions that Bowker was in any way responsible.

Another device designed to blow fuses and stub toes is O'Brien's practice of juxtaposing what we perceive as story and essay. Sometimes he does this as he moves from one chapter to the next. This is jarring in itself. There are other times, however, where he does it within a given story. In the title story, for example, O'Brien switches back and forth numerous times from narrative to lists of equipment soldiers carried (and the weight of each piece). He complicates this correspondence, however, by switching within switches several times. Similarly, in "How to Tell a True War Story," he repeatedly switches back and forth between giving advice on how to tell war stories (essay) and actually narrating stories. And again, he complicates by switching within switches.

In two chapters, "Notes" and "Good Form," O'Brien takes us out of any apparent narrative frame and talks about himself as a writer. And in the latter "story" he bluntly tells us that almost everything we've read up to this point (page 201)—including the death-of-Kiowa sequence—is made up, perhaps especially those moments

107

where he insists "this is true." Then he tells us what really happened, part of which is that he did not kill a thin Vietnamese soldier he earlier admitted—over and over—to having killed. But then he writes "Even *that* story is made up" (203). It turns out he did kill the soldier after all. Finally, he concludes the chapter by answering his daughter's (she too is made up; O'Brien has no children, although he has been asked in interviews how his daughter is doing) question "did you ever kill anybody?" O'Brien's answer is both "Of course not" and "Yes" (204). One of the stories told in "How to Tell a True War Story" concerns the extremely close friendship between Rat Kiley and Curt Lemon. One day they pull the pin on a smoke grenade and play catch. Lemon steps on a booby-trapped 105 round and is obliterated. But at the end of "How to Tell," O'Brien says "No Lemon, no Rat Kiley. . . . It's all made up. Every goddamn detail. . . . None of it happened. *None* of it. And even if it did happen, it didn't happen in the mountains, it happened in this little village on the Batangan Peninsula, and it was raining like crazy, and one night a guy named Stink Harris woke up screaming with a leech on his tongue" (91). Those familiar with the works of O'Brien know that this last occurrence actually takes place in another novel—on the first page of *Going After Cacciato*! So O'Brien confronts us with an exit-less, Borgesian "Library of Babel": we leave one book, only to enter another. But at least we know—O'Brien makes sure of that—that we're in a book. *Carried*, then, is filled with instances of Eastlake's opening *pas vrai* in *The Bamboo Bed*. O'Brien repeatedly turns the reader's "claymore" around and booby-traps the narrative "trails."

To those who still cling to the conventional author-reader contract, who can't let go of the paradigm of realism, these fabulations are irksome. Even some of the reviewers who praised the book found them to be annoying blemishes. The attitude among many readers could be summed up as follows: "I *know* he's making things up, but why does he have to *tell* me?" But O'Brien's sense of self-irony seems to have anticipated this reaction to *The Things They Carried*, and it reminds me of how on more than one occasion in his plays Pirandello denigratingly alludes to the plays of Pirandello. Speaking of Rat Kiley, a fabulator within fabulations, O'Brien writes "Rat had a reputation for exaggeration and overstatement, a compulsion to rev up the facts, and for most of us it was normal procedure to discount sixty or seventy percent of anything he had to say. . . . For Rat Kiley, I think, facts were formed by sensation, not the other way around, and when you listened to one of his stories, you'd find yourself performing rapid calculations in your head, subtracting superlatives, figuring the square root of an absolute and then multiplying by maybe" (101).

Furthermore, another character, Mitchell Sanders, in effect tells O'Brien to stop this fabulation stuff. He wants O'Brien to respect the U.S.-Canadian border, as it were. In "The Sweetheart of the Song Tra Bong," he repeatedly objects to and interrupts the bizarre female heart of darkness story being told by Rat Kiley. Kiley does it all wrong: he keeps breaking the spell, first by interrupting his narrative with editorials, then by admitting that he has no finish and that his information, finally, is thirdhand. Sanders, the prototypical American designated reader, wants the conventions of the "realistic" war narrative to be scrupulously abided by so that he won't see the mere conventions for what they are—filters and circuits. He prefers Peeping-Tom, fourth-wall-removed drama. He demands that the storyteller "get the hell out of the way." Getting in the way ". . . was a bad habit, Mitchell Sanders said, because all that matters is the raw material, [O'Brien's week's worth of facts] the stuff itself, and you can't clutter it up with your own half-baked commentary" (116). [Fully baked by O'Brien himself throughout this "essayed" novel.] Sanders continues by saying that this commentary "just breaks the spell. It destroys the magic" (116). When he discovers that Kiley has no ending, a fully exasperated Sanders says, "You can't do that. . . . Jesus Christ, it's against the *rules*. . . . Against human *nature*. . . . I mean, you got certain obligations" (122). Sanders insists on keeping the seeing mechanism, or medium, transparent so as to avoid seeing theatre as theatre. In the words of E. H. Gombrich, he doesn't want to "watch himself having an illusion" (Iser, 132). He wants the contingencies edited out so that he can experience the seductive pleasures of an unimpeded mimetic pull down "mine-swept" narrative "trails." Unfortunately for all the Mitchell Sanders, O'Brien's stories are *about* those very trails. And he constantly gets in Mitchell's way, thereby frustrating his desire to find the "box" that authentically contains the Vietnam War.

109

O'Brien has told me that "How to Tell a True War Story" is the pivotal "story" in his evolution from a memoirist to a writer of fabulation. Of the twenty-two chapters in the book, this one is the most explicit and insistent about the necessary Dali meltdown of fact and fiction, essay and fabulation. This is what distinguishes *Cacciato* from *Carried*. In the former work there is more of an interplay between fact and fiction, there's no meltdown. O'Brien's three Vietnam books steadily move toward meltdown. Applying O'Brien's words from another context, I think he felt that he had been "held prisoner by the facts" (Lomperis, 46) in *If I Die*. Furthermore, I think the reason he did this series of fabulations in *Carried* is that, in *Cacciato*, he was still working with a Newtonian, Cartesian epistemology, which posits an objective reality "out there" independent of human observation. Thus, in *Cacciato*, O'Brien didn't "get in the way" as much as he would in *Carried*. In *Cacciato*, he was pushing ethnographic realism to the nth degree, and he did it masterfully. But his newest work doesn't push; instead, it is pulled into a vortex of cultural phenomenology, twilight-zone memoir. As O'Brien says in "How to Tell a True War Story," "The vapors suck you in. You can't tell where you are, or why you're there, and the only certainty is absolute ambiguity" (88). Thus, unlike *Cacciato*, *Carried* no longer holds up city limits signs as it moves from past to present, from memory to imagination, from reality to fantasy. Plot, and the continuity and coherence it assumes, is now possible only in "spots in time."

I think O'Brien would be comfortable with the language of Joan Didion in *The White Album*: "I was meant to know the plot but all I know is what I saw: flash pictures in variable sequence . . . not a movie but a cutting room experience" (13). One thing O'Brien does have is a consistent cast of characters—people such as Rat Kiley, Mitchell Sanders, Kiowa, Ted Lavender, Curt Lemon, and Jimmy Cross—but it's a repertory company that O'Brien places in an unstable Heraclitian world. Like the VC, his characters appear, disappear, and reappear again and again. Their costumes and roles largely remain consistent, but performance times vary wildly, as O'Brien swirls back and forth across the borders of time and space.

In *Cacciato*, on the other hand, characters and genres remain distinct, with rather precise job descriptions. The epistemological inventory is shaken but still intact. Not so in *Carried*, particularly not in the seminal "How to Tell a True War Story." The title itself certainly promises an article, not a work of fiction. Yet, as O'Brien has told me, "it is most definitely fiction, not an essay." "How to Tell" is indeed a story, but one that masquerades as an essay, just as "Sweetheart of the Song Tra Bong" is an essay masquerading as a story. Coincidentally, O'Brien informs me, "The Lives of the Dead" is reminiscent of Hawthorne's "The Wives of the Dead," a shadowy tale about the reality of dreams and the dreams of reality. The chapter "Notes" is a story masquerading as a long endnote, which it originally was when published separately as part of the short story "Speaking of Courage." In *Carried*, the story is "mistakenly" placed two-thirds of the way through the "novel." No Vietnam author more fully subscribes to my sixth guerrilla fighting and writing parallel: O'Brien is the war's great rule-breaker. No one is less attached to the conventional job description of an MOS. Listen to his own description of *Carried*: "It's not quite a collection of stories, not quite a novel, not quite a fictionalized memoir. In fact it's a combination of all these—it's being billed as a 'work of fiction,' which is a little tricky, but still accurate."

"How to Tell a True War Story" begins with the words "This is true." ("The Lives of the Dead" begins with "But this, too, is true.") In fact, forms of the word "true" recur approximately four dozen times in this relatively short story. O'Brien and characters such as Rat Kiley and Mitchell Sanders desperately want their audiences to believe in the truth of their stories. O'Brien is obsessed, as are all vets, with telling the truth. Rather than invest his energy in tracing the surface phenomenology of war (the conventional MOS), he invests it in the phenomenology of fiction—particularly in the difference between America's unacknowledged fiction and his own don't-ever-forget-that-this-is-fiction variety. I say this despite the fact that the title and lead-off story, "The Things They Carried," reads like a *Soldier of Fortune* catalog of military surplus, enticingly detailed, both for the gun nut and for the Vietnam authenticity nut. It's a feast of factual ballast. In devilish fashion, O'Brien even gives us precise weights of the things they carried: this item weighs 6.3 pounds, this one 3.5, this one 8.4, and so on. But all of this spurious "precision" is O'Brien's fabrication. His book's metafictional honesty makes a mockery of the reader's easy beliefs when confronted by the veneer of authenticity. One could justifiably accuse O'Brien of playing games here and elsewhere. He is. But they are games with a serious purpose: he has to show the reader how easily he can be set up so that he can then deconstruct his own "confusion of . . . understanding." In a sense, the real subject of *Carried* is the things the reader carries, particularly his appetite for belief.

Thus, as we near the end of "How to Tell," O'Brien startles the "ethnographic realist" in all of us by saying, "in a true war story nothing much is ever absolutely true" (88). O'Brien feels dishonest about telling the truth, at least as Crusoe perceives truth, and that's because the old epistemological inventory no longer is intact, or as he says in the chapter "Spin," "the whole world gets rearranged" (39). "The memory-traffic feeds into a rotary up in your head, where it goes in circles for a while, then pretty soon imagination flows in and the traffic merges and shoots off down a thousand different streets. As a writer, all you can do is pick a street and go for the ride . . ." (38).

I think that the most important new item in O'Brien's epistemological inventory is that "truths are contradictory" (87): "A thing may happen and be a total lie; another thing may not happen and be truer than the truth" (89) "Story-truth is truer sometimes than happening-truth" (203). Sniping at America's "Cuckoo's Nest" sensibility, O'Brien echoes "Chief" Bromden's words of "cultural phenomenology" in Ken Kesey's novel, which attacks the country's bias against invention: "it's the truth even if it didn't happen" (13).

O'Brien again echoes the superior value of fiction truth in "The Lives of the Dead," where the narrator, as a nine-year-old, sees the World War II movie *The Man Who Never Was*. The Allies put an officer's uniform on a corpse, plant fake documents in his pockets, and dump his body into the sea. The currents carry him to the Nazis, and the course of the war is at least somewhat changed. Conceivably an analogue for O'Brien's book, the movie shows how a non-existent person with fictionalized papers alters reality. Lies create a new truth.

There are more contradictory truths: to be courageous requires cowardice. One experiences "falling higher and higher." Hate is love. The linguistic synapse now requires intransitive verbs to carry direct objects. As we've seen, the narrator is at once O'Brien and not O'Brien. "A true war story is never about war" (91). A moral war story has an "absolute and uncompromising allegiance to obscenity and evil" (76). "Order blends into chaos, love into hate, ugliness into beauty, law into anarchy, civility into savagery" (88). In order to present the cool truth you need to heat it up. Silence is deafening and cacophonous. Characters become third persons in their own narratives. A Vietcong glee club and the Haiphong Boys Choir exist in the jungle because they're not there. Sanders has to lie in order to tell the truth. Feelings create facts, not the other way around. O'Brien himself tells a tall tale by writing an article—echoes of Borges. Like Heller's chaplain in *Catch-22*, O'Brien squarely faces the possibility that "he never really *had* thought he had seen what he now thought he once did think he had seen, that his impression now that he once had thought so was merely the *illusion* of an illusion" (276). Again, the language of cultural phenomenology, beckoning us to adapt our critical thinking to it. *Carried* is as different from conventional Vietnam War writing as Brontë's "eccentric" *Wuthering Heights* is different from Austen's "central" *Pride and Prejudice*, to use a distinction made by Carlos Fuentes. The distinction is as old as Western civilization. Thus, O'Brien is to James Webb and John Del Vecchio what Brontë is to Austen, Blake to John Locke, the gothic to the Enlightenment, Hieronymous Bosch to his contemporaries, Heraclitus to Parmenides (again to borrow from Fuentes). O'Brien is inside the tree line, sniping at the onerous assumptions of America's central culture in the clearing.

O'Brien is a good sniper, because, like the VC, he travels light. This probably will strike some readers as a peculiar, even preposterous, claim. Many view O'Brien as the war's most polished (too polished, some would say), intellectual, and even academic fighter-writer. That view has some merit; after all, he does seem to have a lot of stuff up in his "attic." Yes and no. Yes, he does have a goodly number of literary conventions up there; but more often than not, they serve an ironic purpose. Every time he pulls a *"Pas vrai"* on the reader, he's displaying those conventions the way one would pick up a lava lamp, and, chuckling, wonder what it was still doing there, or why it was ever saved at all. In other words, O'Brien uses the attic stuff as a tool for encouraging the reader to travel lighter by deconstructing his own epistemological keepsakes.

Other times, as when Linda compares death to being in a book no one is reading, O'Brien empties the attic. This melts away the illusion of ontological security; but it also frees the writer and reader from a lot of clutter. It opens up a lot of territory for exploration. Crusoe's fences keep danger out, but at the same time they stifle him within. They restrict him to minute, factual descriptions of shadows. Crusoe takes comfort in knowing a great deal about very little—his compound. O'Brien takes a kind of dreadful delight in knowing very little about a great deal.

I began this chapter with the last lines of Graves' poem "In Broken Images." Let me conclude by quoting from a poem so consistent with O'Brien's way of thinking that he has it prominently affixed to a wall in his study where he writes. Another poem by Graves, it is called "The Devil's Advice to Storytellers." In it, Graves writes:

> Lest men suspect your tale to be untrue,
> . . . . .
> Do conscientiously what liars do—
> Born liars, not the lesser sort that raid
> The mouths of others for their stock-in-trade:
> . . . . .
> Nice contradiction between fact and fact
> Will make the whole read human and exact.

Graves' paradoxes run absolutely counter to what Paul Fussell calls the "positivistic pretensions of non-Celts and . . . [the] preposterous scientism of the twentieth century" (*The Great War and Modern Memory*, 206). Those same paradoxes get at the very heart of Tim O'Brien's negative capability.

114

Civilian Perspectives in Peter Straub's *Koko*

You saw at least as much violence outside the normal Milwaukee
tavern as in the average firefight; inside . . . you saw a bit more
—M. O. Dengler, *Koko*

Up to this point we've looked at three writers who spent a year "in
country." All three experienced combat—even the civilian "journalist" Herr. Peter Straub did not. So what's he doing in a book called
Fighting and Writing? How can a civilian possibly write about war?
How dare he claim that special privilege? To this day, many veterans
of the Vietnam War share the attitude that if you weren't there and
you weren't in combat, then you have no business (or ability) writing
about it. I myself have been told that I wasn't qualified to write this
book, because I'm only a Vietnam era veteran. Beyond the obvious
rejoinder that if one wrote only about personal experiences, one
would have very little to write about, it needs to be added that this
I-was-there-you-weren't attitude rests upon an unwitting hypocrisy:
most vets would agree that they hated their Vietnam experience, and
that they were, to one degree or another, disillusioned and trauma-

tized by it. Yet, many of these same vets often hoard those experiences in the safety deposit boxes of their trapped memories. I believe that what the psychologist says to Christian Starkmann in Philip Caputo's *Indian Country* (1987) applies to many vets, whether troubled by PTSD or not: "It's not like you're guarding some deep dark guilty secret. It's like you're guarding a treasure" (398), a line of thinking explored by William Broyles, Jr. in his notorious *Esquire* article, "Why Men Love War." Visits to the Vietnam Veterans Memorial have confirmed my suspicions that many vets love to hate Vietnam. If you weren't there, you can hate it, but you've earned neither the right to love to hate it nor to write about that loving hate. You're a mere Nam "gentile." Letting another onlooker in a faded fatigue jacket know you're a "gentile" will immediately end a conversation. However, provide a battalion and division number and you're guaranteed a conversational litany filled with olive drab place names, jargon, and acronyms. I don't wish to minimize the combatants' experiences in Vietnam; far from it. In fact, by isolating themselves as a kind of damned elect, and by cutting themselves off from the wider ramifications of the war, combatants minimize their experiences and thus remain in exile. They are "held prisoner by the facts of their own Vietnam experiences." The Vietnam vet, if anything, begins his or her writing task at a disadvantage that needs to be overcome. Put more kindly, perhaps it's a disadvantage that can be turned to their advantage.

The disadvantage exists because the Vietnam War was a time of very special, supercharged craziness; it was so utterly different from mowing lawns or sweeping dandelion fuzz from them that the temptation to stare repeatedly at one's personal Vietnam closeups is hard to resist. But when the vet does not transcend those closeups, he and his writing often endure the calcification of Lot's wife looking back on the burning cities of Sodom and Gomorrah. In his 1988 Vietnam novel *Koko*, Peter Straub runs no such risk; for, during the war he was doing such dangerous things as teaching prep school in Milwaukee, going to graduate school, and studying poetry in Ireland. Allegedly, this background should disqualify Straub from any possibility of writing an authentic Vietnam novel. Yet (or should I say "thus?"), *Koko* is possibly the most intensive, complex exploration of the war's imprint on the American psyche yet published, in part because it's written by a nonsoldier. *Koko* is, to modify the words of a minor character, like a CAT-scan seen from the outside and the inside (85). That is, it offers us "tomographic," multiple pictures and cross-sections of the national psyche before, during, and after a My Lai-like atrocity scene at a fictionalized village called Ia Thuc. Whereas most Vietnam writing stays "in country" for a year, *Koko* moves about from the 1950s to the 80s, from New York to Danang, Bangkok to Milwaukee, the United States to Honduras, from texts to subtexts, ever moving "backwards and forwards," as the novel's most persistent leitmotif puts it. The complex "scans" of the novel do more than any other book I know of to project the war's causes, legacies, and opportunities both for being overwhelmed by it and being healed from it.

Koko is essentially an elaborate play of the imagination within the framework of the whodunit genre. The "who" in this case is a character nicknamed Koko. Following the much-celebrated release of the Iran hostages, Koko goes on an apparently random killing spree in Singapore and Bangkok, shooting at least eight people, removing their eyes and ears with a cleaver, then placing in the victims' mouths a playing card with "Koko" written on it.

Upon the occasion of the dedication of the Vietnam Veterans Memorial in 1982, Beevers, Poole, Conor, and Pumo, members of an infantry platoon in 1968, stage a reunion in Washington, D.C. Beevers, the platoon's lieutenant, tells the others that he's sure another member of the platoon—Tim Underhill, now a crime novelist supposedly living in Singapore—is Koko. Three of the vets decide to go to Southeast Asia to stop the killings. However, in Bangkok they finally find Underhill and discover that he can't possibly be Koko. It turns out that Spitalny, another ex-platoon member, from Milwaukee, is Koko. Furthermore, they discover that the killings are not random. All of the victims were journalists who reported on the 1968 massacre committed by Beevers' platoon at Ia Thuc. The homicides are therefore likely acts of retribution against those who printed the story.

Finally, almost five hundred pages into the novel, we learn that yet another character from Milwaukee, M. O. Dengler, is Koko. It turns out that while on R & R in Bangkok, Dengler had mutilated Spitalny's body beyond recognition, switched dog tags, then used Underhill's name while pursuing a Boschean nightmare existence throughout Southeast Asia. After his killing binge abroad, he returns to the States, kills a wealthy yuppie at JFK, then a librarian where Pumo is doing research on the killings, then Pumo himself. Finally, before fleeing to Honduras, never to be heard from again, he lures most of the remaining platoon members to a dark, cave-like basement, cuts off one of Beevers' ears, stabs both Underhill and Poole in the side, and escapes from the police by wearing Underhill's clothes.

In and of itself, this is standard material for the genre of the "airport novel": a mysterious crime, several red herrings to throw us off the trail, and a solution which, like the purloined letter in Poe's story, was right in front of us all along, but our conventional investigative paradigm prevented us seeing it. But Straub parodies the genre self-reflexively to enrich it and indict America's ahistorical, simplistic, "dyslexic" reading of itself and the Vietnam War. On an obvious, literal level, Dengler is the "who" of the whodunit; but Straub treats him less as a solitary maniacal psychopath than as a vengeful victim of an entire systemic chain of exploitation within a dysfunctional culture populated by dysfunctional families. That systemic chain is Straub's purloined letter; as H. Rap Brown once put it, violence is endemic: "as American as apple pie." Even Dengler correctly assesses the endemic nature of violence, which, if anything trivializes the alleged specialness of the Vietnam War. That's why he tells members of the platoon that one saw more violence inside some Milwaukee taverns than in a firefight. Lest we think Dengler is exaggerating, we should remember that during the same time it took for 58,000 U.S. personnel to die in Vietnam, a much larger number of civilians were violently killed by handguns—here at home.

Working with a larger canvas than those used by most veteran writers, Straub's vision parallels Doris Lessing's anatomy of metastacized war and violence in her *Children of Violence* series. "She defines the locus of bellicosity," states the feminist critic Lynne Hanley, "not as a place, a field of battle, but as a habit of mind, a structure of feeling, a cultural predisposition" (7). Similarly, Straub, unlike most veteran writers, views Vietnam not as some kind of American "ur" experience, but as business as usual—exported. It was simply highlighted in the media so that everyone noticed—for a while; then most of America forgot and resumed its ahistorical reading while slipping in and out of semiconsciousness at 35,000 feet between JFK and Heathrow, or at zero feet between home and the office.

As a civilian-by-day, guerrilla-by-night writer, Straub would embrace Michael Herr's conclusion to *Dispatches*: "Vietnam Vietnam Vietnam, we've all been there" (278). But who really believes this? Who is willing to accept a whodunit novel in which Poole and Underhill admit that everyone in the platoon is Koko, that everyone hosts a devil within, a theme that pervades *Koko*? Arguably, *Koko* is 562 pages of rebuttal of those who refuse the culpability that accrues from the messiness of living in history. Poole's wife Judy is their representative. Early in the novel she tells him that "the past is in the past because that is where it belongs. Does that tell you anything?" (6) Indeed it does! About the Vietnam War, she simply states, "when it's over, it's over" (81), whether as a noble cause, as Ronald Reagan would have it, or as an aberrant loss, as George Bush would. It is through Maggie Lah, a richly drawn Asian character, that we see Straub's rebuttal explicitly realized. She insists on the novel's dominant theme: our beliefs and actions can be morally informed only if we are engaged in time that goes "backwards and forwards," a phrase repeated dozens of times in the novel. In a conversation with her lover, Tina Pumo, Maggie asks, "Do you think there is a real point where *then* stops and *now* begins?" And then: "Don't you know that down deep the things that happen to you never really *stop* happening to you?" (143). When Pumo asks her how she knows about the connection between Vietnam and the present, she says "*Everybody* knows about it, Tina. . . . Except a surprising number of middle-aged American men [in other words, the very guardians of the ahistorical culture], who really do believe that people can start fresh all over again, that the past dies and the future is a new beginning, and that these beliefs are moral" (143).

In *Koko*, the key to healing from the war is the simultaneity of travel "backwards and forwards." The really important word is "and." Some characters just go forward; some just go backward. Actually, neither of these character types goes anywhere. Like Stephen Wright's

Trips, they are either suspended in a meaningless present or frozen in an implacable past. Poole represents the first sort. *The Divided Man*, the title of one of Underhill's novels talked about in *Koko*, perfectly describes Poole. There is nothing to connect his past self to his present self. After Ia Thuc and the war, he just forgot it, denied it, and divided himself, or at least tried very hard. A killer of children in the war, he's a pediatrician in the present, treating pampered, healthy children of wealthy ahistorical parents. As Tim O'Brien might say of him, "[Poole] has adjusted too well. . . . I wish [he] were more troubled" (205, 207).

Beevers and Dengler represent the second sort. For Beevers, Vietnam was the last significant experience of his life, his "one golden godlike point," his "hot center" (499). In the present he's a lawyer just going through the motions—not very well, I might add. As the story begins, he gets fired. He's Straub's closet Chuck Norris, aching to return to the scene of glory where he had the orgasmic power (literally) of life and death as he killed thirty children with M-16 fire and burned Ia Thuc to the ground. Even Dengler, in rare moments when he's not engulfed by the past, recognizes that "Harry Beevers was the road backwards" (349).

Unfortunately for Dengler and his victims, those moments are much too rare. To explain this rarity, Straub takes us backward all the way to Dengler's horrible childhood. Using Dengler's father and foster mother as microcosmic Americans, Straub would have us understand that the Vietnam War and its bloody spillover in Singapore, Bangkok, and other places in the East was rooted in Dengler's hellfire Milwaukee home, that it was the inevitable result of the endemic violence rooted in the heritage of Puritan ethnocentric racism, Old Testament religiosity, zealous nationalism, and misogyny. Dengler is born to a Nicaraguan prostitute. Soon thereafter, his father, a hypocritical, racist John, kills her. Throughout his childhood he is repeatedly abused, beaten, sodomized, even locked up in the family's butcher shop meat freezer—all in the name of Christian discipline. His father was both a butcher and a fire-and-brimstone preacher. In naming his shop "Dengler's Lamb of God Butcher Shop," he clearly indicates that he often got the two callings mixed up. Obsessed with a parsimonious work ethic, his father beats into Dengler's head *"We waste no part of the animal."* He wasted no part of the Bible either, at least not the Old Testament, for he forces his son to read it "backwards and forwards." But, coming out of his mouth, the phrase doesn't mean harmonization of past and present; rather, it means regimented learning of proscriptive codes, endlessly repeated. In subzero weather he drags his son to street corners, bellowing out proscriptive demands for salvation or damnation while the child passes the hat.

Straub offers us an analogue for the way Dengler was "shaped" by his parents. For untold years his mother has obsessively duplicated identical kitsch artifacts. She fries purple marbles in Wesson oil (never butter—it burns) until they crack from the inside. Then she glues twentyfour of them to black cloth to form grape clusters, never with the slightest variation from one to another. Well, his parents were "successful" in their child-rearing; Dengler, like many nineteen-year-olds in the sixties, became "cracked" and "glued" to darkness. One of the novel's motifs confirms this. Koko (Dengler) often alludes to Handel's *Messiah*. His favorite line comes from the dark alto solo "He was Despised": "Man of sorrows and acquainted with grief." A cracked grape cluster, Dengler can imagine only a *Messiah* without a messiah. He is unable to balance the "shaking," "purifying," "breaking," and "dashing" "refiner's fire" with the joy of a child being born. He seems to be utterly unaware that the oratorio's opening recitative is "Comfort ye my People," which contains the line "her [Jerusalem's] iniquity is *pardoned*" [my emphasis].

Translated into Dengler's post-Vietnam behavior, *"We waste no part of the animal"* becomes *"I pardon no one who had any part of the Ia Thuc massacre."* Dengler does travel backward and forward, but only between the far distant and distant pasts. As Straub says, "what happened on the frozen banks of the Milwaukee River [his father's murder of his mother] never stopped happening for him, no matter how many times he killed in order to make it stop" (553). Notice that Straub doesn't say that what happened at Ia Thuc never stopped happening. As a nonveteran, Straub has the necessary distance to see a bigger picture. In that picture the Vietnam War is not seen as some sort of uniquely awful, monstrous destruction of American values. The war did not, as common wisdom has it (and I mean *common*), invert or betray American values. Instead, the war was the ultimate

121

manifestation of those "values," which are chronicled in Richard Drinnon's book *Facing West: The Metaphysics of Indian-Hating and Empire-Building* (1980), a book that essentially begins with the Pequot Massacre and ends with its more recent edition at My Lai. Straub reverses the prevailing attitude of teachers, critics, novelists, and psychologists regarding the war. According to that attitude, Vietnam engulfed us in darkness that now needs to be illuminated. Implicit in *Koko*, on the other hand, is the attitude that Vietnam was the light that should have illuminated the dark sub-text of American myth. From this point of view, the war was less a heart of darkness than a "heart of light," or a "heart of whiteness." Vietnam didn't ruin Dengler; *Milwaukee* did.

Milwaukee provided Dengler his basic training. This is where he was inculcated by simplistic, black-and-white notions of good and evil. Even more pathological than Wright's Major Holly or O'Brien's Lieutenant Callicles, he hunts his victims with as much fervor as Wisconsin's U.S. senator displayed in attempting to rid the country of evil Communists. Never escaping from the Old Testament, as it were, Dengler tries to undo or sweep away evil by pursuing a course of retribution rather than atonement. Already as a child, one of his favorite characters in his favorite book, *Babar the King*, is Hatchibombitar, "the street sweeper, a man of no ambition but to keep the streets clean . . . sweeping and sweeping away the filth" (503). So he is now the street sweeper, a role that entraps him as surely as he was locked up in his father's meat freezer.

Throughout *Koko* Straub uses images of caves to express the entrapment of his war vets in a kind of negative womb that procreates evil. The cave motif begins with the primary atrocity at Ia Thuc: the slaughter of the thirty children hidden in a cave. About this cave we read: "[it] folded and unfolded, branching apart like a maze. . . . It began to seem hopeless, they would never find the end of it: it seemed to have no end at all, but to twist back around in on itself. . . . The chamber was filled with a complex odor compounded of terror, blood, gunpowder, and some other odor Poole could identify only in negatives. It was not piss, it was not shit, it was not sweat or rot or fungus or even the reeking dew all animals exude when they are frightened unto death, but something beneath all these" (336–37).

122

Although all of Straub's vets have their sojourns within the "cave" of their war experiences, no one is more committed to the cave without exit than Dengler. His New York basement apartment is repeatedly described as a cave that incubates evil. For example, "Koko sat alone in his room, his cell, his egg, his cave. The light burned, and the egg the cell the cave caged all the light and reflected it from the wall. . . . Dead children clustered round him, crying out, and the others cried out from the walls" (502). Straub "couples," or parallels, this negative yonic imagery with the all-too-familiar phallic destructiveness of Vietnam War literature and testimonials: "Koko went into the cave and into the Devil's arsehole and there met the Lieutenant, Harry Beevers, his surfboard his shovel his weapon out before him, being fingered, being fluted, being shot—shooting. You want a piece of this? The Lieutenant with his cock sticking out and his eyes glowing" (503).

Straub completes his cave imagery with one of Koko's last acts, the stabbing of Underhill and Poole and mutilation of Beevers, in a basement within the cave-like Bowery Arcade on the edge of New York's Chinatown. We never see anything down there in this American Ia Thuc cave; it is pure darkness, disembodied voices, the touch and smell of blood flowing from Beevers, Poole, and Underhill. Connecting this "cave" to the one in Ia Thuc, Straub says, "Sometimes it sounded as if children were speaking or crying out a great distance away. These were the dead children painted on the walls. Again Poole knew that no matter what he might hear in this room he was alone with Koko, and the rest of the world was on the opposite side of a river no man could cross alive" (535).

Fortunately, here is where Poole is wrong. The river separating Vietnam and contemporary America can be crossed. This brings us to Straub's counterpart to caves—bridges. If caves imprison, bridges liberate. But in *Koko*, as with the Vietnam Veterans Memorial, the liberation isn't cheap. The bridge image doesn't provide a mere passive means of getting from A to B, from the memories of Vietnam to an unburdened present. Instead, it relates A and B, literally, in the sense of "carry back." Bridges enable Straub's vets—particularly Poole and Underhill—to transcend both the deadness of amnesia (Poole's pre-bridge life) and the crippling effects of trapped memories (Dengler). Bridges enable Poole and Underhill to remember in a way that heals.

123

Fighting and Writing

In his book *Healing from the War*, Arthur Egendorf traverses the very river that Poole initially thinks is uncrossable. Egendorf argues that we must utilize the pain of Vietnam: "The rarely spoken fact is that however painful they [responses to the war] are, these reactions also may serve as the occasion for men to evolve and update their ways of responding to life" (68). "The tendency among many veterans and the public," Egendorf goes on to say, "is to respond to talk of 'stress disorder' with the seemingly logical but mistaken idea that what veterans need is to reduce their level of stress. . . . which has the unfortunate effect of encouraging veterans to shrink from life. . . . Their horror, rage, guilt, and desperation may be genuine, the signs of a reemerging sensitivity. . . . For once a man grants himself the freedom [i.e., the bridge] to be appropriately upset by what he has seen and done, his reactions subside quite naturally, and he experiences himself as 'more himself' " (69). One final comment by Egendorf that parallels the experiences of Poole and Underhill: "The more amply we reach out to grasp our past [going backward], the more we can look on old pain gratefully, recognizing it as the instigator that provoked us into growing [going forward] to encompass it" (74). In other words, Poole had to grasp his past by descending into this one last "cave" in the Bowery Arcade. Rather than paralyzing him within the evil that was Vietnam, this descent is a ritualized Fortunate Fall. Instead of being a place of inherent evil, the cave becomes a bridge to a bridge.

Poole's initial turning point occurs while he searches for Underhill in Bangkok: "Poole walked beneath a highway overpass and eventually came to a bridge over a little stream. On the far bank was a hodgepodge village of cardboard boxes, nests of newspaper and trash. This warren smelled much worse than the compound of gasoline, excrement, smoke, and dying air that filled the rest of the city. To Poole's nose it stank of disease—it stank like an unclean wound. He stood on the quavery little bridge and peered into the paper slum. . . . A smudge of smoke curled up into the air from somewhere back in the litter of boxes, and a baby cried out" (264–65). Reflecting on the shocking contrast between his comfortable suburban practice and this scene of squalor, Poole experiences an epiphany—his bridge:

His pampered, luxurious practice also felt like a confining pit—[his cave of amnesia] . . . . Westerholm was an evasion of everything. . . . He could not stand finishing out his life in Westerholm. . . . Before Poole stepped off the bridge, he knew that his relationship to these matters had irrevocably changed. His inner compass had swung as if by itself. (265).

Next, Poole echoes Egendorf's sentiments and even some of his words: "He had decided really to be himself in relationship to his old life. . . . If really being himself put his old life at risk, the reality of his position made the risk bearable. He would let himself look in all directions"—backward and forward (266). Somewhat later, we read: "Eight hours earlier, Dr. Poole had crossed over a rickety bridge and felt himself coming into a new accommodation with his profession, with his marriage, above all with death. It was almost as if he had finally seen death with enough respect to understand it. He had stood before it with his spirit wide open, in a very undoctorly way" (304). Then, once again, Straub directly parallels Egendorf's argument: "The awe, the terror were necessary" (304)—his bombshell/jewel. Looking back on this experience much later, Poole reflects "his first moment of real awakening had come on the rickety bridge beside the cardboard shacks. That was where he had started to give things up" (405). So just what is Poole's bridge? It is his decision to spend the rest of his life being "appropriately upset." This will require him truly to connect his *backward* with his *forward*, his killing in Vietnam with his practice in the present. It will mean getting out of his "confining pit," where he "patted heads, gave shots, took throat cultures, comforted children who would never really have anything wrong with them, and calmed down those mothers who took every symptom for a major illness" (265). His practice doesn't connect him to his Vietnam experiences; instead it has had the effect of nullifying them, or at the very least, anesthetizing them. The idea for Poole's bridge comes from the crying Southeast Asian baby in Bangkok. He decides to spend the rest of his life being a store-front doctor. Crossing a bridge each day, "Michael Poole commutes to the Bronx [slums] every day, where he practices what he calls 'front-line medicine' " (560).

Front-line medicine not only establishes the link between Ia Thuc and the Bronx, it also reminds us that his new practice in the crime-ridden slums will involve risks—risks necessary for his healing. Straub underscores this very late in the novel when Underhill flashes back to Vietnam, where he is listening to jazz with a black platoon member, Spanky Burrage. The language used to describe Duke Ellington's rendition of the tune "Koko" utilizes (as opposed to merely "uses") the raw material of experience, whether it happens in Vietnam or on the streets, as a way of being "appropriately upset":

> It is a music of threat. . . . Long ominous notes on a baritone saxophone counterpoint blasts from trombones. A lurching, swaying, uneasy melody begins in the saxophone section. From the darkness two trombones whoop and shake, going *wa waaa wa waa* like human voices on the perimeter of speech. There are noises that jump right out of the speakers and come toward you like a crazy father in the middle of the night [which is precisely what happened to Dengler as a child]. The piano utters nightmarish chords which are half-submerged in the cacophony of the band. . . . [The] bass pads through the band like a burglar, like a sapper crawling through our perimeter. (558)

(Notice that "burglar" and "sapper" further bridge "the world" and Vietnam.) This is the artist utilizing what James Baldwin, in "Sonny's Blues," calls "the risk of ruin, destruction, madness, and death" (79) as building blocks of the imagination. Ellington neither turns away from the risk (as Poole has been doing for years) nor is engulfed by it in Dengler fashion.

Like Fuller's Neumann and Wright's Griffin, Poole will try to rebuild his life from the destruction left in the war's wake. Underhill elaborates on this strategy when he tells of Spanky playing a second version of "Koko," this one by the great Charlie Parker. Again, there are risks; we're told that there's an urgency to the music, that it is unsentimental, fierce, threatening, and tense. "Then,"

> An astonishing thing happens. When Parker reaches the bridge of the song, all that open-throated singing against threat is resolved in a dazzle of imaginative glory. . . . The urgency is engulfed in the grace of his thoughts . . . . What Charlie Parker does on the bridge . . . reminds me of Henry James's dream—the one I told Michael [Poole] about in the hospital. A figure battered at his bedroom door. Terrified, James held the door closed against the figure. Impendingness, threat. In his dream, James does

126

an extraordinary thing. He turns on his attacker and forces open the door [of his cave] in a burst of daring. The figure has already fled, is only a diminishing spot in the distance. It is a dream of elation and triumph, of glory. That was what we listened to in the dripping tent in the year 1968 in Vietnam. . . . we heard fear dissolved by mastery. (559)

On the final page of the novel, Underhill says, "I think of Charlie Parker leaning as if into an embrace into the conditions that surrounded him" (562), and he calls this a "complicated joy." It's an authentic joy because it's complicated, a word that means "folded together," as in backward and forward, Ia Thuc and the Bronx, theme and bridge, cave and opened door, destruction and creation.

The necessary integration of creation and destruction is reminiscent of a story told me by a woman whose brother had returned from Vietnam more than twenty years earlier, when she was still a child. He was sullen and prone to violent acts. She cited as an example the time he pulled off the arms, legs, and head of her favorite doll, then taped the arms where the legs should be, the legs where the arms should be, and the head on backward. To this day, the woman and her parents view this action as a fit of gratuitous violence committed by an understandably traumatized brother and son. It hasn't occurred to them that this act may have been a profoundly creative expression of destruction and madness. You see, this vet had been a medic in Vietnam. As such, he saw more than his share of boys in pieces. Quite likely he had many times come to Ardell's fundamental awareness in David Rabe's play *The Basic Training of Pavlo Hummel*: "We melt; we tear and rip apart. Membrane, baby. Cellophane. Ain't that some shit" (96). Once ripped apart, always ripped apart. All efforts to reattach the pieces, repeated in Sisyphean fashion, are futile. The clumsily, improperly reattached pieces of the doll might have been a richly disturbing expression of the futility and the real price of war. Thus, rather than being a gratuitous act mired in the "theme" of destruction, the doll episode may have been a complicating bridge that leads to healing.

Returning to Dengler, if we think of music (if not all art) as a balance between redundancy (theme) and new material (bridge), we have another way of understanding his tragic life: he's all theme and no bridge, no "variations." Interestingly, jazz musicians (in America, at any rate) universally use the word "release" instead of bridge. When I've asked "release from what?" the answers usually are "monotony," the "old stuff," and the "familiar part." Except in rare cases, however, where a tune has an AB structure, the release is not permanent; instead, it creates a permanent relationship with the theme. The result is a playful interplay between Apollonian, thematic order and Dionysian disregard for that order. The most exciting moments, then, occur during the last bar of the theme and the first bar of the release, the last bar of the release and the first bar of the theme. Lacking the creativeness engendered by this interplay, Dengler therefore removes pieces from people instead of dolls. Simply put, he's a victim of Vietnam War redundancy—*the* shortcoming of most Vietnam literature, which is addicted to the bridgeless theme of combat, destruction, and the tragic victimization of the soldier—set on autoreverse. Like Stephen Wright's Trips, Dengler views the world intensely but simplistically.

Poole, on the other hand, views the world complicatedly and extensively. He complicates his theme as a pediatrician by making Vietnam and Bangkok experiential spaces at one end of a bridge, not as caves without exit. Peter Straub, for his part, complicates his status as "civilian" writer with the tacit admission, "Vietnam Vietnam Vietnam, we've all been there," a fact Underhill and Poole subscribe to. The demon is within all of us. This is their bridge for Dengler's theme, and it connects them to their kin—Ishmael and Marlow, both of whom might well have "jammed" with Parker had they lived in his time.

This is part of Straub's rebuttal of the Judy Pooles of the world. Another part of the rebuttal takes the form of the novel's refusal to buy into a fiction that is particularly American—namely, the Platonic notion that the art of fiction imitates the life of facts. *Koko* is an extremely "authored" novel. Over and over, we see life imitating art in its pages. Straub clearly views imagination—as we will see below—not as a function that spices up or escapes reality but as the means to create it—Wallace Stevens' "supreme fiction." Like O'Brien, Straub is a "fabulator," to use Robert Scholes term. As "fabulation," *Koko* doesn't turn away from reality in escapist fashion. On the contrary, it "attempt[s] to find more subtle correspondences [i.e, bridges] between the reality which is fiction and the fiction which is reality" (8). Like O'Brien, Straub is concerned that we investigate both the reality of story and the story of reality. As Straub's fictional writer, Underhill especially understands this imperative. Knowing as he does that "We have only the shakiest hold on the central stories of our lives" (126), he also knows how imperative is the newly imagined material of the bridge.

Koko does show that the results of life imitating art can be disastrous—not, however, because the sequence is backward. No, the problem arises when characters, particularly Koko (or anyone going to war mistaking a country's fictions for God-generated truth), don't recognize art as art, but as an implacable truth that will not permit editing, revision, or variations. This offers us another way of viewing Dengler. Raised by a mother who fervently believes that "Imagination must be stopped. You're talking about imagination. You have to put an end to that. That's one thing I know" (473), Dengler eventually becomes a fixated cracked marble who eschews the freedom of the imagination in favor of dogma-fettered revelation and the call to sweep the filth off the streets. After Underhill tells Mrs. Dengler that her stepson had been "inventive" in Vietnam, she cuts in and objects: "You think backwards. . . . Oh my. *Backwards*. Inventive? You mean he made things up. Isn't that part of the original trouble?" (473).

As someone who goes only backward, Beevers is another character fettered by his certainty of a fact-fiction split. One of his motives for tracking down Koko is his plan to make lots of money with the "true" story of this crazed serial killer. Like O'Brien's *Savak* colonel in *Going After Cacciato*, he can entertain fiction or nonfiction, but any leaching of one into the other is unthinkable. Thus he tells Underhill "I want your agreement that you won't use any of this Koko material in a work of nonfiction. You can write all the fiction you want—I don't care about that. But I have to have the nonfiction rights to this. 'Sure,' Underhill said. 'I couldn't write nonfiction if I tried'" (340). Later he says, "I don't really know what a 'nonfiction novel' is" (554). Always implicit, and sometimes explicit, in Straub's novel is the question "who really *does* know?" Unlike Beevers, who thinks he knows, Underhill believes "imagination was everything" (304). In one of his three dialogues with himself, he says "I think I saw him [Koko]. I know I saw him. You imagined you saw him? It is the same thing" (125). Poole shares this awareness. Once, while in a cemetery, he sees his deceased child as a twenty-two-year-old man. At first he assumes he had hallucinated him: " 'I didn't see my son,' Poole began, and then his objections dried to powder in his mouth' " (431). "[H]e had authored him" (432), just as Underhill—so we read on the same page—had authored Milwaukee. The trick, as Wallace Stevens once put it, "is to believe in a fiction, which you know to be a fiction . . ." (163).

Stevens' statement would strike Beevers as nonsense. When he shares his research about Koko with the others in the platoon, four times he emphatically asserts "*Consider the facts*" (41–42). So it's not surprising that when Underhill tells about Beevers' eventual suicide, he says "[Beevers'] imagination had failed him. His illusions [regarding fact and fiction] were all the imagination he had—a ferocious poverty" (560). Maggie Lah also sees through Beevers' poverty. She tells Poole, "Your friend Harry Beevers can't act very well" (388). It simply never occurs to the shallow Beevers that he's on Shakespeare's world stage. He is a confirmed Prospero; it never occurs to him that his colonized island of facts not only destroys the world's Calabans, but himself as well. A confirmed Cartesian realist, Beevers is the victim of an unrecognized male fantasy, with no one left to take it out on but himself.

Koko does much more than merely present the arguments of characters regarding the interpenetration of fact and fiction: it *is* an interpenetration, an interlocking series of bridges "between the reality which is fiction and the fiction which is reality." First of all, Underhill is a writer of fiction within a fiction. Of course, there is nothing revolutionary about that. But Straub pushes the interpenetration to a Borgesian level. Underhill is not just a fictional character who writes; instead, his fictions "bleed" through Straub's novel and parallel his plot. Like Griffin's apartment walls in *Meditations in Green*, *Koko* is like a large palimpsest on which previous texts—literally subtexts—rise to the surface to multivocally mingle with others that previously arose, thereby altering the "master narrative" written by Straub. David Eason would call *Koko* a "multi-layered interrogation of communication" (52), a novel that "blurs traditional distinctions between fantasy and reality" (54). Always in the interrogative mode, *Koko* insists on a plurality of authoring and authority.

A case in point occurs when Pumo tells Maggie what happened to Beevers' platoon when it was trapped between a minefield and the NVA in Dragon Valley. His narrative begins conventionally, with Pumo in the first person and the use of quotation marks. However, the reader soon notices that some paragraphs begin but don't end with quotation marks, while others begin and end with them. The reliability of point of view thus gives way to a collage of disembodied voices. To further complicate our reading, these paragraphs are interspersed with italicized passages (Underwood's interpolations) in which Pumo is cast in the third person. Thus, instead of Dengler's obsession with a single, monovocal story, we have versions and variations that pollinate each other.

Some of Underhill's stories don't merely parallel the actions of the novel—they actually induce them. For example, "The Running Grunt" provided Dengler with a scenario in which he mutilates Spitalny and switches dog tags. This scenario, in turn, stems from a previous palimpsestic text, Underhill's first novel, *A Beast in View*. In it, another "running grunt" mutilates a different GI and switches dog tags. Furthermore, we gather that Dengler has read all of Underhill's fiction, including the story "Blue Rose" (about a serial killer who places a card with "blue roses" written on it in his victim's mouth), and the novels *The Divided Man* and *Into the Darkness*. Speaking of the latter, the narrator says, "Koko remembered buying that book because once in another life he had known the author and soon the book revolved and grew in his hands and became a book about himself" (343). To further complicate Straub's "complicated joy," "Blue Rose" is also one of his previous stories.

The palimpsest motif dominates *Koko*. Poole finds Strether, Henry James' character in *The Ambassadors*, bleeding into his life. Jan de Brunhof's Babar stories frequently infiltrate the novel, as do Wordsworth's *Prelude*, Büchner's *Woyzeck*, Conrad's *Lord Jim* and *Heart of Darkness*, Jane Austen's *Jane Eyre*, Kafka's *The Trial* and *The Metamorphosis*, and others. Internally, in Underhill's *The Divided Man*, the Sisyphean sleuth, Hal Esterhaz, follows an endless series of homicides, never getting any closer to solving the crimes. He too is an orphaned son of a fanatically religious butcher. Like Dengler's real mother, Rosita, Esterhaz is found as a child naked and muddy on the banks of a river in Monroe, Illinois, which we're told later is actually Dengler's Milwaukee. Like Dengler, Esterhaz was found trapped in a meat freezer, just as he is now trapped in an endless theme of crime "circling around and around the same cycle of chords" (320). Neither knows how to enrich "the same cycle of chords" with a bridge. *Into the Darkness* is an even more insistent reiteration of the Sisyphean sleuth theme.

Straub doesn't stop with literature; he extends the palimpsest to music on several occasions, most notably in the Spanky Burrage flashback. There we read that in Parker's version of "Koko" (alike in name only to Duke's version), the harmonic pattern of "Cherokee" bleeds through. The chord changes of Stan Getz's tenor solo on "Indiana" bleed through Parker's alto solo on "Donna Lee," but with a new melody. Basie's big-band rendition of "April in Paris" rises to the surface of Monk's quartet version, and so on. These cross-pollinations of tunes offer us one of the keys to reading *Koko*: 562 pages of new melodies added to old harmonies and new harmonies added to old melodies—in a word, complications.

The second key to reading *Koko* is our recognition that Straub offers us multiple *versions* of events. The word literally means the process of change, precisely that which Dengler finds unattainable. It's a word that describes a way of healing from trauma: imagining new "versions" of ourselves, an activity that Poole, Underhill, and Conor Linklater (who now rehabs houses) are engaged in, Dengler not. But the word also describes Straub's activity within the novel—looking at the same blackbird in different ways. In the final chapter Underhill engages in a microcosm of the novel. First, he imagines what happened to Dengler in Honduras: "I saw how it could have happened, and then I saw it happen" (554). As we skip through the pages, we see how the imagination is linked to the creation of versions: "This is one version of how Koko came to Honduras" (554). "I think he closes his eyes and sees a wide plaza. . . . When he closes his eyes he sees a broad sidewalk lined with cafes" (554). "He sees brown naked children . . . burned in a ditch" (555). "Let us say: he hears the dead man's soul. . . . Or let us say: Koko looks straight through the roof of the airplane and sees his father. . . . Or: he instantly feels the dead man's being. . . . [H]e sees a family and recognizes his brother, his sister. . . . he sees a little whitewashed house . . ." (556). Jumping ahead, past the Spanky Burrage flashback, we read "I think Koko. . . . I think . . . . perhaps because. . . . And perhaps. . . . Maybe this time. . . . STOP. PLAY" (560).

Looking back at the flashback, we see, among other things, an analogue of Underhill's literary microcosm—a palimpsestic microcosm within a microcosm. Nothing delights Spanky more than playing multiple versions of the same tune. And he's an absolute whiz at the control panel, pushing FAST FORWARD, REWIND, STOP, and PLAY to quickly juxtapose one version with another: two of "Koko," two of "April in Paris," three of "The Sunny Side of the Street," five versions of "Stardust" in a row, six of "How High the Moon," a dozen blues . . ." (557), and then the phrase that captures the very essence of *Koko*: "Everybody going to the same *well* but returning with different water."

Going back and forth to the well offers us a liberating version of "backwards and forwards." Spanky is as adept at using fast forward and reverse on his reel-to-reel Sony as Dengler is at reciting the identical monotones of scriptural judgment. It is strange that Dengler often sat in on Spanky's sessions yet in the present is utterly incapable of "looking at a blackbird" in more than one way. What happened on the muddy banks of the Milwaukee River and much later at Ia Thuc left him with but one somber tune, repeated endlessly, with only the monotonous hum of the rewind back to the beginning of his univocal apocalyptic quest.

Because Straub calls attention to music as an analogue for his book and for healing from pain, guilt, and fear, it is tempting to mine this vein more deeply. Late in the novel Poole makes a long trip by car and plays a cassette tape of Mozart's opera *Don Giovanni*. We read that the Mozart piano concerto already in the tape player is "the wrong music" (400). It is interesting to speculate what makes *Don Giovanni* the right music and the concerto the wrong music. We're told only that the concerto is "Music of great delicacy and melancholy . . ." (400). The opera in many ways does parallel the form and content of Straub's novel. First, like Parker's "Koko" (as opposed to Dengler's), it bridges tragic import with "grace" and "beauty" (559). Second, it uses mistaken identities to help fuel the plot. Third, it deals with the theme of fantastic retribution: a statue of the commandant pursues Don Giovanni and drags him down to hell. Fourth, like *Koko*, the opera bridges genres. Over the years since the work premiered in Prague more than two hundred years ago, critics have argued incessantly over whether it is a pop-culture opera buffa or a musical drama. Actually, it's both, just as *Koko* is a pop-culture airport novel and a "supreme fiction"—because Straub artfully masters the fusion of genres delimited by the canons of high culture. Fifth, Mozart further breaks down boundaries by using trombones in the orchestra, instruments which until then had been used exclusively in church music. Sixth, *Don Giovanni* parallels Straub's palimpsest theme, not only in that it is another version of an old story, but also in that a piece from a previous Mozart opera, *The Marriage of Figaro*, shows up in the second act. Seventh, like Dengler, Don Giovanni is a serial criminal of sorts, winning and dashing the hearts of a long list of women, a list that is enumerated in the famous "catalog aria."

But there is an eighth connection—admittedly not mentioned by Straub—that is especially germane to the music motif of *Koko*. In the opera's wonderful ballroom scene, Mozart takes Spanky's practice of juxtaposition to a whole new level: he scores three songs (a minuet, a contre-danse, and a waltz), with three different rhythms—to be played simultaneously. And he pulls it off. He dissolves the threatening chaos with mastery, creating a bridge that connects even the incongruity of three-four and four-four meters.

One cannot demonstrate that Poole is in any way conscious of Mozart's extraordinary feat; but one can demonstrate that Poole is a character in a novel that comes close to matching the feat, a novel with a recurrent, eerie statement bleeding through the surface: "God does all things simultaneously." So Mozart's three simultaneous tunes are an apt analogue for Poole's new "complicated joy." To paraphrase the language of O'Brien, Poole and Underhill will neither forget Ia Thuc nor remember it simplistically. They will utilize it, not

134

be used by it. It will be their catalyst for growing up morally and epistemologically. Like the Vietnam Veterans Memorial itself, their lives will be reflected in an imaginative construction that empowers them to be "appropriately upset."

I began this chapter by pointing out that many vets insist—along with Beevers—on having the exclusive rights to the Vietnam story. They need to give this up. It seems to me that if these vets, and Americans in general, are ever going to become "appropriately upset," we all will need to learn how to "read" ourselves more wisely and holistically. This revised reading will entail at least two sobering admissions: First, with few exceptions, veteran-written literature is narrow, white, male-centered, misogynist, and, finally, self-serving in that it typically asks the reader to pity the white, male, American soldier who was tragically misled into a nightmare of evil. Eschewing this narrow-victim syndrome, *Koko* compels us to give the Vietnam War a much more involved reading.

Second, "Vietnam Vietnam Vietnam"—we all *have* been there, both as victims and victimizers. As Lynne Hanley observes, there is a "frightfulness and ugliness deeply embedded in ourselves and our culture" (125). Vietnam was a mere symptom of an endemic state of mind. That means we *all*—veterans and non-veterans, men and women, enlistees and conscientious objectors—have a stake in and a responsibility for remembering, writing, and reading the story of Vietnam in America, America in Vietnam. We need to read the rememberings of all people who are suspicious of and cognizant of the paradigms embedded in our culture. We need more people going to the well. Most important, we need to learn how to invent more versions of ourselves and our country, or else we will continue to produce "children of darkness." Peter Straub—civilian—offers us one bridge between the killing and a new kind of remembering.

SEVEN

Poems "Whittled from Bone"

I write eraser poems on a blackboard soul.
—J. Vincent Hansen

In a two-way interview called "Knots of Wild Energy," the poets Robert Bly and Wayne Dodd agree that much of contemporary American poetry suffers from a "sameness and tameness" brought on by excessive domestication. Dodd points out that young poets are afraid of being scolded by the Establishment for peeing on the rug (Bly, 301, 302). Indeed, there is something generically well-behaved and paper-trained in the "new" poetry I've heard and read in the last fifteen years or so. Much of it is chatty, warm, reasonable, Apollonian, and bloodless—and, as such, little more challenging to one's paradigmatic habits of mind than high-brow greeting cards. Dionysus is M.I.A.; missing with him is anything dark and disturbing: ecstasy, terror, outrage, wildness. In a word, what both Longinus and Burke meant by "sublime," and what the Spanish mean by *duende*.

If we look at the history of the Western world, Apollo generally has had the upper hand. I suspect that most of us, whether feminists,

Marxists, New Critics, or deconstructionists, insist on this most of the time, regardless of our political persuasion. Usually, and at best, we pretend to allow equal time to the token, exceptional Heraclitus and Socrates to offset the prevailing Parmenides and Plato. It has always been the depreciated marginal versus hegemonic central: Pelagius versus St. Augustine; Bruno versus Calvin; the folly of Erasmus versus the earnest reason of Descartes; Blake versus Locke; Brontë versus Austen; Rimbaud versus the Parnassians; Whitman versus Eliot, and so on. Carlos Fuentes expresses this stacked deck in terms of "eccentric" culture's Ship (singular) of Fools versus "central" culture's ships (plural) of the conquistadores (123). There are several other well-known distinctions between poetry on the margins and poetry validated by the dominant culture. For example, in 1949, Philip Rahv designated American poets as either "redskins" (the conquered) or "palefaces" (the conquerors). Later, Robert Lowell used the categories "raw" and "cooked," even though he himself often seems "well done." More recently, in *The Maverick Poets* (1988), Steve Kowit distinguishes between the "defiantly wacky" and the hermetically aloof. Bly himself distinguishes between "wildness and domesticity." In the dominant white, male, American culture, clearly, poets such as Pound and Eliot head the list of the cooked, with offspring such as Marianne Moore, Howard Nemerov, Richard Wilbur, and John Ashbery. Whitman, largely ignored for decades in the university (not at all elsewhere in the world—especially in the eccentric cultures of Latin America), fosters the raw poets, such as Thomas McGrath, Allen Ginsberg, Robert Bly, Jayne Cortez, and Simon Ortiz, who also are ignored in the canon-bound circles of academia. Each of the latter group, in the words of the uncooked Spanish poet García Lorca, "rejects all the sweet geometry one has learned" (93).

How does Vietnam War poetry stack up in this ancient and contemporary conflict? Despite the Furies unleashed by the war, frequently, like most of the fiction, it is a victim of the same widespread cultural domestication and authoritarian control. In *Our Last First Poets* (1981), Cary Nelson argues that even the Vietnam poetry written by established, nonsoldier poets, such as Levertov and Duncan, often is "flat, predictable, and not likely to survive" (2). But what he says about these established poets could be said of virtually all the poets who have written about the war: "Many of them too convincingly master the anguish and anger at their source. They wish to contain and verbally transform their emotion without themselves becoming part of the inconclusive history of their times" (2, 3). "They give us exactly what we most want—consummation, control, and eventual forgetfulness" (3). In a word, they give us "defoliation." Nelson further ascribes to these poets "an apparent ignorance of how history has usurped both their language and their form" (4). Finally, in a statement that needs to be applied to all literature of the war regardless of genre, he isolates the source of their failure in their refusal to "risk more, [to] openly contend with [their poetry's] coeval public history, and [to] court its own formal dissolution" (10).

Often "palefaced," the poetry of veterans and non-veterans alike doesn't require us to process the dark, disturbing contingencies that surfaced during the war, which by now have been lacquered over by the central culture. Paper-trained in its undisguised, preachy didacticism, it frequently rails against the Establishment (in the manner of Ron Kovic) for its ignorance of and indifference to the war. But not without first peeing outside in the prescribed areas and carefully wiping the shoes on the welcome mat. That is to say, its content often challenges the Establishment, but its isolation from what Nelson calls "an incurable spiritual virus, whose disguises for invasion are protean and omnipresent" (10), its reassuring conventional syntax, clichéd observations of war's horrors, linear statements, and its lists of the war's surface phenomenology—all of these flights from chaos make it unnecessary for the reader to experience the discomfort of retooling Doc Peret's perceptual equipment. Instead of watching themselves look at Vietnam, most of the poets just look, unaware of how much the "sweet geometry" conditions that look. In *Thank God for the Atom Bomb* (1988), Paul Fussell says this unawareness has resulted in a Vietnam War poetry consisting of "dribbles of easy irony or easy sentiment or easy political anger" (110).

In his discussion of Vietnam War poetry, John Clark Pratt, the author of *The Laotian Fragments*, facilely accepts the fact that the "only context [of Vietnam poetry] is that of the rice paddy, the landing zone, or the jungle. . . . [T]he majority of [Vietnam] poets know only the now . . ." (*Unaccustomed Mercy*, viii-ix). In other words, they know only combat. This too is a weakness of much Vietnam poetry; narrow in scope, it stays safely over there, in a special place during a special time. It doesn't crash Ozzie's and Harriet's coffee klatch, and it leaves their neighborhood "zoned residential," as D. F. Brown puts it in "Coming Home" (47).[1] Insistently, it remains other. One of the themes of this book is that a narrowness of scope is a widespread shortcoming of most Vietnam War literature. The alleged specialness of this war, its depravity, and its huge destructiveness encourage this narrowness, which, as we will see in chapter 8, results in the Sodom and Gomorrah syndrome—the compulsion to look back at the horror and ecstasy, and to write "pillar-of-salt" literature that induces closet warriors voyeuristically to love the abhorrence. Much Vietnam poetry is as adept at voyeur inducement as is narrative fiction. In fact, many of the poems *are* narratives thinly disguised by short lines. Sometimes the punctuation and syntax are unorthodox; more often than not, however, they would please the grammarian guardians of Prospero's gates.

Lorrie Smith would agree that at least some Vietnam War poetry takes a close look at Peret's filters. For example, she argues that "D. F. Brown goes further than any other poet toward formal dissolution in order to deconstruct the very modes of thought and speech [the wires, filters, and circuits] that permitted our involvement in Vietnam and perpetuate war's mystique" (58). I couldn't agree more with this statement—if we're talking about D. F. Brown or some of the poems by John Balaban, Walter McDonald, Yusef Komunyakaa, Bruce Weigl, Marilyn McMahon, and a few others. A large number of poems, however, do not deconstruct the cultural paradigms; they both accommodate them and are informed by them. The fox guards the chickens.

Of course, I don't wish to imply that there is anything consciously

---

1. Quickly going out of print, original publications of Vietnam poetry books are extremely difficult to locate. For this reason, unless otherwise specified in context or in parentheses after quotations, citations will come from *Carrying the Darkness*, an anthology edited by W. D. Ehrhart. In addition, because some of Yusef Komunyakaa's poems appear only in his own collection *Dien Cai Dau*, this book will be the sole source for his citations.

insidious going on with many of the "poetic" rememberings of the war. Still, they often are unwitting examples of eating one's cake and having it too. One of our most insidious cultural paradigms is the unquestioned belief that we can divide what and how, content and form, subject and treatment, that one can be "deconstructed" in Vietnam, and then return to write literature that is reconstituted in only temporarily mothballed modes of thinking and expression. I call this division proper misbehavior, because it's like a quarrel between brother and sister—they'll probably make up; and even if they don't, they're still family. The poets' brutal honesty talked about by Pratt often is merely apparent; when they don't risk staring at the mediating implants in America's cultural narrative, they actually serve to suppress honesty and encourage simplistic remembering. They and the reader are then let off the hook too easily.

The Vietnam War should have resulted in a body of honest, extremely disconcerting poetry, and in some cases it does. In fact, it goes "off location" more than Pratt seems aware of. We've seen that no war veteran has more succinctly expressed what war should do to the arrogance of linguistic hegemony than Robert Graves. If he were alive today, no doubt he would conclude that, unfortunately, many Vietnam poems—and many post-Vietnam poems and literature in general—are written by the "He" of his poem. To reiterate, the problem with "He" is that he knows too much, or thinks he does. Confusion for him is but a temporary state that must be overcome. Linguistic order must be quickly restored. This confused understanding leads to what Virginia Woolf called "scoring the floor of the earth with chalk marks" (105). The image calls to mind the trenches of World War I and the violent shifts of power and national boundaries in an insane world of *realpolitik*. But it also calls to mind the "civilized" gridiron warfare fought on athletic playing fields, where the strategy is to infiltrate the chalk marks owned by the other side. Finally, Woolf's image might very well point to the most sinister kinds of warfare which "learned" teachers play on blackboards as they propagate a rage for order and symmetry in the next generation. Elsewhere I call this rage "linguistic Agent Orange," and it is precisely this habit of mind that responds to natural confusion by waging war. It is a predisposition dictating that mysteries shall be solved, not articulated; ignorance shall be overcome, not delineated; stress and guilt shall be eliminated, not utilized; confusion shall be eradicated, not understood. In short, the philosophy of American education, K through post-graduate.

The most responsive and responsible poets recognize that after war, poetic vision will necessarily find itself in a state of radical crisis as it collides with an intractable historical reality. In "After Our War," for example, John Balaban asks, "Will the myriad world surrender new metaphor? / After our war, how will love speak?" (16). In "For Mrs. Cam, Whose Name Means 'Printed Silk,'" he asks, "How does one start over?" (17). He knows he'll have to "study things which start from scratch" (18). In his latest collection, *Words For My Daughter* (1991), he sees apocalyptic ramifications of the war for the poet: " . . . this time when all assertions are suspect, / to this century when assurances are mute." It's a time when poets "gag on words like sour meats / . . . So, pity the poets, whose work is words, / reduced to blather or fiery silences, / When God who breathed the Word expired" (69).

Yusef Komunyakaa senses that the perceptual paradigms were so shattered that even—or especially—the seeing-in-the-dark starlight scope leaves us myopic, at best watching shadows lift shadows (8). In recognition of the damaged wires, circuits, and filters, he titled his collection of Vietnam poems *Dien Cai Dau* (1988), Vietnamese for "crazy" in the head.

With allusions and epigraphs, D. F. Brown aligns himself with one of the worst-behaving poets of all time—Arthur Rimbaud, whose "Seven-Year-Old Poets" "wash [themselves] from the day's [civilized] odors" (77)—in outhouses. Like Rimbaud, Brown turns away from the Christian heaven and toward *A Season in Hell*, which he echoes on more than one occasion. A "Child of Ham," he puts himself on the margins of culture, whose center he feels is contaminated by patriarchal insistence upon Cartesian clarity. He seems to feel that one cannot be sort of connected to the center, no more than one can have an adjunct relationship with the mafia. Thus the great breadth of his leap away from the linguistic, syntactical, grammatical conventions of that center. As he puts it in his long unpublished poem, "Napalm Elegy," he's "Going vocal hand to hand with history," doing "Ear to ear resuscitation."

Bruce Weigl, one of the better misbehaving poets of the war, tells

141

us in his pastoral "Song of Napalm" that "Nothing / can change . . ." the image of a napalmed girl running down the road—"not your [his wife's] good love and not the rain swept air / and not the . . . Pasture unfolding before us can deny it" (274). Therefore, it will bracket everything he writes. In Weigl's poetry, America's destruction of pastoral in Vietnam precludes mitigation by the at-home variety. Weigl misbehaves on the rug even more in "Burning Shit at An Khe," where he likens his poetry to finger painting with shit:

> Only now I can't fly.
>   I lie down in it
> and finger paint the words of who I am
>   across my chest
> until I'm covered and there's only one smell,
>   one word. (264)

Marilyn McMahon, a Navy nurse during the war, views the task of the poet in terms of how to treat a very serious wound:

> *Wounds heal from the bottom up*
>   *and from the outside in.*
> *Each must be kept open,*
>   *must be probed*
>   *and exposed to light.*
> *Must be inspected*
>   *and known.* (Van Devanter, 85)

On a metaphorical level, the last five lines accurately describe the agenda of much Vietnam writing. The first two lines, however, would seem to ask us to rethink healing from war. "Bottom up" and "outside in" direct our attention away from the "inside" of Vietnam toward wounds more radical, sinister, and anterior to the war.

Throughout his haiku-like poetry, the little-known writer Jerry Hansen (*Blessed Are the Piecemakers*—the spelling is correct) insists on probing, exposing, inspecting, and knowing—from the bottom up. Thus, in "Upon Entering a Montagnard Hamlet," he writes: "We were Americans first then, / soldiers second. / Americans first, / on our linear way from Wounded Knee / to only God knows where" (55). At the foundation of Hansen's poetry lies a perennial acceptance of America's historical guilt. No doubt he would readily concur with

Dennis Swain, who in 1986 asked "Can't anyone see that we *deserve* to feel guilty?" (108) Hansen sees us "advanced / deep / into / the dark forest" (19), always a scary place for America's Western mind-set. How to exit this heart of darkness? According to Hansen's stunning rewrite of the Hansel and Gretel story, the only way out is the way back in, rather like Maya Lin's exitless memorial. For him, art offers no possibility of linearity and expiation, only ongoing self-irony, because in that same forest we Americans left

orphans
in
our wake
like bread crumbs
that
we might find
our
way
back again
to
innocence. (19)

Rather than replacing darkness with the clear images of day, Hansen tries to see the smudges in the dark. Thus, in his book's "overture," "Infrared," he announces his tactics and strategy:

On
dark nights
allied
with guilt
and
a
Blue Nun,
I
write
eraser poems
on
a
blackboard soul.

Finally, Hansen's "blackboard soul" has no patience with the widespread agenda of honoring the vet while despising the war. In

143

"Americans" he characterizes this practice as being analogous to the boy "who killed his parents, / then asked the court to / go easy on him because / he was an orphan" (95).

In my final example of how the war should deconstruct the solipsistic "assertions" and "assurances," Steve Hassett brings the poet inside the parlor, with—as yet—unsoiled rugs:

> And what would you do, ma,
> if eight of your sons step
> out of TV and begin
> killing chickens and burning
> hooches in the living room
> stepping on booby traps
> and dying in the kitchen
> beating your husband and
> taking him and shooting
> skag and forgetting in
> the bathroom?
> would you lock up your daughter?
> would you stash the apple pie?
> would you change channels? (131)

The problem is that many of the veteran writers, whose wisdom adolescent America so desperately needs to see developed, often "change the channel" themselves. They let America off the hook when they do so. Apple pie, perhaps a bit more tart, then remains the nation's favored mythic dessert. Even Bill Ehrhart has been a channel-changer. It bothers me terribly to say this, for Ehrhart is not only a fine, generous person, but also, arguably, the poet laureate of the war. He may not be the greatest poet of the war, but he is its most important one, both in terms of the sheer volume of published poems and his indefatigable efforts to anthologize a poetic rendering of the war and its legacies. He has coedited with poet Jan Barry the anthology *Demilitarized Zones* (1976), which includes the voices of one hundred poets. He is also editor of the collection called *Carrying the Darkness* (1985), plus the "best-of-the-best" anthology *Unaccustomed Mercy* (1989), a title taken from Bruce Weigl's poem, "Monkey." No Vietnam War writer has tried harder to keep America conscious of what happened in Vietnam from 1959 to 1975. He is rightfully applauded; for, without him, it is doubtful that much of anything would even exist for the public. Again, I feel uneasy saying anything negative about a person of Ehrhart's importance. Actually, however, he himself gave me the courage to do so in his poem "Letter," in which he writes, "Oh, we're still haggling over pieces / of the lives sticking out / beyond the margins of our latest / history books—but no one haggles / with the authors" (99).

Yet one needs to interrogate his emphatic assertion made at a conference in 1985, called "The Vietnam Experience in American Literature": "I don't give a goddamn about art. I'm not an artist. I'm an educator . . ." (Lomperis, 32). Apparently, Ehrhart doesn't believe that art can be a powerful form of education. This is consistent with a general cultural bias, and it is rather commonplace among some Vietnam War literary scholars suffering from Platonic hangovers: art is contrived, artificial, somewhat effete, even dishonest; speaking straight from the heart or the gut expresses real, unvarnished truth.

At a recent academic conference, a "scholar" argued that Ron Kovic's *Born on the Fourth of July* is more important than the postmodernist *Going After Cacciato* because the former "comes from the gut." We were supposed to overlook the facts that the book develops very literary symbolic motifs and time distortions, and that it was at least partially cowritten by a ghost writer.

This preposterous anti-artist bias fails to take into account what should be absolutely obvious: whenever we don't monitor, edit, revise, and deconstruct what comes straight from the gut, we're most prone to repetition of the paradigmatic, binary habits of the mind. We overaestheticize precisely when we impute honesty. Because the gut is the repository of more civilized mental habits than many would like to admit to, there's a very short step, indeed, between "Less Filling! More Taste!" and "I'm not an artist. I'm an educator." Knowledge of how dangerous it is not to recognize how the gut is imprinted prompts Michael Herr to say in *Dispatches*, "Not much chance anymore for history to go on unselfconsciously" (44). But it still does. We continue to argue with rhetorical counter-cheers, oblivious to the watered-down, compromised beer we're arguing about.

Ehrhart's civilized, nonartistic poems are his weakest, because this

145

is when he is most victimized by a patriarchal tell-it-like-it-really-is attitude. His best poems are those in which he boldly and self-consciously attacks the "truths" of his time and his gut. (He readily admits that it was his gut that sent him on a John Wayne mission to Vietnam.) These are poems in which he is an artist, an artist who would seem to concur with Donald Hall's emphatic assertion: "We must learn to make art. Art is long and life is short . . ." (79). One such poem, "Christ," perhaps predictably shows up only in the early Rottmann-Barry-Paquet anthology, *Winning Hearts and Minds* (1972). In all three of the Ehrhart-edited books, the poem is omitted. "Christ" takes us well beyond the political, historical dissidence of some of his poems. Here the ramifications are existential and eschatological.

> I saw the Crucified Christ three days ago.
> He did not hang upon The Cross
> But lay instead on a shambled terrace
> Of what had been a house.
> There were no nails in His limbs;
> No crown of thorns, no spear wounds.
> The soldiers had left nothing
> But a small black hole upon his cheek.
> And He did not cry: "Forgive them, Lord;"
> But only lay there, gazing at an ashen sky.
>
> Today, on the Resurrection,
> Angelic hosts of flies caress His brow
> And from His swollen body comes
> The sweet-sick stench of rotting flesh—
> Three days old. (38)

Self-evident, the poem requires no explication. Although the poem is direct, it is not simple or shallow. Since the first time I read this poem fifteen years ago, I have never been able to think of the number 3 the way I used to. That in itself may seem to be too trivial to mention. However, the poem took me to a place I had never been before. It reminded me that we can study our own filters and change the way we think. We need not be paralyzed by perceptual paradigms. Because I was raised in a Christian family, "3" always had a special resonance for me. It was a number of wholeness (the Trinity), universal redemption, rebirth, victory, three strikes, three outs, a triple, a field goal, the sonata allegro form, *amo, amas, amat*. Ehrhart turns all of this upside down. The "assertions" and "assurances" are spilled like the contents of Weigl's bedpan in "Monkey." Frankincense and myrrh trade places with putrefaction. The poem is actually a blockbuster of a theological reversal: the sacrifice that was supposed to put an end to sacrifice—the Crucifixion—not only hasn't panned out, but has through the centuries actually *induced* continued sacrifice of the "other," this time a Vietnamese, a "godless Communist." For Ehrhart, that sacrifice is now as absurd as the original one. "The Word was made flesh" alright, but not in the way St. John envisioned! This is a fine poem—a work of art. And its enormous ramifications are vastly disproportionate to its length.

Ehrhart has written several other fine poems, such as "A Confirmation," "The Blizzard of Sixty-Six," "A Relative Thing," and "To Those Who Have Gone Home Tired." At his artistic best, Ehrhart opts for a broad, non -Sodom and -Gomorrah canvas, which enables him to contextualize the war as a horrible symptom of a more horrible disease. In "A Confirmation," for example, the war is a backdrop to its continued enactment in the forests of Washington, where Douglas firs are being slaughtered and the sacred land of the Klamath Indians defiled. The broad canvas makes it possible for him to say "goodbye" to the patriotic simplifications and distortions of "Tom Paine and high school history" (101). Like all good poetry, this poem complicates and enriches the speaker's and reader's perceptions. It opens channels to the healing messiness of paradox: "ignorance shattered" can lead to the "frail hope" of "implacable wisdom"; our "shame" can make us "holy" (102). In none of his poems does Ehrhart come to a greater sense of peace with a new understanding of his confusion.

Nevertheless, the much greater brevity and fine craftsmanship of "To Those Who Have Gone Home Tired" make it one of Ehrhart's most powerful poems. It's a brevity painted with wide brush strokes on a very large canvas. The poem is literally about making connections, which often are unrecognized in Vietnam War literature, or, as in this poem, by America's conscience. Ehrhart writes,

147

After the streets fall silent
After the bruises and the tear-gassed eyes are healed
After the consensus has returned
After the memories of Kent and My Lai and Hiroshima
lose their power
and their connections with each other
and . . . (97–98)

Following this "and," the poet names eight other things that should
be connected to Kent, My Lai and Hiroshima:

and the sweaters labeled Made in Taiwan
After the last American dies in Canada
and the last Korean in prison
and the last Indian at Pine Ridge
After the last whale is emptied from the sea
and the last leopard emptied from its skin
and the last drop of blood refined by Exxon
After the last iron door clangs shut
behind the last conscience
and the last loaf of bread is hammered into bullets
and the bullets
scattered among the hungry.

Rather than stare narrowly at Vietnam, Ehrhart watches himself—as an American citizen—look. What he then sees is that Vietnam was a domino in an ongoing policy of extermination, exploitation, and greed. Vietnam was a domino America toppled, long after it initiated the process. As we've seen, Michael Herr dates the beginning of the Vietnam War back to when "the proto-Gringos . . . found the New England woods too raw and empty for their peace and filled them up with their own imported devils" (51). But America doesn't make this connection; the "iron door clangs shut." In "Letter," upon the occasion of the Bicentennial, Ehrhart writes " . . . we've found again our inspiration / by recalling where we came from / and forgetting where we've been" (99).

"Gone Home Tired" can be viewed as a kind of pedagogically innovative history quiz in which the student is asked to match Kent State, My Lai, and Hiroshima with sweaters made in Taiwan, the last Indian dying at Pine Ridge, extinct whales, and so on. The student is asked to remember "where we've been." The poem gains its effectiveness and makes its point by virtue of the fact that many readers would not ace the "quiz," and many more would likely fail it—certainly those who are impoverished by the high school history texts and classes Ehrhart says goodbye to in "A Confirmation."

But who else is saying "goodbye?" Because "no one haggles / with the authors," our youth still find their inspiration in the myths of our pioneer kin, but remain ignorant of the ethnocentric butchery that accompanied their exploits. They remain blind to the bullets-for-bread sleight-of-hand ruse that is passed off as humanitarian aid. Ehrhart penetrates this blindness with the very grammar of "Gone Home Tired." Fifteen times as he catalogs the connections to the killings at Kent, My Lai, and Hiroshima, he refuses to bring his introductory, dependent clauses to closure with a main clause. The words "after" and "and" do a not-yet dance throughout the poem. Moreover, if we look back at the first four lines, each of which ends without a comma, we can read them both as a series of adverbial clauses and as adverbial clauses of adverbial clauses. Thus, the "streets fall silent / After the bruises . . . are healed," and so on. This creates the effect of the concluding line of "The Blizzard of Sixty-Six": "And the snow keeps falling" (105). The grammar of "Gone Home Tired" reinforces the inertia of America's real domino history, an unstoppable blizzard of violent events leading to Vietnam, hooked together tail to mouth.

Ehrhart may well have learned a lesson from Allen Ginsberg's poem "Wichita Vortex Sutra"; it too sees a different set of coordinates charting the march to Vietnam. Recalling the time when temperance leader Carry Nation was smashing saloons in Wichita, he writes, "Carry Nation began the war on Vietnam here / with an angry smashing axe / attacking wine—/ Here fifty years ago, by her violence / began a vortex of hatred that defoliated the Mekong Delta . . ." (131). Like Ginsberg's poem, Ehrhart's is a truer version of American history than one gets in "high school history" because it interrupts the "clear images" of assuring main clauses with the dependent clause interrogations of "broken images." And when the poem finally reaches the main clause, "What answers will you find / What armor will protect you / when your children ask you / Why?" (98) it does not even honor the first question with a question mark. Even that piece of punctuation represents Lorca's "sweet geometry." In this, one of his finest poems, the only word Ehrhart allows himself to punctuate is the final—sighed, I suspect—unanswered "Why?"

Ehrhart's poem is richer, more complicated than Graves' because he asks *us* to come to a new understanding of our confusion. We have to articulate and make the connections between Taiwan sweaters and My Lai. We have to become more adept at admitting and articulating dependent clauses, and more instinctive at mistrusting the main clauses of the classroom, the political forum, and the recruiting slogans.

Of all the Vietnam War poets, John Balaban is the most insistent on translating the war—on both a figuratively literal and a literally figurative level. On the first level, he includes his own translations of Vietnamese and Bulgarian poetry in his 1991 collection *Words For My Daughter*. This helps make his poetry avoid the pitfalls of solipsism and parochialism. On the second level, Balaban insists on "translating" (which literally means "carrying across") Vietnam to America and America to Vietnam. Thus, in many of his "Vietnam" poems, America bleeds to the surface. And in his poems about hitchhiking through the American Southwest, the horror and ravages of Vietnam sometimes penetrate his consciousness percussively. As a translator, Balaban eschews the boundaries of "clear images."

There are no chronological boundaries either. Balaban refuses to let the war end, not because he is fixated on it, as is too often the case, but because it simply has not ended. In "After Our War" we are surrealistically reminded of that fact:

> After our war, the dismembered bits
> —all those pierced eyes, ear slivers, jaw splinters,
> gouged lips, odd tibias, skin flaps, and toes—
> came squinting, wobbling, jabbering back.
> The genitals, of course, were the most bizarre,
> itching along roads like glowworms and slugs.
> The living wanted them back, but good as new.
> The dead, of course, had no use for them.

. . . . .

Since all things naturally return to their source
these snags and tatters arrived, with immigrant uncertainty,
in the United States. It was almost home.
So, now, one can sometimes see a friend or a famous man talking
with an extra pair of lips glued and yammering on his cheek,
and this is why handshakes are often unpleasant,
why it is better, sometimes, not to look another in the eye,
why, at your daughter's breast thickens a hard keloidal scar. (15–16)

If we combine the deformity of the extra pair of lips and a daughter's "keloidal scar," we come up upon the phenomenon emblematic of the war's continuation—Agent Orange. Nothing keeps the Vietnam War in the present tense like this deadly chemical. Scrambling the DNA codes of life—especially for the Vietnamese people, but in America as well—"lunatic genes" ("Atomic Ghost") develop monstrous fetuses, like faces located by the navel. As a conscientious objector field representative in Vietnam for the Committee of Responsibility to Save War-Injured Children, Balaban dealt almost exclusively with traumatic injuries, such as amputations, napalm and white phosphorus burns. But his poetry is more an exploration of the chronic injuries endured by people everywhere connected to the war. In fact, one could aptly designate Balaban's work the literature of the keloidal scar. "Yammering lips" and long-hidden injuries from Vietnam appear everywhere in his poetry of troubling juxtapositions. For example, in the middle of a rather recent poem about his childhood, which he narrates to his daughter, he "interrupts" himself with

Worse for me is a cloud of memories
still drifting off the South China Sea,
like the 9-year old boy, naked and lacerated,
thrashing in his pee on a steel operating table
and yelling "Dau. Dau," while I, trying to translate
in the mayhem of Tet for surgeons who didn't know
who this boy was or what happened to him, kept asking
"Where? Where's the pain?" until a surgeon
said "Forget it. His ears are blown." (*Words For My Daughter*, 11)

After this "translation" of Vietnam into the United States, Balaban cuts to a tender, fatherly scene with his daughter on Halloween. Then

151

we cut back to Vietnam when a trick-or-treat child rings the doorbell, wearing a tiny Green Beret uniform.

Conversely, in "Dead For Two years, Erhart Arranges to Meet Me in a Dream," Balaban "translates" the United States into Vietnam:

> So the cyclo driver,
> mantis eyed in mirror glasses,
> straddling his blue-and-orange,
> pin-striped, lawnmotorized chair—
> met me at the corner just as Erhart said.
> Neither the driver nor I—slightly fuddled
> from having been awakened by the call—
> registered much surprise: In dreams,
> nearly every night, the dead ring up
> and Vietnamese cabbies hustle U.S. streets
> in one's postwar, American sleep.
> So I just plunked down on the vinyl cushion
> and he varoomed a blue cloud all the way to Saigon. (19)

Balaban also translates Vietnam and America with his global perceptions. This is not at all surprising, since he is a linguist and speaks several languages, including Vietnamese. Rather than falling victim to the Sodom and Gomorrah syndrome, he repeatedly views events, including those in Vietnam, in a macro context. Standing atop a conceptualized Blue Mountain ("Crossing West Nebraska, Looking for Blue Mountain"), he writes,

> one can see everything clearly:

> In humming fields, beetles, aphids, weevils, ants.
> Fox pups frisking in bluebells before their burrow.
> A naked boy and girl dogpaddling an inner tube
> in bayou waters, off a levee near Big Mamou.
> Subterranean rock grinding in the San Andreas Fault.
> A Malay fisherman, perched on a spit of rock off Penang,
> hurling a circling net into surf at sunset.
> A bloated mare giving foal in a clover field in Kent.
> A blindfolded teenager, shoeless, slumped against a tree
> as the firing squad walks off in Montevideo.
> Missiles hidden like moles in Siberian silos.
> A black man, in red cotton shirt and khaki pants, his skin

alive with protozoan welts, sipping coffee in a Congo shop.
An eel sliding through a corpse's yellowed ribs
in a Mekong swamp where frogs croak and egrets fish.
  (*Words For My Daughter*, 17–18)

Balaban's global perceptions necessarily usually take us to the level
of the systemic violence of what he calls "our helpless tribe" (*Words
For My Daughter*, 12). For example, "April 30, 1975" marks the end
of the Vietnam War. But the end of hostility is only an illusion; not
only will it continue for many more years in Indochina, it continues
here at home:

City lights have reddened the bellies of fumed clouds
like trip flares scorching skies over a city at war.

In whooshing traffic at the park's lit edge,
red brake lights streak to sudden halts:
a ski-masked man staggers through lanes,
maced by a girl he tried to mug.
As he crashes to curb under mercury lamps,
a man snakes towards him, wetting his lips,
twirling the root of his tongue like a dial.

Some kids have burnt a bum on Brooklyn Bridge.
Screaming out of sleep, he flares the causeway.
The war returns like figures in a dream.
In Vietnam, pagodas chime their bells.
"A Clear Mind spreads like the wind.
By the Lo waterfalls, free and high,
you wash away the dust of life." (18–19)

The conclusion of the poem might seem to offer hope and consummation. In fact, in *Re-Writing America*, Philip Beidler, eager to see
America recover from the war, views these last lines as "mythic transport" and "the start of a new going" (152). But this "re-writing" is a
misreading of the poem. At the very least, it ends on an ambiguous
note, for "dust of life" is a translation of *bui doi*, which refers to
the wasted lives of the war's children, in particular, the Amerasians
left behind to live their lives as permanent outcasts, accepted neither
here nor there. Yusef Komunyakaa says of the latter (which he mistakenly spells "Dui Boi") that they "were born disappearing" on their

153

"inchworm's foot of earth." "I blow the dust off my hands / but it flies back in my face" (58). Seen in this context, the sound of the bells becomes a death knell, the pastoral Lo waterfalls, a nightmare stream of blood.

In the title poem of *Words For My Daughter*, Balaban again begins on a pastoral note: "About eight of us were nailing up forts / in the mulberry grove behind Reds's house" (9). But Balaban quickly juxtaposes the pastoral with the systemic violence of dysfunctional families. Reds, fourteen, beats his drunken father with a hammer: "We heard thumps like someone beating a tire." Another kid comes home "to find / his alcoholic mother getting fucked by the milkman," whereupon he cuts the milkman with a broken bottle. The kids are violent amongst themselves as well:

> Once a girl ran past my porch
> with a dart in her back, her open mouth
> pumping like a guppy's, her eyes wild.
> Later that summer, or maybe the next,
> the kids hung her brother from an oak.
> Before they hoisted him, yowling and heavy
> on the clothesline, they made him claw the creekbank
> and eat worms. I don't know why his neck didn't snap.   (10)

Despite the fact that Balaban sees "our helpless tribe" "twisted in shapes of hammer and shard," he remains one of the war's most hopeful poets. He tells his daughter "I want you to know the worst and be free from it. / I want you to know the worst and still find good" (12). No poem better demonstrates Balaban's agenda of finding good *within* the worst than "For Mrs. Cam, Whose Name Means 'Printed Silk.' " It begins with a self-imposed strike against itself:

> In Vietnam, poets brushed on printed silk
> those poems about clouds, mountains, and love.
> But now their poems are cased in steel.
>
> . . . . .
>
> The war has blown away your past.
> No poem can call it back.
> How does one start over?   (17)

Balaban's answer to this question is the same one given by Fuller's Neumann: with fragments. The speaker in the poem finds an analogy of his job as poet while walking the beach in Southern California,

> marveling at curls broken bare in crushed shells
> at the sheen and cracks of laved, salted wood,
> at the pearling blues of rock-stuck mussels
>
> all broken, all beautiful, accidents
> which remind you of your life, lost friends
> and pieces of poems which made you whole. (17)

Instead of being overwhelmed by the accidents and the broken things, the poet makes a new use of them as "bargaining chips" of the imagination, like a sculptor welding together cast-off items in a junkyard or like a grieving person using the pain of loss to engender new reverence for life. Why waste waste? We all need a form of alchemy that finds its analogy in the poem in the process by which pearls are created:

> Nicely like a pearl is a poem
> begun with an accidental speck
> from the ocean of the actual.
>
> A grain, a grit, which once admitted
> irritates the mantle of thought
> and coats itself in lacquers of the mind. (18)

Irritation, usually thought of as something that blocks or impedes progress, is here seen as a cause of progress. It is precisely this kind of paradox that makes Balaban a "redskin," a poet looking for planned accidents.

Like Balaban, Walter McDonald is an alchemist who sifts through the waste for his building materials. In "The Food Pickers of Saigon," he begins with a simile that represents his poetic tactics: "Rubbish like compost heaps" (*Unaccustomed Mercy*; ed. W. D. Ehrhart, 106). Like a compost heap, his poetry achieves "fertility" through destruction. This is precisely what happens in one of his strongest poems, "Once You've Been to War." The poem focuses on the interplay between creation and destruction, fertility and barrenness. The speaker was a pilot who dropped incendiaries on the rain forests of Vietnam. But we don't find this out until half way through the poem. The first fourteen-and-a-half lines reveal a protean fertility in the speaker's dreams:

> There are times when everything I touch
> turns to leaves, my plot of earth breathing
> like women who seem to be always fertile,
> their nurseries teeming with mouths,
> flower-print dresses forever bulging.
>
> Whatever I plant at night in dreams
> by dawn has rooted, ferns like veils,
> orchids, fuchsia tendrils reaching for trees,
> my secret back yard dense as the front,
> three canopies of rain forest
>
> chattering with spider monkeys,
> toucans, orange and black minahs,
> birds of paradise. And there are times
> deep in my pillow below three canopies
> of rain forest (193)

Then comes the transition to destruction, with the last half of line fifteen and the first half of line sixteen reading ". . . I did not plant / but helped to burn. . . ." Except for the last line, the remainder of the poem only yields images of the wasteland: ". . . sand blows over everything." "Concertina wire"; "Roaches . . . the size of condors"; "parched riverbeds" where "fish keep flopping" in the "lightning without rain" (194).

So, are these two kinds of recurring dreams opposites? On an obvious level, of course they are. One kind of dream offers images of things taking root; the second kind focuses on things being uprooted by rockets, napalm, and B-52 strikes. But McDonald subtly impresses on us that they are closely related, much like Balaban's "translations" of Vietnam to America and vice versa. Notice that in line thirteen, as he moves from dreams of fecundity to those of sterility, he says "And there are times," not "but." He does so in the middle of a stanza that begins by continuing the litany of fecundity. Furthermore, when he does use "but," it almost seems to reinforce the connection between planting and burning. He accomplishes this by ending a stanza with "plant"—without punctuation. The momentum thus pulls us directly into "but helped to burn." In general, McDonald provides a sense of seamless interconnectedness by not finishing the grammatical structures of four of the six five-line stanzas. The result is a poem that refuses to forget or remember Vietnam simplistically in tidy categories of the mind; instead, it creatively complicates it by utilizing the composted heaps of destruction.

The final image of the poem, "like flutes whittled from bone," completes the complication. The poem neither forgets Vietnam with the flute's soothing, pastoral tones, nor is engulged by it, like Straub's Dengler. The implicit argument of the poem is that we can create new life if we find new ways to use the rubbish of Graves' "broken images." I think McDonald would concur with my answer to the question, What are good "war poems"? They are "flutes whittled from bone." The flutes of bone are the bridge between "flower-print dresses forever bulging" and the burning rain forest. The new use of "bone" links "breathing" and "bulging" to "burn," "burst," "blows," and "bombs." As McDonald says in "The Food Pickers of Saigon," we can reimagine the burning rubbish as "Moses' holy bush / which was not consumed." Like the burning bush, the veteran's war experiences can actually point the way to emancipation from the tyranny of both paralysis and amnesia.

It appears that all Vietnam poets, including Yusef Komunyakaa, would opt for Graves' well-behaved illuminating "clear images," were that possible. Indeed, many of them write as if it were possible. Of course it is superficially reassuring to climb out of the Platonic cave of the war and escape the shadows into the clear light of day. It's an extremely tempting ascent. As Komunyakaa says in "Missing in Action," "Sunlight presses down for an answer" (54). And in "Facing It," while looking at the Vietnam Veterans Memorial, he admits he's "depending on the light / to make a difference" (63). But more often than not in Komunyakaa's poetry, Plato's truth-revealing light is like a "flashlight . . . into the void" (5), or it is simply blinding, or it is disappearing in a "Sunset Threnody." Admitting up front in the title of his book that he, she, we, they are crazy in the head (*dien cai dau*), Komunyakaa directly repudiates and inverts the wisdom of

Plato, and for that reason he would be one of the very first poets to be banned from the ideal republics of those with valuable rugs. Komunyakaa seeks truth precisely where Plato and Western "enlightened" cultures find falsehood and illusion: in shadows, "invisible ropes to nowhere" (10), "titanic darkness" (19), "half-lit rooms" (33), the "indigo mystery" in the "labyrinth of violet" (37), and the "letters of smoke" etched in the "black mirror" (63) of the Vietnam Veterans Memorial. An African-American writer, Komunyakaa quite literally is not among the palefaces.

Perhaps more consistently than any other poet of the war, Komunyakaa embraces dark spaces in his search for truths that transcend the wilful "clear images" of mapmakers. Everywhere in his Vietnam poems we find images "disappearing," "blurred," "splintered," "blinded," "dissolved," and "shattered" in "shadows," "darkness," "mist," "dust," "dusk," and "smoke." His poems are about seeing and not seeing. In fact, a great many of them contain the very words "see" and/or "eye." Some of the poems' titles indicate Komunyakaa's preoccupation: "Camouflaging the Chimera," "Starlight Scope Myopia," "Seeing in the Dark," and "Eyeball Television."

The "I" of Graves' poem, Komunyakaa views the "He" with a good deal of skepticism. He confronts even the high-tech, infra-red, see-everything starlight scope with an oxymoron counterattack. In "Starlight Scope Myopia" he wonders if the Viet Cong, ever at one with the darkness, are calling the American "He" "*beaucoup dien cai dau*" (9). And well they might be, for what was the Vietnam War if not the American imperialistic insistence upon LET THERE BE LIGHT!? Conversely, Komunyakaa insists on searching for the kind of "darkened illumination" made accessible to us by Maya Lin's "black mirror," where a woman "trying to erase names" and "brushing a boy's hair" (63) form a creative dialectic of darkness and light, erasure and fullness.

A maker of anti-maps, Komunyakaa insists on seeking adventure "under our eyelids" (8). A poet of insight rather than sight, he says "I close my eyes & I can see" (29). As a poet of insight, he gains the freedom to explore subterranean, prerational landscapes. This results in a poetry of rich, surrealistic, disturbing associations: in "'You and I Are Disappearing'," he rushes frenetically through ten similes (as if to say no one simile, or five, or even ten will adequately express the searing memory), likening a napalmed girl to "a sack of dry ice," "the fat tip / of a banker's cigar," and "a shot glass of vodka" (17); he visualizes a burning Buddhist monk as turning blue pages (18); "Booby-trapped pages" float through dust (25); a voice is "shiny as a knife / against bamboo shoots" (54); the odor of perfume is described in terms of color; a "moon cuts through / night trees like a circular saw / white hot" (7); a woman holds "the sun / in her icy glass" (52).

This is but a small sampling of Komunyakaa's efforts to penetrate the deep interior life lurking beneath "sweet geometry." It gives his poetry a strangely vital, nightmarish quality. Never coming to a resolution (in "Sunset Threnody" he writes "& I'm a man fighting / with myself. Yes, no, / yes" [51]), his poetry at its best strikes an ambivalent balance between irretrievable loss and glimmers of hope, as when standing in front of the Vietnam Veterans Memorial, he sees "In the black mirror / a woman's trying to erase names: / No, she's brushing a boy's hair" (63).

The Spanish would say Komunyakaa's poetry has *duende*, for which we have no one-word translation. Roughly, it refers to the pre-rational wild spirit of death, darkness, and blood. Keeping company with it results in a profound form of misbehavior. In a lecture entitled "Theory and Function of the *Duende*," García Lorca explained it best:

> *Duende* is "the roots thrusting into the fertile loam known to all of us, ignored by all of us, but from which we get what is real in art. . . . To help us seek the *duende* there is neither map nor discipline. All one knows is that it burns the blood like powdered glass, that it exhausts, that it rejects all the sweet geometry one has learned, that it breaks with all styles. . . . We have said that the *duende* likes the edge of things, the wound, and that it is drawn to where forms fuse themselves in a longing greater than their visible expression. . . . The *duende*—where is the *duende*? Through the empty arch comes an air of the mind that blows insistently over the heads of the dead, in search of new landscapes and unsuspected accents; an air smelling of a child's saliva, of pounded grass, and medusal veil announcing the constant baptism of newly created things. (91, 93, 100, 103)

I have quoted Lorca at length because his words perfectly describe Komunyakaa's poetry, not to mention the best of the other poets under consideration here. Many of his poems "fuse themselves in a longing greater than their visible expressions." Among them are "A Greenness Taller Than Gods," "You and I Are Disappearing," "Re-creating the Scene," "2527th Birthday of the Buddha," "Missing in Action," and "Nude Pictures." But in what I think is his greatest poem, "Eyeball Television," Komunyakaa fuses *duende* with a cultural critique and a repudiation of Graves' "He." True to form, the poem explores the motifs of sight, vision, eyes, and darkness. Again, although the poet might opt for "clear images" if he could, he can't. Because he can't, he sees instead behind the eyes, thereby offering a complicated critique of the narrow way the war is perceived and written about.

The persona of the poem is a POW limited to a "pinhole of light" as he "sits crouched in a hole / covered by slats of bamboo." While there, he recalls television shows, ". . . hundreds of faces / from *I Love Lucy, Dragnet, / I Spy, & The Ed Sullivan Show*," plus ". . . *Roadrunner* on channel 6" (39). He tries to maintain the imposed structure of a reassuring TV world. But his inner "focus" shows a world that is crumbling. What he sees is reminiscent of the wild sequences in Dali's and Buñuel's *Un Chien Andalou*:

> Holding the world in focus
> in his solitary cell, he sees
> Spike Jones' one-man band
> explode. Two minutes later
> Marilyn Monroe is nude
> on a round white sofa
> that dissolves into a cloud.
> Shaking his head to get her pose
> right again, he finds himself
> pushing vertical & horizontal hold
> buttons, but only Liberace's
> piano eases into the disconnected
> landscape. (39)

"Pushing vertical & horizontal hold buttons" describes not only the soldier's efforts to make sense of a surreal experience, but worse, the efforts of the military, political, and media Establishments to mediate the war in tidy packages of "clear images." In this poem, Komunyakaa deconstructs all packages. Eventually, even the senses melt like Dali's clocks:

> He hears deliberate
> heavy footsteps of the guards
> coming for him. The picture
> fades into the sound of urine
> dripping on his forehead,
> as he tries to read the lips of Walter Cronkite.

The poem's final line is supremely ironic, for it implicitly attacks America's ultimate "He"—Walter Cronkite, a man, who surrounded by epidemic madness, could nevertheless confidently say during the entire course of the war, and without laughing, "That's the way it is." On CBS, yes, but not in Komunyakaa's *dien cai dau, duende* poetry. In fact, one way of getting a handle on his poetry is to juxtapose Cronkite's confident objectivism with the ten frenetic similes of "You and I Are Disappearing." Cronkite's broadcasts came to a self-deluded *end*, whereas Komunyakaa, as Vince Gotera says, ". . . simply has to *stop*" (292) [my emphasis].

If we look at the poets being discussed in this chapter, we see a pattern: each of them—at his or her best—has had to find a way to navigate the treacherous terrain between the two powerful temptations to either put the war behind or remember it the way Lot's wife remembered her favorite cities. At their best, the Vietnam poets use the war like an alchemist. Making sure that all the suffering isn't wasted, they sift through the waste themselves, scrounging for the "pieces of poems that [make] you whole." Jerry Hansen's very title bestows an uncertain blessing on those who try to make something from these pieces, and respect them *as* pieces. Komunyakaa sifts through the debris of *dien cai dau*, searching for things "molded from ashes." D. F. Brown seeks "renovated," not replaced "rubble," aided in his effort only by "tattered summations" and "shredded language." McDonald whittles flutes from the bones of war. Balaban tries to fashion pearls from the profound irritation that was Vietnam. Ehrhart tries to refashion shame into holiness. Weigl, as we will see, tries to create music from napalm.

Nor is this alchemical effort limited to the poets discussed here. In his deeply troubling-hopeful poem "Rice Will Grow Again," Frank A. Cross, Jr. writes about a soldier who wantonly kills a rice farmer in Vietnam. The farmer's defiant dying words, according to an interpreter, are "Damn you / The rice will / Grow again!" (78). Indeed, years later this same defiant farmer plants rice around the murderer's bed—at home in Kansas, the very heart of America. It's a complicated alchemical operation seeking rebirth from revenge and remorse. Growth will come from the unrooted rice shoots clutched in the farmer's hands as he dies, or it will not come at all.

In a similar vein, Basel T. Paquet describes a desperate, if futile, CPR effort on a dying soldier in terms of the art of prosody: "I've scanned the rhythms of your living, / Forced half-rhymes in your silent pulse, / Sprung brief spondees in your lungs, / And the caesura's called mid-line, half-time, / Incompletely, but with a certain finality" (218). Surely, part of Paquet's point is that you can't turn war and murder into spondees. Just as surely, however, the art of poetic memory must be viewed as a tactic to resuscitate a nation's consciousness.

This pattern continues with Bruce Weigl. The very title of his most important collection of poems says it all: *Song of Napalm* (1988). This title is a powerful, oxymoronic expression of the war poet's difficult predicament: How *do* you make poetry out of war? How can you possibly make music from—of all things—napalm? Irving Howe has asked similar questions about the holocaust in "Writing and the Holocaust" (27–39). How can you write about the unspeakably horrifying without somehow domesticating it and making it nonthreatening to rugs? The answer to the first two questions probably is "you can't." Perhaps we need to view these poems as necessarily failed attempts to whittle flutes from bones and to compose songs from devastating incendiaries. I don't mean to minimize the achievements of these poems. On the contrary, their achievement—their music—resides in the very fact that they fail in the right way: they are rug-threatening. As in Steve Hassett's poem, the horrors will come into our living rooms and our landscapes. They will "sing," but as Galway Kinnell puts it in *The Book of Nightmares*, it will be "music blooming with failure" (35), and the violin will be bowed with "the sliced intestine of cat" (74).

Such is the case in the title poem of Weigl's *Song of Napalm*. Although it is set amid pastoral beauty, the war bleeds through:

After the storm, after the rain stopped pounding,
we stood in the doorway watching horses

walk off lazily across the pasture's hill.
We stared through the black screen,
our vision altered by the distance
so I thought I saw a mist
kicked up around their hooves when they faded
like cut-out horses
away from us.
The grass was never more blue in that light, more
scarlet; beyond the pasture
trees scraped their voices into the wind, branches
crisscrossed the sky like barbed wire
but you said they were only branches. (273)

Looking at the poem as a whole, we see an ongoing, anguished vacillation between pastoral rebirth and the rebirth of Vietnam nightmare. After the lines already quoted, Weigl twice tries to turn his eyes away from what he saw in Vietnam:

I turned my back on the old curses. I believed
they swung finally away from me . . .

But still the branches are wire
and thunder is the pounding mortar,
still I close my eyes and see the girl
running from her village, napalm
stuck to her dress like jelly.

After his second effort at denial, the poet writes

But the lie swings back again.
The lie works only as long as it takes to speak
and the girl runs only as far
as the napalm allows
until her burning tendons and crackling
muscles draw her up
into that final position
burning bodies so perfectly assume. Nothing
can change that, she is burned behind my eyes.

Those who wish to put Vietnam behind them likely would accuse Weigl of cynicism, of a wilful refusal to simply enjoy America the beautiful. Indeed, he does superimpose the horrors of Vietnam on a delightful bucolic scene. But one should not forget Paul Fussell's wake-up call in *The Great War and Modern Memory*: "Since war takes place outdoors and always within nature, its symbolic status is that of the ultimate antipastoral" (231). As easy as it would be to be paralyzed by this antipastoral, Weigl finds ways to utilize it. He doesn't sing to forget or to assuage the pangs of Vietnam, but to sing of it. It's not that he is paralyzed by the image of the napalmed girl; he just refuses to *waste* her suffering. Weigl may fail to complete his "dispensary," but at least he convinces us where it must begin and of what it must be built. He shares Yeats' conviction that he "must lie down where all the ladders start, / In the foul rag-and-bone shop of the heart."

Insistent on the place where ladders start, Weigl starts his surrealistic "Monkey" with two complete conjugations of the verb "to be." We need to read this opening in a couple of ways. Generally speaking, we can infer that Weigl is announcing at the top that language is in trouble. Epic materials are simply unavailable to the Vietnam poet. (They've never been available to any war poet, including Homer and Virgil; they've simply culturally imposed on the sheer madness.) Weigl's conjugations suggest that like stroke victims we need to relearn how to speak, to start from scratch, as Balaban puts it. And that means going back to the primary building block of language—*being*. Thus, on one level, the poem seems to suggest that we must assess the fallout of war truthfully, and that means accepting an ontological crisis as our starting point. Furthermore, the repetition of *I, you, he, she, it, we, you*, and *they* underscores the complicity of all Americans in the Vietnam War. In a sense, Weigl begins "Monkey" the way Michael Herr ends *Dispatches*: the war belongs to all of us.

As rudimentary as this beginning is, it at least possesses the order of recognized syntax. But in most of the remaining 117 lines, syntax gives way to surreal juxtapositions and shards of broken language:

> The snakes are thirsty.
> Bladders, water, boil it, drink it.
> Get out of your clothes.
> You can't move in your green clothes.
> Your O.D. in color issue clothes.
> Get out the plates and those who ate,

Those who spent the night.
Those small Vietnamese soldiers.
They love to hold your hand. (268)

As Lorrie Smith observes, the rapid-fire succession of lines is "seman-tically tied to the logic of nightmare" (57). Even when Weigl does recover syntax, it doesn't last:

Good times bad times sleep
get up work. Sleep get up
good times bad times.
Work eat sleep good bad work times. (269)

The syntax that does hold together is only of the most elemental, Dick-and-Jane sort, which echoes Herr's LURP story:

There is a hill.
Men run top hill.
Men take hill.
Give hill to man.

. . . . .

Men take hill away from smaller men.
Men take hill and give to fatter man.
Men take hill. Hill has number.
Men run up hill. Run down. (271)

With the ontological crisis his starting point, Weigl offers the reader none of the guardrails provided by narrative, and even by most Viet-nam poetry. This is risky, because there is a fine line between sifting through the debris of war for building materials and sheer nonsense. There is a fine line between deconstruction and destruction of lan-guage. Weigl succeeds because, in a sense, the unifying "subject" of "Monkey" is the failure of language and logic to express the fallout of war. He laudably defies the sentimental compulsion to impose lin-guistic control on America's mythic history. Thus his attitude toward language is necessarily ambivalent. He knows that when poets are not ignorant "of how history has usurped both their language and their form" (Nelson, 4), they can no longer cleanse language of its complicity by merely being "quick, thinking in clear images." Only Graves' "He" can blindly claim that prerogative. The only prerogative the honest postwar poet can claim is using language and the habitual structures of thought against themselves.

In "Monkey" one of the victims of this necessary internal strife is a cardinal point of Western sense making—causality. Thus, at one point (270) Weigl repeats "because" five times, not to communicate causality but to point to the mysterious, non-articulated space between cause and effect. It's a dangerous space that Weigl designates "a field of claymores." Where those claymores are positioned, and in which direction they are aimed, the reader can only guess. That's because the poem is virtually devoid of grammatical subordination. When Weigl does employ it, as with the five uses of "because," it dissolves into the logic of nightmare. Knowing what to subordinate to what is a luxury that only the "He" of Graves' poem insists on claiming. Weigl's wisdom, by contrast, consists of his courageously articulated confusion. Walking through the minefield, the reader, too, is forced to assume the role of a stroke victim having to rethink how to move and speak.

Obviously, the monkey is another unifying device, an objective correlative for Weigl's ambivalence and confusion. It is at once everything he hates and everything he desperately needs—like language itself. He beats it; and disembowels it, yet it "came here from heaven / to give me his spirit" (271). He even credits the monkey with saving him from punji sticks and mines. So it is at once the Vietnam monkey on Weigl's back that he can't shake off and an emblem of his fortunate fall, his necessary shadow. It's his flute whittled from bone. Weigl expresses what he hopes to accomplish in "Monkey" with the epigraph from James Wright: "Out of the horror there rises a musical ache that is beautiful." Does Weigl achieve a beautiful ache? Can something beautiful rise from finger-painted shit or from a "survivor . . . spilling his bedpan?" Can napalm be alchemized into song? A *duende* poet in his own right, Weigl, I think, would answer: "If it doesn't, it doesn't mean much, does it?"

So far, we've looked at five poets who occasionally sound a "musical ache." No Vietnam poet does this more consistently or disturbingly than D. F. Brown. As some of his epigraphs and allusions indicate, one of Brown's external resources is the French nineteenth-century *poète maudit*, Arthur Rimbaud—from the nineteenth century.

166

Like Brown, Rimbaud, who probably misbehaved more than almost any poet in history, was deeply disturbed by the well-behaved sameness and tameness of the poetry of his time. In his meteoric career he strove to create a new, sensuous language of *duende*. Knowing how deeply engrained the Cartesian rationalist paradigm was in the Western psyche, he searched for a poetry that would be altogether different in *kind*, rather than degree. Recognizing the stranglehold of his "filthy education of childhood" (205), he called for the "derangement of all the senses" (307), and "looked on the disorder of [his] mind as sacred" (195). Eschewing the tidy parlors of bourgeois France, his "Seven-Year-Old Poets" "wash [themselves] from the day's [civilized] odors" (77)—in outhouses. In similar fashion, Brown turns away from the Christian heaven and looks to Rimbaud's *A Season in Hell*. Like Rimbaud, Brown makes a radical break from the *New Yorker* poetry of his time. A "Child of Ham," he puts himself on the margins of a culture, whose center he feels is contaminated by patriarchal insistence on clarity. He knows one can't be partially connected to the center. Thus the great breadth of his leap away from the linguistic, syntactical, and grammatical conventions of that center.

Brown offers us a preamble to his postwar poetry in "Coming Home," which confronts us with a message quite different from that of the movie with the same title. His relationship to the assumed values and what Lorrie Smith calls the "linguistic hegemony" of the central culture will be that of a "vagrant / A culprit at home nowhere / Or everywhere / Dancing stealth / Into living rooms." He ends the poem by issuing a warning of sorts to America's suburban, amnesiac rage for order: "Someone has stacked his books / Records, souvenirs, pretending / this will always be light / and zoned residential" (47). More often than not, Brown's poems are not zoned at all. One of Stephen Wright's descriptions in *Meditations in Green* parallels the "unmapped" terrain of Brown's poems: "The runway buried in sand. . . . The basketball court sunken and cracked. . . . A rotting T-shirt on a nail. . . . A nodding table fan plugged directly into the void."

Readers who subscribe to Philip Beidler's notion that a "sense making" remythologizing effort lies at the center of Vietnam literature will be disappointed by Brown's poetry, but not for any fault of

Brown. Brown uses his poetry to confront a culture obsessed with understanding, with demystification, with answers, with packaging. In response to this dangerous obsession, Brown denies the reader conventional syntax and linear development. As he once told Lorrie Smith, "The absence of narrative drive in the poems requires another sort of investment from my dear reader. . . . The understanding syntax provides retards the understanding I desire" (Smith, 59). This different understanding will come, if at all, without the grammatical presence of picket fences and sidewalks.

Brown's Rimbaudian rebellion takes several forms. He mixes verb tenses, as in the title "When I Am 19 I Was a Medic," which makes a mockery of George Bush's reassurance that we've progressed beyond the "Vietnam syndrome." His use of the parts of speech is ambiguous: adjectives, verbs, and gerunds ignore each other's no-trespassing signs. He also frequently seems to use dashes to interrupt main clauses, but then rarely uses a second dash to indicate resumption of the apparent main clause. Like Weigl, Brown seems to view subordination with a great deal of skepticism. Furthermore, his punctuation often seems tied more to the uncertainties of Khe Sahn than to the verities of ancient Athens and Rome. Sometimes, as in "Returning Fire," there is no punctuation whatsoever.

As the Language Poets would say, Brown writes lines, not sentences. According to this school of poetry, the sentence is an imperialistic, territorial marker. All these poets certainly would concur with Grace, a character in Joan Didion's *A Book of Common Prayer*: ". . . the consciousness of the human organism is carried in its grammar" (234). And that grammar bears close watching, for as Ron Silliman argues, traditional grammar merely creates "the lie of clarity" (183), which Steve Benson says leads to a "system of organization hegemonically dreadful" (196). Another language poet, Lyn Hejinian, has strongly influenced Brown; in his latest poetry he has taken her manifesto to heart: "I have lost faith in what I can say in a sentence" (191). One can easily infer that Brown sees how the territorial consciousness of the sentence led to the Cold and Vietnam wars. America saw itself as a grammar-confident subject and verb reacting to a misbehaving Communist direct object. Brown's poetry thwarts this grammar at every turn. In fact, in "Bluto Addresses the Real," he explicitly confronts grammar and Rimbaud's "filthy educaton." He writes "Education / works they like to say" (*Returning Fire*, 15). Throughout Brown's poetry, however, "they" corresponds exactly to Graves' "He." Like the title of Ron Silliman's language poet manifesto, Brown, the dispensary builder, is endeared less to the sentence than to "Terms of Enjambment" (183). Lorrie Smith, who has closely followed Brown's career as a poet, sums up the reader's experience with his poetry: "The reader walks point through an open linguistic field of slippery signification, abrupt drops, syntactical dislocations, and elisions. . . . These are poems that deny interpretation and ask instead to be experienced as kinetic, disturbing moments of thought" (62, 64). Brown doesn't write about nightmares; he *creates* them. In "Eating the Forest," which begins with the Rimbaud epigraph, "*If I am alive in the morning / then I am alive in the dream*," he writes,

We think we are
ready awake
all night the dead
snap back on legs
they had the day before
bleached into dreams
we talk sweet for them
working their slow way around
new at being dead, young
and nervous kick
the dirt, try wiping
off mud, and still
they carry everything—
ammo, the charges, flares
cut sharp floating
angles, they don't kill
shadows, we are cut-outs,
the dead stay for contrast

. . . . .

in the great, late All-Night
they keep track in our sleep

—visibility
far off standing
light thick sound
tracked each flash
crosses soldiers,
trained to sleep
where the moon sinks
and bring the darkness home. (55–56)

In this darkness there is, as Smith says, a good deal of "slippery signification." We need read no further than the first two lines of "Returning Fire" to experience it: "what we think / we remember" (48). Recalling Peret's vicious cycle, this opening can be read either as what we think, we *remember*—or as we remember *what* we think. The ambiguity presents a frontal assault on America's Monopoly-loving Major Hollys. However we read the first two lines, we are denied the cleanliness and closure we sought and failed to impose on Vietnam. Brown confronts us with what T. S. Eliot called "the sin of language." Because we are our language, we can so easily be deluded into thinking that it is purely neutral, that it is preexistent to thought. Thus, when we fail to recognize the "sin," we fall into the "Peret Trap": we think what we remember and remember what we think. Brown alerts us to the potentially dangerous sin of language by denying us the order-forcing power of the sentence and by deterring the closure of conventional grammar. His poetry breaks and enters the closed and unconscious linguistic habits with which one confidently maintains himself as Graves' "He." Most readers are so entrenched in the paradigms of grammar that they feel lost as they read "Returning Fire," a poem devoid of the punctuation they rely on to hierarchically order thought. Our very awareness of how desperately we want the missing commas put back in makes us admit that we normally organize our thoughts according to the "natural law" of subordination and the hierarchy of power inherent in the conventional clear images of sentence-making.

The Vietnam War should have made us more comfortable with discomfort. It should have made us more tolerant of "plantain in the mess hall" and "lotus in the latrine." It should have made us more

170

adept at being " . . . slow, thinking in broken images." It should have made "raw" verse as common as Chevrolets. Yet the national culture continues tamely to think, as it were, in eighteenth-century heroic couplets. The Vietnam poets can do nothing about the suffering the war produced; but they can do something about our propensity to waste it. In their best "songs of napalm," they do just that.

The Theatre of Doing It Wrong, Getting It Right

Take the glamour out of war! I mean, how the bloody hell can you do that? Ohhh, what a laugh! Take the bloody *glamour* out of bloody war!

—Tim Page, *Dispatches*

The story is told of one of Marcel Marceau's performances in which he mimed playing a cello. After the performance a somewhat bemused spectator—a *real* cellist—informed Marceau that his movements had been all wrong, that if anyone actually fretted and bowed a cello that way the sound produced would at best be peculiar. He then volunteered to show Marceau the correct way to mime cello-playing, and Marceau taped it. After viewing the tape, both agreed that it simply did not look like someone playing a cello. Somehow, by doing things wrong, Marceau had made it look right, whereas by doing things right, the cellist had made it look wrong.

My contention is that even highly considered Vietnam War narrative literature and cinema usually get Vietnam wrong because they do the fretting and bowing "right." Conversely, there is a handful of works that get Vietnam right by doing it all "wrong." One could argue, as I will, that most of them belong to war's neglected genre—drama. I might add that poetry is faring little better in attracting an audience. The epic and its modern offshoot, the novel, have traditionally dominated "box office" sales. The paradoxical premise of this chapter is that drama is best suited for grappling with the Vietnam War (or any war) precisely because it is the least suited. It is the best equipped for doing so because it is the least equipped. Most of the war's plays could be called the same thing the VC were during the war: "Those raggedy-assed little bastards" (Sheehan, 205). Necessarily "traveling light," the genre of drama is richly endowed with the resources needed to show the underbelly of the cliché "war is hell" precisely because it has so little "firepower." But, as I discuss below in this chapter, even theatre can fret and bow "correctly" by denying that it is theatre. As of this writing, Broadway's *Miss Saigon* has been doing just that for four years. It has spent millions to create the illusion that it isn't theatre. Theatre is real because it is so blatantly artificial. And, because the fretting and bowing are wrong, we hear richly disturbing music that is muffled, sometimes silenced altogether, by those who do it right.

This book is about how to "get" the Vietnam War right. It is now time to question my own fretting and bowing, maybe even to booby-trap my own "trail." In calling for a narrative accounting of America in Vietnam that is rooted in grave epistemological doubt, have I deluded myself into the belief that *I*, at any rate, am looking for my wallet where I lost it—in the dark? All the serious critics agree, to one degree or another, that the "postmodern" experience of Vietnam becomes seriously distorted when forced into the tidy perimeters of realism. These "Chuck Norris narratives" both do and get Vietnam wrong. On the other hand, my contention has been that skewed, ironic narratives are far more capable of expressing the disjunction between the official "reality" and what really happened to us and to Southeast Asians during the war. In his book *Walking Point*, Thomas Myers argues that this official reality flourished in order to force the war to dovetail with America's mythic identity. He and others have called this deluded identity America's "master narrative."

But can any narrative ultimately connect the reader or viewer responsibly to the Vietnam War? Edward Said says "no." According to him, all narratives are inextricably tied to imperialist impulses. He claims that the aesthetics of the "highly regulated plot mechanism" (71) bear a chicken-egg relationship to conquest. Imposing the structure of the novel on the naturally disordered flux of experience, and imposing one's cultural will on "backward" Third-World countries—both actions, says Said, stem from the very same "consolidation of authority": "The novel, as cultural artefact of bourgeois society, and imperialism are unthinkable without each other. . . . Imperialism and the novel fortify each other to such a degree that it is impossible . . . to read one without . . . the other" (77, 70–71).

Furthermore, isn't what Irving Howe said of Holocaust writing applicable to Vietnam narratives as well, despite my own arguments elsewhere in this book? Aren't even the skewed postmodernist narratives, like Michael Herr's *Dispatches* and Stephen Wright's *Meditations in Green*, a perpetuation of a traditional aesthetic problem?

> that the representation of a horrible event, especially if in drawing upon literary skills it achieves a certain graphic power, [will] serve to domesticate it, rendering it familiar and in some sense even tolerable, and thereby shearing away part of the horror. The comeliness of even the loosest literary forms is likely to soften the impact of what is being rendered. (Howe 29)

In Iris Murdoch's way of thinking, even horrific representations, because they too are "consolations of form," lead to caricatured memories. Therefore, as Howe and Said would have it, aesthetic decisions, whether good or bad, have moral and political ramifications.

It seems to me that this aestheticizing of the war obscures a deeper, far more radical problem—again, like Joseph Heller's Yossarian fastidiously treating Snowden's superficial hip wound. We need to take our cue from William Broyles, Jr., from whose article, "Why Men Love War," we can infer that one can properly loathe this war and be attuned to all of its monstrous atonality; one can correctly see all the stupidities, the genocides, the racisms; one can weep and rage—but still love it! "War is not an aberration," Broyles says; "it is part of the family, the crazy uncle we try—in vain—to keep locked in the basement" (56).

174

If I may extrapolate from Simone Weil's famous essay "The *Iliad*, Poem of Might," in war narratives "the intolerable afflictions either of servitude or war endure by force of their own weight, and therefore, from the outside [the reader's point of view] they seem easy to bear; they last because they rob the resources required to throw them off" (170). Weil goes on to say that whether you win or lose a war makes no difference, for pride and humiliation are equally intoxicating (179). (See the intoxication of the POW/MIA myth in chapter 9.) It makes no difference if a war story is written with patriotic zeal or disillusioned irony; both are predicated on the assumption that the human condition is largely rational and that, at its worst, the Vietnam War was a temporary disruption of sanity. Thus, both are false expressions of the misfortunes of war. To write with patriotic zeal is to deny any wounds; to write with disillusioned irony is to treat the superficial wounds. Either way, the act of bottling war in narrative form is a tacit admission that no radical change in the writer's consciousness has taken place. Either way, as Bertolt Brecht would have it, the spectator is projected into an event rather than confronted by it (3). Either way, to use the words of Weil, it is the "subordination of the human soul to might, which is, be it finally said, to matter," the intoxicating matter of war (179–80).

The problem with the movies and novels that get war wrong by doing it right is that, to use the words of Janine Basinger, they "have it both ways with the audience" (170). They offer jeremiads and trenchant criticisms of the war but at the same time engage us by appealing to our voyeuristic appetites. They tell us how terrible it all was, while at the same time they directly tap into the "pornography of popular desire," as Beidler aptly phrases it in "Bad Business: Vietnam and Recent Mass-Market Fiction" (64). In "Charlie Is a She: Kubrick's *Full Metal Jacket* and the Female Spectacle of Vietnam," Krista Walter argues that *Full Metal Jacket* (and I would suppose also Gustav Hasford's *The Short-Timers*, on which it is based) is an exception, that it cuts the voyeuristic "orgasmicord" by eliminating most of the staples of the traditional war story: the characters are psychopaths, so we can't identify with them; they have no mission, so there's no plot to sweep us along; and the Mickey Mouse ending is anticlimactic. But no matter how skewed or starkly ironic this narrative

175

may be, there is a much more powerful master narrative in counterpoint—a hungry narrative that will eat what is available. It does not like the taste of irony but will gladly eat it in order to get at the camera's seductive power to evoke the beautiful sexuality of combat, death, and massive destruction. This movie, too, has it both ways. In Howe's language, we are enthralled because we are appalled. Kubrick makes war deeply repulsive and deeply attractive. For popular audiences, the latter, arguably, wins out: Army enlistments rose sharply after this film was released.

In his fascinating essay/story/memoir/chapter, "How to Tell a True War Story," taken from his genre-crashing "novel" *The Things They Carried*, Tim O'Brien seems to point the way beyond glamorizing war and having it both ways: "If at the end of a war story you feel uplifted . . . then you have been made the victim of a very old and terrible lie" (210). Indeed, we have. But what if the lie satisfies? And what do we do with O'Brien's *Going After Cacciato*, a novel so exquisitely written that I felt uplifted after reading it? The narrator of Larry Heinemann's *Paco's Story* draws our attention to this problem when he says: ". . . most folks will shell out hard-earned, greenback cash, every time, to see artfully performed, urgently fascinating, grisly and gruesome carnage" (4). O'Brien's narrator also tells us that a true war story has an "uncompromising allegiance to the obscenity and evil of war" (210). Very good; but then so do Kubrick and Hasford in *Full Metal Jacket*. Again, O'Brien says, if you believe a war story, be skeptical. This is excellent advice, but it's a bit like being told by a pathological liar that he or she is lying. Finally, O'Brien tells us that some war stories are "just beyond telling" (210). But aren't they all? Couldn't it be argued that the very act of telling is exemplary of getting it wrong by doing it right?

Vietnam War writers and critics need to find a way beyond silently accommodating—like an alcoholic's hidden bottle—Tim Page's glamorous vision of war:

> Take the glamour out of war! I mean, how the bloody hell can you do that? Go and take the glamour out of a Huey, go take the glamour out of a Sheridan. It's like trying to take the glamour out of sex, trying to take the glamour out of the Rolling Stones. . . . I mean, you *know* that, it just *can't be done!* . . . The very *idea!* . . . Ohhh, what a laugh! Take the bloody *glamour* out of bloody war! (Herr, *Dispatches*, 265–66)

The glamour of the master narrative is hard to kill. Perhaps we need to admit that more than the family quarrel or in-house revolt of ironic narrative is required. Perhaps we can't fix war narratives by tinkering with war narratives. Maybe we can no more fix the wrong tool by using that tool than we can lift our left arm with our left arm. In John Arden's brilliant antiwar play from England, *Serjeant Musgrave's Dance* (1977), this is exactly what the title character tries to do. He wants to use the arts of violence to end violence. He tries to use what he calls his "book" (the British edition of the master narrative that encourages and dignifies the horrors of war) against itself. But, as a fellow soldier says: "You can't cure the pox with further whoring" (108).

In a sense, this is the error repeated by the most gripping of the Vietnam War anti-master narrative books. What Herr calls Vietnam's "dense concentration of American energy" screaming out in "hundred-channel panic" is powerfully seductive. The urge to plug back into that energy is a powerful come-on. The writer and the reader are enticed to give America's smoking Sodom and Gomorrah one more "eye fuck." To paraphrase Larry Heinemann's narrator, destruction is terrible, but it also is beautiful.

In my introduction I ascribe a degree of madness to the best Vietnam narratives. But can they ever be mad enough? C.D.B. Bryan, author of *Friendly Fire*, would say no. In response to a question about what the true Vietnam book will be like, he says: "I think it would have to be a Mystery, a Political Exposé, a Horror Story, a War Novel, a Tragedy; it would have to be fantastical, hallucinogenic, nightmarish black comedy born of rage and despair and betrayal and, yes, love. It would not be available at bookstores. Instead it would be helicopter-assaulted onto readers' front lawns; it would come videotaped, computerized, and Dolby-stereoed, with acetate overlays and a warning that eight or so years after being exposed to it, the reader stood a good chance of getting cancer" (72).

Leaving to the reader the question of what narratives might or might not be available at bookstores, one can say with certainty that a different species of war remembrances are available; they are the books that do take the bloody glamour out of war. Doing Vietnam all wrong, they are written by error-prone "mimes" of the Vietnam War—playwrights such as Tom Cole, Terrence McNally, Stephen

Metcalfe, John DiFusco, and, of special importance, Emily Mann, David Rabe, Amlin Gray, Arthur Kopit, and Steve Tesich.

Each of these playwrights seems to have realized that being on location, in country, for very long is dangerous for writer and reader alike. Irving Howe comes to this same conclusion in his article about Holocaust writing. Saying that some things are too terrible to be looked at or into directly, he urges the writer to learn a lesson from Perseus, who would turn to stone if he looked directly at the serpent-headed Medusa. But he could look at her through a reflection in a mirror. This is what the Vietnam dramatists tend to do. They look at Medusa through the mirror of self-conscious artifice. For example, in John DiFusco's collaborative play *Tracers* (first performed in 1980), a pantomimed post-battle scene, called a "blanket party," is staged. Four grunts are assigned the task of stacking invisible dead bodies scattered all over the stage. Soon they begin locating invisible fingers, arms, and various unrecognizable body parts, which they then try to mix and match with the stacked bodies. A "food fight" ensues. Finally, they place all the invisible human fragments on an invisible blanket, and with each character holding an invisible corner, they exit to the sound of "The Unknown Soldier" by the Doors. To use Jerzy Grotowski's phrase, this is "poor theatre" at its best. By not looking at the bodies directly, we actually see them more absolutely. In their palpable absence they become the Idea of carnage. Because the spectators can't see the individual bodies, they find themselves in the overwhelming presence of the Idea of death.

The actual genesis of this chapter was my perplexity over why this pantomimed scene in *Tracers* had a much more unsettling effect on me than the scene of mass carnage at the end of the movie *Platoon*. The sight of death is strangely wonderful because it is not one's own. This reaction to death is frequently documented in the novels and memoirs of the war. What makes the "blanket party" so chastening is that we can neither stare at death voyeuristically nor close a second, protective eyelid to shield us. Instead, we stare at the ultimate incarnation of death: emptiness filled with itself. The indirect look at death becomes painfully direct through the ritual of flaunted make-believe: theatre.

One of the most important differences between Vietnam narratives and plays is that none of the latter looks at Vietnam directly. Very few

178

even take place "in country." (By contrast, almost all Vietnam fiction and cinema do.) Only *Tracers*, Terrence McNally's *Botticelli* (1968), and Amlin Gray's *How I Got That Story* (1979) are set in Vietnam. And of David Rabe's four Vietnam plays, only *The Basic Training of Pavlo Hummel* (1971) is set in Vietnam, and then only briefly. Furthermore, even those that are "on location" are, like *Tracers*, so blatantly artificial and stylized that there is no possibility of seduction. There is no rerunning of the war.

This frees the playwright to reflect the subtexts of the war, to raise what James Reston, Jr., calls "generational questions" about the master narrative, to confront Americans with their own duplicity and complicity. As Emily Mann says in a note to her play *Still Life* (1980), Vietnam War plays are pleas for examination and self-examination of our own violence. The battles that these playwrights fight are not the ones in Khe Sanh, Pleiku, or An Loc. Their battlefield is one located between the war and the home-front epistemology that started, maintained, and lost it. Their battlefield reflects the conflicting realities of the master narrative, now out in a new edition, and the anti-novel that was Vietnam. Using a metaphor from Rabe's *Sticks and Bones* (1972), the Vietnam playwright traces either the fallout or the roots of the war back to the myth of innocence enshrined in Harriet Nelson's kitchen of immaculate deception. The Vietnam plays bring the war back home where it started and is still being waged. In some cases, "back home" is not some back alley in our crime-ridden coastal cities. Instead, it's the heartland of America. Emily Mann's *Still Life* is based on interviews in Minneapolis. In *How I Got That Story*, Amlin Gray's reporter hails from Dubuque, Iowa. Arthur Kopit's *Indians* (1969) deconstructs the cultural myths of America on its storied plains. Steve Tesich's *The Speed of Darkness* (1989) is set in the "Indian Country" of Sioux Falls, South Dakota. David Rabe's *Sticks and Bones* takes place in an archetypal middle-class family home. We could give these plays the composite title of Paul Hoover's novel, *Saigon, Illinois*, Bobbie Ann Mason's *In Country* (where "in country" means America), and Terry Allen's collage "Laos, New Mexico." To emphasize this connection between home and Vietnam, Rabe, in two of his plays (*Pavlo Hummel* and *Streamers*), calls for a stage that slants downward, rather threateningly, toward the audience.

And what a different "movie" we get when the "cello" is removed from the stage; when the screaming Phantoms just above tree level, the thudding rotors of the Huey, the vision of multicolored flares and tracers are all edited out. Most important, what a different "movie" we get when combat is edited out. Theatre simply cannot do combat without being plain silly. (Neither can cinema, but it has the technology to create the illusion that it can.) But this "VC" limitation is one of theatre's strengths, because trying to get Vietnam right by spending millions of technological dollars on the latest special effects is tantamount to fighting the wrong war, wrongly again.

Theatre gets into trouble when it tries to mimic Hollywood. This is precisely what happened in one of Broadway's smash hits—*Miss Saigon*. Just as the Pentagon unleashed its vast resources to do the Vietnam War right, to win it with ever more technological "toys" of war, so "the brass" of *Miss Saigon* "lost" their story by winning over kitsch-hungry audiences. And on Broadway the latter rarely, if ever, happens without state-of-the-art glitter, razzle-dazzle, and three-story spectacle. A contemporary retelling of the tragic tale of *Madame Butterfly*, the story behind the production of *Miss Saigon* is terribly important. I feel certain that Claude-Michel Schönberg (composer), Alain Boublil (lyricist), and Nicholas Hytner (director) really wanted their musical to raise American consciousness regarding the tragic plight of the thousands of Asian lovers, wives, and Amerasian children left behind in Vietnam. They operate on the correct premise that the war didn't end when it ended, in April 1975; for many, the end was the beginning. The reader will recall that the Vietnamese name for the Amerasian offspring is *bui doi*, which "can be translated," says Larry Engelmann, "as 'Dust of Life' and refers generally to anyone who belongs to no one" (28).

In a painful, more elaborate description of a *bui doi*, Tran, a Vietnamese character in Robert Olen Butler's *A Good Scent From a Strange Mountain*, says, "I was a child of dust." Comparing such children with drawings one can buy in Saigon bookstalls, she adds, "You look once and you see a beautiful woman sitting at her mirror, but then you look again and you see the skull of a dead person, no skin on her face, just the wide eyes of the skull and the bared teeth. We were like that, the children of dust in Saigon" (66).

Because of America's continued embargo on Vietnam, there's little chance of a *bui doi* ever being united with mother and father. So the war goes on, almost twenty years after it ended. There never was any linear closure, despite the rhetoric of our leaders. The play calls attention to this lack of closure by beginning in April of 1975, shooting ahead to a limbo time in 1978, then going back to 1975, and finally "ending" back in 1978. Appropriately, the final words of the play come to us in the form of a disturbing, ironic question. A dying Kim (the Madame Butterfly of the play) asks Chris (the new and morally improved version of Pinkerton): "How in one night have we come so far?"

There is another feature of the play that would seem to encourage a Brechtian spirit of audience self-examination: its indictment of consumerism and the American Dream. The vehicle for this indictment is the slimy, entrepreneurial pimp called the Engineer. Feeding his ego and purse with wasted, prostituted lives, he's a parody of neon, materialistic greed. With a huge tail-finned Cadillac a dominating presence on stage, he croons "Make me Yankee, they're my family." The problem with the play is that it tries to indict consumerism by gorging on it itself. Even in the somewhat scaled-down version of the touring show, twenty-eight tractor trailers are needed to contain the set and the machinery to run it. Even if we assume the best of intentions, the result is another kind of seductive prostitution, another form of having it both ways with the audience. Just as the cinema voyeur will "eat" irony to get at the food of choice—technology's intoxicating power of destruction—so the commercialized, "culinary" theatre voyeur will put up with a bit of consciousness-raising if he's rewarded with sufficient doses of the dazzling power of high-tech spectacle. By the end of the show, I believe, the raised consciousness sinks to its previous level.

This happens because, instead of "alienating" us (Brecht's *Verfremdungseffekt*), the play mesmerizes us; instead of challenging us, the medium massages us with its extravagance. Busy as an air-traffic controller, the stage manager manipulates an arsenal of "Vari-Lights," "Digital Light Curtains" generated and monitored by the latest computer wizardry, motorized pylons, infrared monitors, a body-vibrating sound system analyzed and controlled by "SIM" ("Source Independent Measurement"), twelve breath-taking breakaway sets, and "through-composed" music that exchanges serious thought and dialogue for hackneyed rhymes sung in a never-ending succession of sentimental, seductive harmonic thirds, regardless of the situation. The Fall of Saigon scene is a classic instance of "rich theatre" flaunting its wealth. The show spent tens of thousands of dollars—and a lot of dry ice to conceal the "strings"—to create the illusion of an actual helicopter landing on top of the embassy roof. This particular pretense of reality was the main reason —so it clearly seemed—that many of the people sitting around me had been willing to pay one hundred dollars a seat for a bit of Disneyworld titillation. During the intermission, one of them said, "That helicopter shit *better* be good!" Lest anyone think that the Broadway Theatre was innocent of "neon complicity," he or she should bear in mind that the theatre inverted the normal sixty/hundred dollar ticket prices for mezzanine/orchestra seats. Why? Because the former offered a better view of the helicopter.

If theatre is to have a lasting effect on its audiences, what is needed is a guerrilla genre. Unlike the military planners and Hollywood producers, who have so many toys that they try to play with all of them at once, this genre—when it is not trying to become a different genre—is quite satisfied with a rice ball, a little *nuoc mam*, and a carbine. Unlike the narratives of cinema and fiction, theatre, as Grotowski says in *Towards a Poor Theatre*, is like sculpture (39). The playwright and the director reveal essence by taking away, not adding on. They remove what is concealing the essence instead of building it up. They reveal by removing Snowden's flak jacket. What is left after their sculpting is the elemental stage. If we apply what Peter Brook says about Elizabethan theatre, we end up with "Absence of scenery [in the theatre of the Vietnam War] is one of its greatest freedoms" (86).

The paucity of scenery on the Vietnam stage creates a new relationship between author and audience, a new contract with new responsibilities for both parties. Once we no longer have a cello decorating the stage, we have a whole new agenda that differs radically from any on-location war narrative. Without the dead bodies, the jobs of the playwright and spectator become quite different from those of the narrator and reader or the moviemaker and spectator. The narrator enables the reader to see the seen, whereas the playwright enables the spectator to see the unseen mythic tracks that led to Vietnam and back to Harriet's split-level. Whereas the rich narrative is very user-friendly in that it does a great deal of the work for the passive reader as it fills in the Medusan Vietnam canvas, the poor theatre is user-disturbing; eliminating the wealth, it requires a great deal from the necessarily active spectator.

There is a sense in which both actors and spectators are vulnerable in the absence of scenery. That absence signifies that what happens in this theatre is active presentation and investigation, not passive representation; enactment, not reenactment. It is live, disturbingly so, because everyone involved (including the audience) knows that in production, theatre can easily go wrong if either party fails to embrace the special contract demanded by the genre. Distinguishing between the artifice of cinema and theatre, Brook says:

> The cinema flashes on to a screen images from the past. As this is what the mind does to itself all through life, the cinema seems intimately real. Of course, it is nothing of the sort—it is a satisfying and enjoyable extension of the unreality of everyday perception. The theatre, on the other hand, always asserts itself in the present. This is what can make it more real [getting it right by doing it wrong] than the normal stream of consciousness. This also is what can make it so disturbing. (99)

Brook argues that theatre is disquieting because the spectator cannot get beyond the medium itself. The medium is the message. The authentic Vietnam theatre is about theatre, about making the unseen seen, about how we see. It is artifice that flaunts its artificiality and poverty. Compare this to what Northrop Frye says about the artifice of narrative. He likens it to a plate-glass window between shoppers and a department store display. The glass is so clean and polished that the shoppers are unaware of it. Unconsciously they pass right through its invisibility to the costly consumer items on the other side (265). This is what happens to the readers of most Vietnam War narratives. Enticed and distracted by the content, they are unaware of how the intervening form (like Thomas Myers' "neutral camera") is processing and translating that content. Polished and repolished by long use, narrative—and language itself—seems completely natural and neutral, as if created by God. Seeing only the seen, readers are unaware of the intervening filtering lens. In a word, Vietnam narratives can very easily become what Roland Barthes means by myth, "a way of thinking so deeply embedded in our consciousness that it is invisible" (Postman, 79). In other words, events seem real only to the extent that they are organized into a plot. Meanwhile, the processing medium goes about its window washing—unseen; the interpretive tool becomes the mythic reality, and the unseen artifice of realism actually is identified as "authenticity," the buzzword of critics and veterans.

In these post-Vietnam years, we can ill afford to ignore how dangerously easy it is to remythologize the war, which I think Michael Herr, for example, has done—quite unintentionally—with his magnificent book. The Vietnam playwrights seem to have recognized this, for they are demythologizers of war's glamour, of militarism, of violence, of machismo, of the whole apparatus of Bildungsroman, of the media that process us and tell us who Americans are. On their relatively bare, detechnologized stages they never let us forget the artifice and the illusion of transparency. We never get around or through the opaque medium; it takes up all of our time. To translate Brecht again, these playwrights "alienate" us at every turn, breaking all the rules of verisimilitude. Blatantly tossing away any pretense of being real, they insist on the being of real pretense—the imaginary cello.

Emily Mann's *Still Life* is one of the most effective examples of a play as the being of real pretense. It consists of three characters: Mark, a guilt-ridden Marine combat veteran, now a struggling, tormented artist; Cheryl, his willfully politically naive, passive-aggressive wife; and Nadine, Mark's somewhat cynical older friend, artist, and social activist. Soon after the play begins, Mark says, "I don't want this to come off as a combat story" (222). One can infer that he has done very little but rerun intoxicating combat stories since his discharge, and he knows that these stories simply plug him back into something he can't process: nostalgia, and therefore guilt, for the seductive power of having been able to do horrible things—legally—while in Vietnam. The point is, Mann doesn't allow her play to turn into a combat story. She cuts the "orgasmicord" by staging a Brechtian play loaded with alienation effects. Somewhat reminiscent of Beckett's play (simply called *Play*), *Still Life*'s characters speak—much to our discomfort—directly to the audience; and, rather than speak to each other, they speak about each other in the third person. Rarely do they even seem aware of each other's presence. Their voices collide with each other and overlap, undermine, and deflect each other ironically. Occasionally they even drown each other out. Also, because the audience is repeatedly and directly told that we are *all* implicated in the Vietnam War, we have a fourth "voice" added to this polyphonic collage of traumatic memories of the 1960s and 70s and explorations of an untenable present.

What Mann achieves with the contrapuntal voicings is that no single voice can ever build up narrative momentum and stake out a claim for the spectator's sympathy. The content of this play is not any or all of the voices; instead it is the charged, silent spaces between the voices. Almost like a musical score, this play is an investigation of consonant and dissonant relationships. Thus, Mark can share fragments from his Vietnam experiences without the play becoming his univocal "melody." Many of these fragments are slides of war photographs that Mark projects on a screen throughout the play. As such, they are offered up as still lifes, operating on the spectator's mind in conjunction with the "still lifes" of Nadine and Cheryl. I emphasize "still" to distinguish Mark's Vietnam slides from the movement and life of narrative art. Whereas narrative art presupposes either linear or nonlinear continuity, the still lifes underscore rupture.

Mann's point is that the tangled, ruptured voices allow (and force) the audience to see the real theatre of Vietnam where we all were "it." The real Vietnam is not *other*, not an isolated, sickly surreal aberration of the American identity. Instead, as Mann presents the war it is a logical continuation, a mere symptom of violence masked by seemingly respectable values, marriages, fatherhood, motherhood, even the church. Dysfunctional families and social institutions are seen here virtually as basic training for Vietnam. For Mann and for the Vietnam playwright in general, the Vietnam War was not a short circuit. Rather, it was all systems go; everything went according to plan. The crazy uncle simply had to walk up the stairs. He did.

Mann's collage of domestic voices *is* Vietnam. It is its formula. Of course, this collage once again does Vietnam all wrong: it muffles the universal siren call; it pulls it off location; it devotes two-thirds of the play to women; it is written by a woman who hasn't set foot in Vietnam; finally, it is an internal-affairs investigation, not an adventure. Mann's stage directions call for a "poor theatre" set that looks like a conference room or a trial room.

Mann concludes her play with a microcosmic slide projected on a screen. It is Mark's still-life collage, and it reveals the Vietnam that can exist only when the one done right is replaced by the one done wrong. At first it looks like a classic Zurbarán still life: wholesome grapefruit, an orange, delicious fresh bread. But with her melody-destroying improper "fretting and bowing," Mann also includes a grenade, a broken egg, and a fly on the fruit. In the production I saw, the director called for a fast-changing series of slides that began with "sweetness and light" but quickly degenerated into a picture of America that America would rather not recognize. That fly, broken egg, and grenade are not meant simply to represent the ticking trip-wire Marine veteran suffering from post-traumatic stress disorder; they are also a commentary on the dangerous American mythic jungle. If anything, Mann would have us see the fruit and bread as Mark's, the rest of the collage as Nadine's, Cheryl's, and the audience's. "We've all done it." Mark's final line—"I didn't know what I was doing"—reminds one of Friedrich Dürrenmatt, who upon surveying the first fifty-four years of the twentieth century, declared, "In the Punch-and-Judy show of our century . . . everything is dragged along and everyone gets caught somewhere in the sweep of events. We are all collectively guilty, collectively bogged down in the sins of our fathers and of our forefathers . . ." (31).

All of David Rabe's Vietnam-related plays—*The Basic Training of Pavlo Hummel, Sticks and Bones, Streamers,* and *Hurlyburly* (1984)—are seemingly incongruous collages of the voices that led us to Vietnam. Once again, it is Brechtian juxtaposition, not continuity, that forms their structure. Even his seemingly conventional *Streamers* is Brechtian. As I have said, the stage threatens to spill into an implicated audience. Beyond that, although the play might seem at first simply to be a study of characters nervously awaiting reassignment to Vietnam, it is actually something quite different. The main character is not Richie, Carlyle, Billy, Roger, Cokes, or Rooney. Instead, it is the claustrophobic physical space of the theatre in which Rabe confines them and us. Rabe denies the master narrative the open space it needs to thrive. For audience and actors the play thus becomes a no-exit confrontation without, as it were, the mitigating backgrounding of Samuel Barber's tear-jerking Adagio in *Platoon*. Without giving anyone any cover, Rabe thrusts the myths of male initiation and barracks camaraderie into the foreground where they self-destruct.

Rabe refuses even to write an anti-Bildungsroman, for that would still give us the seductive continuity of so many Vietnam War narratives: naive young man's initiation leads not to new wisdom but to cynicism. Rabe will have none of that in his plays. In effect, he announces this to his audience one minute into *Pavlo Hummel* by having his "hero" die the first of several deaths. The beginning is the end. The title character is Rabe's new American mythic Everyman: a creature who dies over and over, pointlessly and absurdly. As Ardell, his stud alter ego, says, we're "thin as paper. We melt; we tear and rip apart. Membrane, baby. Cellophane. Ain't that some shit" (96). It is as if Pavlo is caught in the middle of the very chaotic game of hurly-burly, and Rabe's collage-like structure reinforces this. If Mann gives us a Dali still life, Rabe gives us one of Jean Tinguely's motorized, self-destructing sculptures, coughing, hissing, belching, lurching, and smoking, with the grinding of unaligned gears. *Pavlo Hummel* is frantic and frenetic. I know of no play that makes such a shambles of Aristotle's three unities. Action, place, and time are so scrambled that sometimes we are in Vietnam in the jungle, in a whorehouse, in a hospital; we are at Fort Gordon, in a day room, in the physical training area, in a barracks, at the rifle range; we are in New York, in Pavlo's brother's apartment, in Pavlo's mother's apartment—all virtually simultaneously, with no significant set changes. At one point Pavlo undresses, dresses, has a prostitute undress him in his brother's room, which is his mother's place, which is a Vietnamese whorehouse, where a wounded GI calls to Pavlo from his hospital bed while Pavlo's drill instructor yells training instructions, and so on. Of course cinema can do these same cuts (in fact, it can do them much better), but this wealth often is its poverty. Whereas in cinema the cuts are demarcated from one discrete space to another, in *Pavlo Hummel* the dirt is dragged from space to space, until they merge, messily, in a mise-en-scène collage of fractured space and time that properly contextualizes the war.

Whereas, in *Still Life* the voicings are a tenuously controlled polyphony, in *Pavlo Hummel* they are strident, raucous, and cacophonous. The volume is set at fortissimo, the tempo at prestissimo. Paradoxically, all these quick movements and sharp juxtapositions bring the play to a silent halt. They destroy any possibility of momentum. Appropriately, following eight staccatoed, crescendoing repetitions of the word "shit," Rabe's composition climaxes with a very long, sustained note, a note that sums up the lessons learned from the experience that supposedly turns boys into men—Pavlo's basic training. Dying for the fourth time, Pavlo howls "SHHHHHHHHIIIIIIIIITTTT-TTTTTTttttttt!" certainly the most protracted use of the word in the history of the theatre. How do we interpret this moment of "epiphany"? We can infer from Rabe's note to the play that Pavlo, one of many thousands of middle-class kids who went to Vietnam, finally comes to the realization that he is lost and always has been lost. But he does not learn "how, why, or even where" (110).

Like most of Rabe's characters (David Nelson, in *Sticks and Bones*, is somewhat of an exception), Pavlo finds himself in a world where linguistic certainties no longer obtain. His line, "I DON'T KNOW WHAT YOU'RE TALKING ABOUT!" (97) expresses the extremely limited point of view of these characters. Similarly, what Rabe says in his afterword to *Hurlyburly* reminds one of *Still Life*, and it applies to all of his plays: "It has no 'mouthpiece' character. [What play responsible to its genre does?] No one in it knows what it is about. It has no character who is its spokesman. The main character [Eddie] does not understand it" (169). Rabe's characters search for an author, for anything that will locate them in a world where language meaningfully connects them to a seemingly accidental sequence of events, for which Vietnam was the "ON" button. In fact, one could say that Rabe's plays are Tinguely accidents, not constructed plots. They are the antithesis of narrative. Trapped within that antithesis, we find characters on an elemental stage who, like stroke victims, need to start from scratch, without sustaining props, to rediscover language, voice, and movement. To draw attention to this loss of language, Rabe, in *Hurlyburly*, has his characters fill silence by repeatedly being reduced to uttering such phrases as "whatchamacallit," "thingamajig," and "blahblahblah." As Rabe says in his stage directions, "These are phrases used by the characters to keep themselves talking and should be said unhesitat-

Doing It Wrong, Getting It Right

ingly with authority and conviction . . ." (13), as in A squared plus B squared equals whatchamacallit.

But if Rabe does not allow his characters to pilot their way through a linguistic wasteland, he does allow his spectators to come to some understanding of how, why, and where America got lost. He allows this by *not* allowing us to make the mistake that Magellan makes in Sergeant Brisbey's story. Brisbey, a minor character who loses both legs and an arm to a Bouncing Betty, says to Pavlo: "I keep thinking about ole Magellan, sailin' round the world. . . . So one day he wants to know how far under him to the bottom of the ocean. So he drops over all the rope he's got. Two hundred feet. It hangs down into the sea that must go down and down beyond its end for miles and tons of water. He's up there in the sun. He's got this little piece of rope danglin' from his fingers. He thinks because all the rope he's got can't touch the bottom, he's over the deepest part of the ocean. He doesn't know the real question. How far beyond all the rope you got is the bottom?" (89) Of all Vietnam War literature, the genre of drama has the best track record for compelling audiences to contemplate what occupies the space between the end of Magellan's rope and the bottom. Even some of the longer "ropes" of narrative are somewhat limited to the duration of the writer's immediate war experiences. Rather than measure depth, they measure the short length of a year or less in most cases. As such, they lack an appreciation for what Owen Gilman calls "deep history."

Changing the attitude of the "rope" from horizontal to vertical, Rabe frequently makes contact with the same submerged phenomenon of America's identity and epistemology: Hollywood. Not for nothing does the refrain, "I don't think I'm going to like this movie" echo throughout Vietnam War literature. Hollywood is in the background (the foreground in *Hurlyburly*) of all Rabe's plays. Talking about Hollywood, a character in *Hurlyburly* says,

> They take an interesting story, right? They distort it, right? Cut whatever little truth there might be in it out on the basis of it's unappealing, but leave the surface so it looks familiar—cars, hats, trucks, trees. So, they got their scam, but to push it they have to flesh it out, so this is where you come in, because then they need a lot of authentic sounding and looking people—high quality people such as yourself, who need a buck. So like

189

every other whore in this town, myself included, you have to learn to lend your little dab of whatever truth you can scrounge up in yourself to this total, this systematic sham—so that the fucking viewer will be exonerated from ever having to confront directly the fact that he is spending his life face to face with total shit. (29)

Later he adds, "Phil, you're background, don't you know that? They just take you on for background. Don't you know that? You're a prop" (114). A prop in a mythic landscape immaculately conceived by Hollywood.

In *Pavlo Hummel*, Rabe would have us see that Hollywood infiltrates and poisons the family, where mothers and fathers pass on a schizophrenic legacy to their children. In fact, in this play Hollywood becomes a father substitute. After Pavlo asks his mother who his father is, she answers, "You had many fathers, many men, movie men, filmdom's great—all of them, those grand old men of yesteryear, they were your fathers" (75). Rabe's plays are explorations into the mythic landscapes where he searches for connections between the network of trails and voices that led to Vietnam. In *Sticks and Bones* he pinpoints one very important source: the TV, spic-and-spanned, Tidy-Bowled, lemon-pledged, Aunt-Jemimad, perfectly middle-classed home of Ozzie and Harriet Nelson. David Nelson, a combat veteran blinded in the war, says, "I am—a young . . . blind man in a room . . . in a house in the dark, raising nothing in a gesture of no meaning toward two voices who are not speaking of a certain . . . incredible . . . connection!" (162). Not so paradoxically, like Tiresias, David does come to see the connection precisely because he is blind. Being blind, he gets Vietnam right. He is no longer distracted by the seductive, "systematic sham." Because he is blind, only he can see the tortured images of his Vietnam War home movie. Because he is blind, only he can see the specter of a dispossessed Vietnamese girl floating through the walls of Ozzie and Harriet's home. Because he is blind, only he can see that the walls of his parents' home are constructed from coffins filled with the war-dead. He sees the total complicity of his Hollywoodized family. And now he understands the hows, whys, and wheres. Now he sees the collage of voices that led to Vietnam. He says: "There were old voices inside me I had trusted

190

all my life as if they were my own. I didn't know I shouldn't hear them. So reasonable and calm they seemed a source of wisdom" (177). We hear all these voices within the Nelson home. They are the voices of racism, xenophobia, ethnocentrism, technology, consumerism, sexism, patriarchal theism, and narrative revisionism.

Rabe's Nelson family of the 1970s certainly is less innocent than its counterpart in the 1950s: Harriet expresses overt racism; Ozzie uses x-rated language; Rick talks about sexual exploits, and so on. Fundamentally, however, the family is as inane, unaware, and morally obtuse as ever. Rabe shows us the underbelly of sit-com innocence, and it's not pretty. Behind those respectable walls is a family that in Neil Postman's words is "amusing [itself] to death" in America's "brave new world." As Rabe says in his note to the play, Ozzie, Harriet, and Rick

> must not physically ignore [their complicity in the Vietnam War] . . . —turn their backs, avert their eyes, be busy with something else. The point is not that they do not physically see or hear, but that they psychologically ignore. Though they look right at things, though they listen closely, they do not see or hear. The harder they physically focus and concentrate on an event, the clearer their psychological state and the point and nature of the play will be, when in their next moments and speeches they verbally and emotionally ignore or miss what they have clearly looked at. (225)

David certainly understands that this is a family that has stayed "sane" only because of virtual "hard-wired" fraudulence (170). It has stayed mindlessly happy because it has drugged itself on "E-Z Sleep" and repeated bulimic raids on the kitchen. If Rabe is right, families did not become dysfunctional because of the Vietnam War or because of returning vets. If anything, the war happened because of dysfunctional families bowing down to the combined shrines of consumerism, zealous patriotism, and a frontier mythology.

The Nelson family measures its existence with a very short rope. Thus, Rabe says: "A major premise of the play is that stubbing your own big toe is a more disturbing event than hearing of a stranger's suicide" (226). David tries to incite his family to lengthen its rope

191

(interestingly, my students of the 1980s and 90s invariably have found David to be a selfish, ungrateful ogre) and to widen its vision beyond the posed snapshots that Rick endlessly takes with his Instamatic. He can no more accomplish this, however, than he can expect them to see anything more than flickering shades of green in his "home" movie of the war. Figuratively speaking, the only thing he accomplishes is to rearrange the family furniture so that Ozzie, Harriet, and Rick stub their big toes as they walk in spiritual darkness.

Rabe may grant David a bit of understanding that he denies Pavlo in *Pavlo Hummel*, Billy in *Streamers*, and Eddie in *Hurlyburly*, but he is no sentimentalist. The myth of the master narrative is indestructible in *Sticks and Bones*. It contains its own antibodies which destroy any bacteria that threaten its healthy sickness. Finally, even Ozzie has to admit the presence of Vietnam in his house of coffins. When he does finally see Zung, David's Vietnamese lover, he strangles her to death and drags her out of sight and mind. Even Harriet comes to see that David's presence will undo her fudge-and-cookie bulimic regimen. So she fetches the silver pans and the kitsch towels with roosters on them and watches, with growing contentment and calm, as David slits his wrists. As David's blood flows, the voices of Ozzie, Harriet, and Rick almost literally begin to purr. Their brave new world, which would become even further institutionalized during the Reagan era, is once again intact. The ever-ready supply of soma will keep it oblivious to its complicity.

Amlin Gray's *How I Got That Story* is ultimate "poor theatre," and this very poverty enables Gray to expose the artifice behind the Hollywoodization of the Vietnam War. Although the play shows us an entire war-torn society in Vietnam (called Am-Bo Land here), it uses only two actors. One plays a naive Iowa reporter whose previous journalistic feat was to cover the western part of East Dubuque. The other plays the entire Historical Event, which involves twenty-one different roles, including soldiers, both American and Vietnamese, peasants, a crazed Tim Page-like photographer, a nun, prostitutes, and the Am-bo Land Empress, Madame Ing—all without makeup. Furthermore, this actor does all the sound effects: rock music, gunfire, a self-immolating monk, an airplane dive-bombing. As one can easily imagine, this is all done quite wrong!

But as Jack Kroll said in his review of the play, Gray's "impulse is not so much to see as it is to see through—everything and everybody" (68). What Gray sees through is the myth that war can be truthfully rendered into war stories. The irony of *How I Got That Story* is that there is no story. [1] As the reporter puts it, "All I found out as a reporter was I'd never find out anything" (107). How can you write a story about something that dissolves even as you begin to write about it? How can you write about a labyrinth where the walls change position with each step you take? Gray's reporter thinks he will get his story. He arrives in country with the traditional bag filled with linguistic Agent Orange. He thinks he has all the necessary weapons. He has names for them: truth, reality, document, fact, objectivity, news, answers. But as he desperately searches for a hook, an angle, a way to render the war in narrative form, he is totally done in by the protean Historical Event. There simply are too many masks and dissembling voices between the reporter and reality, too many layers of artifice between him and the edifice. To call attention to this, Gray puts Vietnam's backstage upstage, in Brechtian fashion. The opaque, artificially contrived medium becomes the message of the play, just as it was the unacknowledged, subtextual message of the war itself. Thus, Gray implodes rather than explodes the falseness of the whole Vietnam endeavor, the duplicity, and the overlapping entangled contingencies. Gray's message is that Vietnam was a farce, not a tragedy, and certainly not a narrative. The story that Americans did

---

1. The very title of Gray's play is an ironic inside joke, for it is identical to that of a 1967 self-congratulatory book edited by David Brown and W. Richard Bruner in which thirty-six foreign correspondents tell of the intrepid cunning they practiced in order to get their exclusive stories from various hot spots in the world. Compare the disillusionment of Gray's reporter with the dauntless confidence with which many of these correspondents conclude their stories about their stories: "We sat down on two boxes, used a trunk for a desk, and wrote the story." "And once more Mac had proved that the word 'impossible' is nonsense." "I had taken 'the bull by the horns'—and a big one at that—and won." "I had the satisfaction associated with getting out a story nobody else had. Every newsman and woman knows the feeling!" "I had realized the newspaperman's dream of a lifetime—a world scoop." See also Evelyn Waugh's *Scoop*, a novel about an uncorrespondent acclaimed for his unstory about an unwar in an uncountry.

get back home was therefore less real than the Historical Event crumpling paper to imitate the sound of a monk on fire. So, by seemingly doing everything wrong, Gray gets the war right, as perhaps only the playwright can.

Reporter Michael Herr and Amlin Gray's Am-bo Land reporter both come to the conclusion that they went to cover the war but that the war ended up covering them instead. The difference is, Herr eventually got a story of sorts, whereas Gray's reporter did not. As the play comes to an end, we see the photographer, now legless and one-armed because of his insane efforts to do Vietnam right, pulling himself forward on a dolly. He sees the reporter dressed in peasant pajamas, crumpled on the floor in "a position that suggests a drunken stupor or a state of shock" (117). Delighted by the presence of this former reporter in search of a narrative, he takes a flash photo. At the same instant, a picture of the reporter appears on a screen. "It is the head and shoulders of a body in the same position of the reporter's, dressed identically. The face is that of the Event" (117). The coverage now complete, Gray pushes his irony one final step: a new slide appears on the screen, bearing the words HOW I GOT THAT STORY. Then, blackout. Narrative is expunged.

One of the implicit lessons of this and many other Vietnam War plays is that when a nation's mythic hunger twists a farce into narrative, real people start dying from real bullets and bombs. The real war would never even have started were it not for the fact that Americans saw themselves as the protagonists in that most linear of narratives: the Domino Theory. Long before the war started, we were a people pretending to be characters in a false, superimposed genre. When this paper genre disintegrated, we left hundreds of thousands of Vietnam veterans without a book and without an author. Not for nothing does a character in *Tracers* say that he feels like a character out of Pirandello. To his credit, he at least gets the genre right.

Earlier I alluded to Thomas Myers' book, *Walking Point*. As a critic, Myers himself does an outstanding job of walking point. The metaphor itself seems apt. Like most of the point-walking novelists he discusses, Myers has a keen awareness that "the point man seldom knows the strength or the location of his adversaries. In the thick

194

undergrowth of mythic space, however, the enemy is clearly positioned and well equipped, a foe of prodigious power with a familiar face" (8). Myers has a pretty good nose for this mythic undergrowth. He is about as wary of what is on his flanks as one can be: the myths of popular culture on one side, official airbrushings and reifications on the other.

But let him and us keep our eyes on the rear. And let all of us be on the alert for friendly fire, fraggings, and the long-term effects of Agent Orange—in short, our own mythical ordnance. Let us wonder about Myers' very masculine metaphor of being the point that penetrates the jungle. And wouldn't "listening posts," where soldiers observed, rather than fought, be a better analogy for a critical study of Vietnam War literature? Let all of us not overestimate the firepower and effectiveness of the predominate Vietnam War "field weapon"— narrative. Let all of us realize that the "foe of prodigious power with a familiar face" has a more familiar face than we may have first thought. And especially, let all of us realize that the point man, as watchful and responsible for others as he was, sometimes was allowed to pass in order to trap the entire patrol within the enemy's field of fire.

These lessons are powerfully investigated in two plays, Arthur Kopit's *Indians* and Steve Tesich's *The Speed of Darkness*. *Indians*, part historical reenactment and part farce, covers the seven-year period from the creation of Buffalo Bill's "Wild West" show in 1883 to the assassination of Sitting Bull and the massacre at Wounded Knee in 1890. But, by including in his play an entire stable of Western "heroes"—such as Wild Bill Hickok, Ned Buntline, Annie Oakley, and Billy the Kid, and American Indians as spatially and tribally discrete as Sitting Bull, Geronimo, Chief Joseph, and Tecumseh—Kopit enlarges his canvas to include and indict the whole history of American frontier "regeneration through violence." As the play's cover blurb says, ". . . the legend of the Western hero bravely taming a savage land is shown to be a fraudulent mythologizing of greed and stupidity—just as the Wild West Show itself was."

Written in 1969, *Indians* sweeps us forward to the more recent "Indian War" in Vietnam, and to the 1968 version of Wounded Knee—

My Lai. True, Kopit's play never enters the twentieth century, much less mentions anything about Vietnam, but the parallels between Indian wars fought in the Wild West and in Vietnam—"waged by myth-haunted heroes out of date, waged in all the wrong ways for all the wrong reasons in a grand tragedy of mass cultural misperception" (Beidler, 69)—are too obvious to ignore. The climaxes at Wounded Knee and My Lai are troublingly similar, committed as each was by angry, weary, edgy, scared soldiers involved in an enterprise to save "Indians" by killing them. Beidler points out additional parallels. For example, in one scene a Russian duke desperately wants to become inscribed in the Frontier Myth by killing a Comanche. Because there are no Comanches in Missouri, he kills a Sioux instead, figuring any Indian is close enough, a scene Beidler plausibly claims is prophetic of the TOG rule: "They're Only Gooks" (67).

But there is another way we can imagine *Indians* as an allegory of the Vietnam War, and that is by looking at the actual history of Cody's Wild West Show from 1883 to 1917. We can gather from reading Richard Slotkin's account of this history in *Gunfighter Nation: The Myth of the Frontier in Twentieth-Century America* (1992), that the show was both static and dynamic. It was static in that, for many years in cities all over America and even in Europe, it persistently dredged up Custer's Last Stand, attacks on wagon trains, Rambo-like rescue missions of white captives, and so on. Long after the Frontier was safely closed, these staged events continued to offer food, unseasoned with irony, to millions of people with ravenous, insatiable mythic appetites.

However, the show was dynamic as well. It may not have led nine lives, but it led several. As Custer's Last Stand finally began to lose luster, Buffalo Bill simply found new locations and events in different Indian countries. His myth-making show quickly learned to cross open water and regenerate itself in Cuba and the Philippines. Teddy Roosevelt's charge up San Juan Hill became the hottest new chapter of the myth. The show even appropriated China's 1901 Boxer Rebellion, and in an extremely prophetic move, Cody had Indians play the role of the oriental Boxers. Finally, near the end of his and the show's life, Cody created a show to propagandize the need to enter World War I.

196

The most important aspect of Cody's actual show, however, is that it helped create an insatiable symbiotic feeding frenzy; the show fed off whatever events came along in Indian Country that would improve its ratings, and the historical events fed on the show's ratings to transform themselves into the stature of myth. Once mythologized, the events gained the procreative power to actually shape reality. Once again, we're back to Doc Peret's unbroken cycle. Twentieth-century American history and popular culture offer ample evidence that it may be unbreakable as well as unbroken. Cody's show went under for good in 1917, but the Frontier Myth and the appetite for it was about to become more powerful than ever—through the new medium of cinema. Hollywood destroyed the show, but would soon turn the myth into a mega-industry that would enchant more people in a week than Cody reached in a year.

This unbroken, perhaps unbreakable cycle of self-regenerative violence lies at the center of Kopit's play. The internal mythic ordnance is overwhelming, and it results in a seamless, mesh of myth and history. Slotkin's comments on Cody's show illuminate Kopit's primary thrust:

> The landscape [of the Wild West] was a mythic space in which past and present, fiction and reality, could coexist; a space in which history, translated into myth, was re-enacted as ritual. Moreover, these rituals did more than manipulate historical materials and illustrate an interpretation of American history; in several rather complex ways, the Wild West and its principals managed not only to comment on historical events but to become actors [in history] themselves. (69)

Kopit underscores the seamless, unbroken cycle by refusing to demarcate the beginning and ending of his play with a curtain. The play "begins" even as the audience is walking in. Moreover, the play ends just as it began, with yet another beginning of the Wild West show. As in an endless fugue, the apparent end is actually the replaying of the principal theme. In a brilliant move, Kopit demonstrates that the myth will not only continue to be unstoppable and omnivorous, but omnipresent as well. Throughout the show's life, Cody strove to believe that the fraudulent myth of the warrior hero was true and empirically verified. For this reason, he always insisted on the title Wild

197

West, rather than Wild West *Show*. (His concern would surface again in those critics who denigrated the metafictional preoccupation of Tim O'Brien.) So, in the play he is horrified when he discovers that Wild Bill Hickok has manufactured dozens of Buffalo Bill replicas who can perform and do "WHAT MY BELOVED COUNTRY *WANTS!* (41), namely, "relieve its conscience" (35), in many cities simultaneously. Enraged, Cody begins to shoot the replicas, who fall down dead and then get right back up again. Hickok had the "right" idea, just the wrong vehicle. It wouldn't be long before film—much better suited to myth-building than any other medium—surpassed his wildest dreams. It wouldn't be long before millions of Americans started idolizing matinee heroes everywhere at once as they killed Indians, rescued white virgins, shot it out on Main Street, and stormed the beach, falling down and getting back up again. Already aware of the myth's omnipresence in the 1880s, Kopit's Sitting Bull tells Cody, "I never killed you . . . because I *knew it would not matter*" (88). He knew that Cody existed principally as an idea, not a man. He knew that an idea, no matter how baseless and fraudulent, was unkillable.

I should add that it does not matter in the least how baseless and fraudulent the idea might be. In fact, Kopit does any number of things to emphasize that showing the fraudulence for what it is in no way detracts from its power: terribly rendered canvas drops are rolled up to reveal terribly rendered canvas drops; caricatures of mechanical horses plop about the stage. In a patently ludicrous play-within-a-play presented to the Ol' Time President (clearly, LBJ, who has bought a mechanical horse of his own with which to hunt buffalo and kill Indians), the Indians speak with German, Italian, and Brooklyn accents. During the play-within-a-play, Hickok incredulously asks the President and the First Lady if this embarrassing "dude-written sissyshit" (41) is really what they want to see. They are ecstatic in their affirmation. Kopit's point is that no matter how absurdly disconnected myth is from reality (as it was in Vietnam, and as it continues in the religious fervor of the POW/MIA issue), our leaders will force the connection. And, as they nail the coonskin to the barn door, with or without an actual coonskin or barn door, millions of Americans will buy it.

This is not to say that *Indians* shows myth as being unassailable. In fact, one can see the very beginning of the play as America in 1969, a time when its mythic narrative was in shambles. The play captures this by beginning in dim light, with lifeless frontier relics enclosed in three sterile glass cases. While the house lights fade to dark, and we hear strange, disorienting music, even these sterile cases "glide into the shadowy distance and disappear" (1). We are now left with a frightened, demythologized America. With an eerie light now on stage, "dim spotlights [searching for a mythic fix] sweep the floor as if trying to locate something in space." We briefly hear fractured, distorted snippets of Western American music. Echoing everywhere in the theatre comes a voice invoking the return of myth: "Cody . . . *Cody . . . Cody!* . . . *CODY!* And in a very short time the invocation is answered. Buffalo Bill and his white stallion appear, rodeo music sounds, lights begin to blaze, and Buffalo Bill proclaims, "Yessir, BACK AGAIN! . . . Yessir . . . Should o'known here's where I belong" (2). Compressing history prophetically, Kopit in a few moments shoots us forward from 1969 to 1991, when the lights blazed again and America sold out of flags, yellow ribbons, and recall.

Near the end of the play, the Frontier Myth is once again jeopardized. Buffalo Bill himself can't help but see, following the massacre at Wounded Knee, that the myth had assumed its natural ugly shape. He says, "I'm scared . . . I dunno what's happenin' anymore. . . . Things have gotten . . . *beyond* me" (77). Already in the play-within-a-play, he had been walking around the stage stunned because Hickok, caught in a myth-history interphase, refuses to play his role in the "sissyshit" play. Irate because Ned Buntline didn't give him the promised Bat Masterton part, he kills him. Then he commits the unpardonable sin against the Frontier Myth: he sexually molests the very maiden he was supposed to rescue from the allegedly lustful Pawnees. The situation has gotten "beyond" Cody, because in Hickok's blasphemous "deconstruction" of the perennial captivity narrative, he now is forced to recognize the big lie of that heart-and-soul national story: White Americans kill, maim, and rape; they're not a special "City on the Hill" at all. Because of his temporary disenchantment with mythic America, Cody somewhat reverses Hamm's opening words in Beckett's *Endgame*: "Me—to play." Instead of playing, he now wants to end the play: "AND NOW TO CLOSE! AND *NOW TO CLOSE!*" (89).

Then we hear him regenerate the myth, not quite sure how to proceed at first: ". . . I would . . . first . . . like to . . . say a few words in defense of my country's Indian policy, which seems, in certain circles, to be meeting with considerable disapproval" (89). In very little time he reaches the point where, in perfect adherence to the organizational procedure of the Frontier Myth, he projects white violence against the Indians of the world onto the Indians. He slams "so-called humanitarians . . . for their aiding and abetting such horrid crimes as the indians have perpetrated on our people" (90). Within minutes the rodeo music blares and the lights blaze yet again. The final stage directions announce that the ritual of "regeneration through violence" is beginning: ". . . Lights return to the way they were at the top of the show, when the audience was entering. The three glass cases are back in place. No curtain."

The meaning of the Steve Tesich's title *The Speed of Darkness* is open for debate, but I submit that it may well refer to the speed with which America rehabilitated its mythic identity, thereby forgetting both the causes and the legacies of the Vietnam War. With the glass cases back on stage, we again find ourselves in the heartland of America, in the Indian Country of Sioux Falls, South Dakota. As with the Nelsons, we once again have a "respectable" family—husband Joe, wife Mary, and daughter Anne. In fact, Joe is so respectable that during the course of the play he wins the South Dakota Man of the Year award. He's a war hero, a philanthropist, civic leader, and a builder of homes that are as strong and respectable as those constructed by Paul Berlin's father in *Going After Cacciato*. But we slowly discover that these respectable homes are less for protection than for concealment of complicity. Hiding under the ruses of civic pride and economic "surge[s] of vitality" (35) lies a nasty secret, which, like Ozzie and Harriet, the residents can look at but cannot see: toxic waste—in both a figurative and literal sense.

While in Vietnam, Joe and his now vagabond friend Lou are caught in a storm of friendly fire—napalm, likely. After being exposed to the toxic fumes, they are rescued. But they're no better off for this rescue

200

than is the maiden in *Indians*. The army "cures" them by eradicating the poison in their systems with radiation and chemicals. Unfortunately, the "cure" leaves them sterile. This is but the first instance in the play of responding to one form of death with another form of death. Had the play merely focused on this and on the bitter legacy Joe and Lou had to endure for the rest of their lives, it would have failed in its "cello playing." What makes the play work is Tesich's implicit echoing of Mark's words (*Still Life*), "we all did" Vietnam. Tesich insists that toxic waste, the war, America, and the way it does business are endemically intermeshed. He inextricably links Vietnam as America's chemical dumping ground to the parallel practice here at home. One instance of this practice occurred years before the action of the play begins—in the cracks and crevices of a huge, undeveloped mesa outside Sioux Falls. The mesa is at once a microcosm of America's endangered wilderness and a counterpart to the chemically assaulted landscapes of Vietnam.

Being invisible to Americans who had no desire to know what we really were doing in Vietnam—to the landscape, wildlife, soil, water, civilians, and soldiers on both sides—Joe and Lou can't find jobs when they return from war. But, as they discover, if they maintain their MOS, as it were—namely, exporting our technological and chemical destroyers of life—then there's work to be had; very profitable work, in fact. In their rage over their treatment in Vietnam and back home, Joe and Lou make lots of money illegally dumping barrels of contaminants down the crevices of the mesa, thereby polluting the soil and water in perpetuity.

The way Joe talks about the "fine, upstanding companies" that hired Lou and him to dump the waste clearly completes a loop from Vietnam to Sioux Falls and back again. The "few good men" these companies were looking for comes straight off military recruitment posters; and the fact that these few good men "didn't ask any questions" expresses the depersonalized, hierarchical paradigm of both corporate and military bureaucracy. (For a full analysis of this corporate-military linkage, see Loren Baritz's book *Backfire*, particularly the chapter "Bureaucracy at War.")

In describing how he and Lou dumped the waste, Joe further emphasizes the Sioux Falls–Vietnam loop. He says, "We were getting even. It was war again, only this time we were dumping stuff on our own" (111). This time they were the perpetrators of friendly fire. Tesich identifies the two instances of "friendly fire" even more closely with his choice of verb tenses. In the more distant first instance, in Vietnam, he uses the present tense repeatedly, whereas in the less distant second instance, atop the mesa, he exclusively uses the past tense. Endemic proclivities, not linear progression or progress, are Tesich's concern in *Speed of Darkness*. Lou refers to the traveling scale model of the Vietnam Veterans Memorial as "Son of Wall." Handling verb tenses in this linearly warped way, Tesich makes a subtle case for the Vietnam War being "Son of Sioux Falls." After all, America had been engaged in chemical warfare against Lou's "Mother Earth" or Joe's "Mother Country" long before the Vietnam War came along.

Joe therefore understands that Vietnam was nothing special in American history. He even calls it "a piece of cake." Granted, there's a good deal of denial going on in that statement; but there's also recognition that Vietnam was business as usual. It's just that the business was more obvious in Vietnam, less sneaky and less gradual. This makes good copy. At home, on the other hand, the soil on farms surrounding Sioux Falls—or anywhere in the United States, for that matter—is good for little more than holding plants up. Du Pont makes the plants grow in the sterile soil it made sterile—another instance of treating death with death. But that doesn't show up in headlines, not like the "Son of Sioux Falls" atrocities did. "We've managed to ruin everything," Joe says; "around here with our "surge of vitality" (35). But, because it has happened so gradually, while feeding people's greed, either the ruination isn't seen or it is applauded as a sign of growth.

Tesich's paradoxical treatment of growth—and, conversely, destruction—forms the nucleus of *The Speed of Darkness*. It is precisely the economic growth of Sioux Falls (to which, as a builder, Joe has made huge "contributions") that culminates in the destruction of the mesa. All in the city but Lou, Mary's boyfriend, and Joe's family have closed their eyes to the downside price tag of their material growth. Joe finally forces them to open their eyes at rezoning hearings concerning a proposed luxury building project on the mesa. He tells the people everything. He bitterly reminds them: "Before I got into the

202

construction business I was in the garbage business" (49). In fact, he bankrolled the former (growth) with the latter (destruction): "It was your trash and filth and waste that you wanted taken somewhere, anywhere, and buried out of sight that gave me my fresh start in life" (49). When we bear in mind that the literal walls he has been constructing all these years have figuratively concealed a deadening lie, we have another instance of treating death with death, which the citizens perceive as growth.

Years earlier, when they are dumping the toxic waste, Joe and Lou indulge in a drunken, nighttime ritual. It's an ugly, hate-filled, Satanic ritual, but it clearly shows their awareness of the destruction of growth. It's a scene where they quite literally try to impregnate the death represented by the waste they've poured down the yonic openings of the mesa—with their dead semen. Joe says,

> There was more venom in us than in all those oil drums put together. The kind of hate that desecrates life. Some eternal hate is what we wanted. To get even for everything. And on our last night up there, we found a way to hate. We stood on top of these empty oil drums. We were grinning at each other, as we dropped our pants down around our knees. We grabbed ourselves and we cursed while we did what we did. "Here you go, Mom. Here you go!" And we shot our dead seed into those dark holes, full of death already. "Here you go, Mom! Let's see the children that are born from this. Here's your next generation, Mom. Let's see how you like these sons and daughters." (111–12)

Throughout the play, Mary enacts a parallel ritual. As part of her high school sex education, she and Eddie must carry with them wherever they go an eleven-pound sack of dirt—their earth baby. As Mary says, we must carry it "to school. To movies. Pep rallies. Everywhere. To show us what it's like to have a baby, just in case we're tempted" (16–17). She and Eddie even make a ceremony of scooping up virgin soil right at the moment of sunrise. It's plausible to conclude that the soil is actually the mesa's soil of death. To "fertilize" this soil of death, she places snapshots from her family's and Lou's pasts inside the sack of dirt. But these pasts were constructed of despair, betrayal, and deceit. So this sack of polluted dirt and dead pasts will remain just that, until in a drunken rage Joe scatters it throughout the floor of his home—Tesich's counterpart to the coffin-constructed floors and walls of the Nelson's home. At the far end of the loop—in Vietnam—we see the other parallel ritual: American technology masturbating on the landscape and on the human instruments of death that a nation sent to do its dirty work. Add to this the fertilization of ignorance, racism, euphemism, and doublespeak and you have "Son of Sioux Falls."

But, like all of the scrounger artists viewed in this study, Tesich offers us a flip side to destroying by building; we also can build from destruction and by destroying. Explaining this paradox to Joe, Anne offers the orthopedic recommendation already noted:

> We were so happy to learn that our broken parts could mend, that we really didn't care how they mended. I think in our rush to love and be loved, we mended crooked. Around a lie. . . . You know I love you, but there's this . . . feeling: I want to love more. And it feels like the only way we can make room for that love to grow is to get all broken up again and try to mend right. It's like a living child inside of me. . . . (66–68)

Instead of treating death with death, Anne wants to create life through necessary destruction, to mend by breaking. This takes the courage to imagine mesa holes and bomb craters as fish ponds.

We can extrapolate from this—and I believe we must—that in its desperate eagerness to heal from the Vietnam War, America "mended crooked. Around a lie." It misused the craters as "landfills." We hear the truth in Joe's and Lou's battlefield prayer: "Save us. Please. Save us from our own" (109). We also hear the truth when Joe responds to Eddie's statement that in Vietnam, "The worst part, I hear, from the little I know, was not knowing who the enemy was" (100): "No. The worst part was finding out. See. For all you know, I'm the enemy" (101). Finally, we hear the truth when Joe admits everything at the hearing, at the conclusion of which he says to the citizens, "And I . . . forgive *you*" [my emphasis] (114).

By committing the radical act of presenting "in country" as Sioux Falls, South Dakota (a Saigon-in-the-heartland), Tesich gives us the opportunity "to get all broken up again and try to mend right." And in Tesich's one-set "poor theatre," we never need to leave—we must not leave—our own living rooms and front lawns to destroy and re-create ourselves. If we pay attention, we will see that this is where C. D. B. Bryan's helicopter assaults were really taking place long before Americans ever heard of Vietnam. Yes, this is yet another example of doing things wrong.

Predictably, none of those who gets things right by doing them wrong receives much attention from Vietnam War literary critics. They're certainly not among Myers' pantheon of point walkers. This is saddening. It is the point walkers turned civilian dramatists who most need to be watched and listened to. We need to watch and listen as they do the cello without a cello, so wrong and so right.

NINE

The Paralysis of Uniqueness

> You have connived at murder, and you thrive on it, and that fact is
> too unpleasant to face except rarely.
>
> —Paul Fussell

Texts like *Koko, Still Life, Words For My Daughter, The Speed of Darkness,*
and "To Those Who Have Gone Home Tired" remind us forcefully
that the war was as normal and close to home as a generic Mrs. Stone
sweeping away dandelion fuzz in Fort Dodge, Iowa, Sioux Falls,
South Dakota, "Laos, New Mexico," or "Saigon, Illinois." Colletti, a
character in Robert Stone's *Dog Soldiers*, reminds the reader that "Everywhere it's Chicago" (38). In the same novel, Converse says of Vietnam, "This is the place where everybody finds out who they are. . . .
We didn't know who we were till we got here" (56, 57). Vietnam
didn't change Americans; it showed them who they always were. But
almost everywhere one turns to "learn" about the Vietnam War, one
reads that this war was unique, somehow outside American history.
It's a familiar litany: We're told that the Vietnam War was the only
one we've ever lost, or at least didn't win. (The War of 1812 never

happened? The Korean War was a mirage?) We're told that it was the only war in which there was no front, and the soldiers couldn't tell friend from foe. (The Philippine Insurrection didn't happen?) We're told that the Vietnam War was a uniquely evil war, in that it involved the massive slaughter of civilians. (Dresden was not firebombed? Hiroshima was not obliterated? During the war with Mexico, General Winfield Scott didn't have to cringe because he didn't see American soldiers commit atrocities "to make Heaven weep"? The massacres on the island of Samar never happened? Wounded Knee? Sand Creek? Mystic River?) We're told that it was the only war after which the soldiers weren't welcomed home with honor and caring commitment. (Daniel Shays and many other farmers didn't lose their farms to foreclosure because they couldn't pay back taxes accrued while they were fighting the war for independence?)

I use the parentheses to make a point: much of American history is tucked away between them—if indeed it was even recorded so that it can be tucked away. The material camouflaged by the parentheses is buried under sensational headlines and thirty-second "news" stories. Of the single child dramatically rescued from drowning and the ten thousand left to starve slowly, the former always gets our attention. And so it goes with the fighting-writing memories of Vietnam and other wars; we respond to nostalgic caricatures but overlook the parentheses.

In their outstanding book, *The Wages of War* (1989), Richard Severo and Lewis Milford turn parenthetical material into the main clauses of American history. Their primary thesis is, "If the soldiers of Vietnam thought there had never been a group of veterans so ignored, abused, and betrayed, it was not because they tried to rewrite history, but because they knew so little about it" (419). Rather than repeat ahistorical clichés about Vietnam, they tell us that from the Revolutionary War to Vietnam, the U.S. government has responded to its returning vets like a "slippery insurance company" (16). Near the end of their book, Severo and Milford say:

> The failure of Government to treat soldiers and veterans equitably after Vietnam was a failure of memory. Most of us were not aware of the wages of war that had not been paid in the past, and so we were more willing, as a people, to tolerate Government's shoddy behavior. We tended to regard

207

it as something that had not happened before and probably would not happen again. We thus behaved as our forebears did after our other wars, for they did not remember either. It is unseemly for people so proud of their heritage to be so unaware of the dark side of it, the side that holds not our dignity, our sense of honor, and our generosity, but our greed, lack of compassion, and shortsightedness. (425)

Lacking any sense of Owen Gilman's "deep history," many critical and fictional books view the Vietnam War as a terrible but singular glitch to recover from. Happily, Gilman's *Vietnam and the Southern Imagination* (1992) is not among these books. He views the innocence of America as a whole as its weakness. Not anchored in the "condition of defeat" (as are Southerners, Native Americans, African-Americans, and women), most North Americans, according to Gilman, ". . . approach Vietnam as an anomaly—a weird mutation on the otherwise spotlessly good American record in war. The southerner knows better" (15).

As I have tried to make implicit and explicit in this study, no permanent healing can take place without a broader awareness of American history and interrogation of it. For one thing, Vietnam vets will be less traumatized if they know they're not the first victims of their government's crass and sinister neglect. Millions of soldiers from previous wars have already been there. They will cease to be paralyzed by self-pity once they can see they were not—as one repeatedly hears—betrayed by the American people and their government. They betrayed themselves by knowing so little about their country. How many times do soldiers have to be betrayed in the same ways before betrayal is called ignorance instead?

These are harsh words, I know; I say them because I believe that, with a greater sense of complexity and irony, our Vietnam vets can become America's invaluable, master "teachers." They can help America grow up. To heal—for America to heal—will require them to couple their direct experience of war and its aftermath with Foucault's "insurrection of subjugated knowledges." They'll need to look inside the ignored parentheses and footnotes to find those knowledges. If they do this, they could become America's great deconstructionists—and I don't mean the paralyzing, arid deconstruction that often goes on in the academy. I mean the nuts-and-bolts deconstruction that leads to what Paul Fussell, borrowing from George Orwell, calls the "power of facing unpleasant facts." Fussell says that this power ". . . is necessary not just to any writer but to any honest thinker. And it's notably a *power*, not merely a talent or a flair. The power of facing unpleasant facts is clearly an attribute of decent, sane, grown-ups as opposed to the immature, the silly, the nutty, or the doctrinaire" (*Thank God*, 81). In Walter Truett Anderson's words, our Vietnam fighters-writers could offer immeasurable inspiration to "make us better at gathering bad news" (264), much of which will consist of discovering the shortsightedness of America's dark side. Unfortunately, as Michael Herr reminds Americans in his interview with Eric James Schroeder, ". . . we're not great at telling the truth about certain kinds of national behavior. The war sure twisted us. We haven't felt the same about ourselves since Vietnam. We're haunted by it, but we won't name the shape of the ghost; we won't say what it is" (38). *The Wages of War* is certainly a big step in the right direction, for its good news is all "bad news." After reading it, a person will be deeply changed. He or she might still tie yellow ribbons around trees and wave miniature flags, but never again on the shaky foundation of chauvinistic ignorance.

Severo's and Milford's "bad news" is of two kinds. First, they document that horror, mutilations, and massacres were not unique to Vietnam. They devote an entire chapter just to the atrocities committed by Americans in the Philippines. You won't find this bad news in the history texts read by America's youth—for that would destroy Vietnam's unique status as our only bad war. Notice the familiar ring in the following sentences.

> Smith [Brigadier General Jacob H. Smith] and his fellow officers were being asked to fight an enemy that forever lurked deep in thick forests and insisted on conducting guerrilla forays that cost many American lives. There was no front. Only the guerrillas. . . . Rifle fire came from unexpected places. . . . It was not a war that the Americans really knew how to fight, and the guerrillas were as implacable as the jungle itself. (212–13)

The year was 1899. But the jumpy, frustrated military's response dates back to the Pequot Massacre of 1637, and forward to 1968 at My Lai 4: kill everything and everyone. The orders given to Lieutenant Calley, and the orders he passed down to his infantry company of the American Division on March 16, 1968, are virtually identical to those given seventy years earlier by General Smith: "I want no prisoners. I wish you to kill and burn—the more you kill and burn the better you will please me. . . . The interior of Samar must be made a howling wilderness" (213). He then gave the order to kill everyone over ten years old. Smith's orders, in turn, were a mere replay of George Washington's orders in 1779, to "lay waste" the Iroquois.

And so began the murder of children, men, and women, the looting, desecration of religious buildings, burning, the summary executions with pistol shots to the head at point-blank range, and even the widely used "water cure." Moreover, the destruction, as it was in 1779 and as it would be in Vietnam, was all highly racist. One representative private said, "The weather is intensely hot, and we are all tired, dirty, and hungry, so we have to kill niggers whenever we have a chance, to get even for all our trouble" (219). Having observed the atrocities, one soldier wrote home saying, ". . . I have seen enough to almost make me ashamed to call myself an American" (217).

Others wrote home as well—to an incredulous, complicity-denying and history-denying America. The leaks eventually prompted a congressional investigation that closely resembled the "Winter Soldier" hearings during the Vietnam War. Not only had other soldiers "been there before," their desire to teach America about itself was equally thwarted in both cases. Hands got slapped, and in the case of Vietnam, a solitary scapegoat—Calley—was offered up for sacrifice on the altar of blind innocence. Protesting voices were silenced, then forgotten—like Lieutenant Colonel Anthony Herbert's, seventy years after the Philippine Insurrection. As commander of the 173rd Airborne Brigade, he had seen VC suspects who wouldn't talk being thrown out of helicopters. Again, Americans were incredulous, disdainfully so in the case of Barry Goldwater, who was then chairman of the Senate Armed Services Committee.

It is this forgetting that *The Wages of War* seeks to undo with its "bad news" about American atrocities. The second kind of news, however, is the primary focus of the book: a two-hundred-year history of returning soldiers being ignored and abused. As these two words suggest, the poor treatment always has taken two forms, passive aggression and active aggression. The most passive form of aggression has taken place after every American war: civilians simply want to forget the war and those who fought in it. They don't want to hear *anything* about the dark side of humanity. This form of aggression makes Vietnam anything but unique. For example, as Severo and Milford remind us, the homecoming of World War I soldiers was "savagely indifferent" (289). This indifference has always been the rule.

Somewhat less passively, Americans and their government have regularly responded to returnees like that slippery insurance company. During the Civil War there were vicious congressional fights between conservatives and liberals over granting pensions to veterans, which made one of them conclude, "After years of toil, privation and hardship, you are turned out to graze on short feed like a broken down mustang" (137). And how does one square America's alleged honor of the soldier with the fact that those who fought in the Civil War quickly discovered they had little chance of getting a good job if they admitted they were vets? How do we measure the stinginess of offering to amputees $75 for a lost leg, $50 for a lost arm? How do we fathom hospital conditions so deplorable that soldiers feared them more than getting wounded? And this infamy took place in the North, where the towns, cities, and economy were largely intact. In the devastated South, conditions were much worse. In the history of warfare, few soldiers have ever come home to less.

The cognizant response today to such receptions should be, "So what else is old?" There are many recent versions of the same neglect. A motif sounded throughout Severo's and Milford's book is that the architects of this neglect are invariably the same people who were ". . . among the most vociferous, moist-eyed flag wavers before the war" (258). These people usually are our public officials. Severo and Milford quote William Edler, who, following World War I, wrote: "Congress little realizes that its creature, the Veterans' Bureau, has probably made wrecks of more men since the war than the war itself took in dead and maimed" (259). A World War II vet says, "I would rather be on Iwo Jima Island with our Marines, than be in a veterans' hospital. . . . I could certainly fight back there, but here you can't" (305). And, in *Born on the Fourth of July*, Ron Kovic tells us how during nights in a VA hospital rats ate the toes of paraplegics.

211

What, then, about the "good war," World War II? Granted, they got their parades. (In view of having learned of war's horrors, why would any soldier want a parade? It seems utterly incongruous.) But the authors dig up bad news here as well. They point out that conservative politicians, who have historically been among the most hawkish, bitterly fought against the passage of the GI Bill. They like war, but they want the warrior to go away after each war concludes. Clergymen preached from the pulpits that returning soldiers would try to corrupt the country. As we've seen, the VA hospitals were a disgrace then as now. Lynda M. Van Devanter, a Vietnam nurse, tells a very old story about women not being able to get even the most elemental of gynecological services, such as pap smears and breast examinations (303). Following World War II, women participants were not even acknowledged as having served. Because World War II was not simply a good war for veterans but rather, in many ways, an all-too-typical one, this failure to acknowledge women anticipates the year 1987, when Vietnam nurses were told that the Vietnam memorials were complete—without them. On Veterans Day, 1993, twenty years after the war ended, Glenna Goodacre's memorial to the American women in Vietnam finally made it to the Mall.

Silvero and Milford also cite examples of active aggression against soldiers, and they date back to the greedy injustices inflicted on those who had fought in the Revolutionary War. Some of the active aggression throughout American history has taken the form of invective. While it is true that Vietnam vets were stereotyped as baby killers, it also is true that no veterans received more verbal abuse than did those of the Korean War. Routinely, they were considered (and called) cowards for losing a war that was designed to be unwinnable, as well as traitors and Communists for not being John Wayne POWs.

Worse, however, than irresponsible stay-at-home rhetoric is the physical abuse soldiers have endured during and after wars. In one of the worst cases of active aggression, in Vietnam the U.S. sprayed thousands of soldiers with dioxin. Like every form of abuse that Severo and Milford talk about, this one, too, has precedents, usually deleted from the national memory. For example, following the Korean War the Army secretly fed LSD to soldiers to see how susceptible they would be to brainwashing. Many lives were left in ruins. Because of recent publicity, we now know that, in 1944, the Navy used as many as 60,000 of their personnel as guinea pigs to test the effects of mustard gas. One of the victims, interviewed on *60 Minutes* in 1993, said: "We were used, abused, and lied to." So what else is old?

How does one reconcile this abuse with the fact that Saddam Hussein's use of mustard gas on the Kurds became a hysterical rallying point for starting the Gulf War? Millions of Americans shuddered when they said or heard the two dreaded words "chemical warfare," because only a demented monster would ever use it. Indeed—19 million gallons of chemicals weren't dropped on South Vietnam, a country smaller than Missouri—by the USA? Americans also became patriotically paranoid about Hussein's nuclear capabilities; yet, from 1945 to 1963, the Army deliberately exposed large numbers of soldiers to radioactivity—as a psychological test. Untold numbers died prematurely as a result. As was the case with Agent Orange and mustard gas victims, compensation efforts had to run a gauntlet formed by flag-waving Americans.

The most distressing chapter in *The Wages of War* is a horror story of abuse that happened after the Spanish-American War. The story chronicles the shiploads of soldiers ". . . who were shipped from Cuba to Montauk and left at the tip of Long Island to die in the summer of 1898" (420). Thousands of the combatants in Cuba came down with such infections as typhoid, yellow fever, and malaria. Undaunted, the surgeon general of the United States said the fevers were "mild," that only a few days would be required for recovery (193). An adjutant general claimed they had no diseases at all; they were merely sick from "homesickness" and "nostalgia" (199). Secretary of War Russell A. Alger actually blamed the soldiers who were sick for overcrowding the transport ships that brought them home (196). Doctors, both military and civilian, were no help either: "Asking the obvious and answering disingenuously became as epidemic among doctors as the fevers were among the soldiers" (195). To compound matters, many became sick on the ships, largely because of the absence of food and drinking water. What food they had "would have sickened well men" (194). The hardtack they were served after they disembarked in the United States was filled with worms. The bottom line in this

213

story is that Montauk ". . . became more of a killing ground than any battlefield in Cuba" (204). Hundreds who died were crammed into five-dollar pine coffins, their limbs broken so they would fit (209).

Ironically, infantrymen who hadn't managed yet to die were given a parade in New York. Rather like Alden Pyle, the cheering thousands couldn't even see that the paraders were "pathetic . . . emaciated, hollow-eyed and enfeebled" (208). Not so ironically, after the Montauk crime started to recede into forgetfulness, the media were given the blame for having a "baneful and pernicious effect" on the soldiers because of "careless and exaggerated" statements about the incident. This same cowardly fantasy would be repeatedly used as a red herring after Vietnam. It "worked": huge segments of the population still believe the media helped lose the war. People may have smelled a rat for a while, but the herring quickly and lastingly sent them back to the kennels.

Severo and Milford end this chapter with some sentences on the Montauk disaster that sound chillingly familiar:

> . . . James Fitch of Troop F, 1st Regiment, Illinois Volunteer Company, was rejected in 1914 for a pension because the Government told him he had not proved he got 'malarial poisoning, disease of the stomach and diarrhea' while in the Spanish-American War. Fitch, whose home was in Muncie, Indiana, was apparently convinced that he could not have contracted malaria there. Fitch's widow, Lula, kept applying for war benefits into the early 1960s, when she died. (210)

Like so much parenthetical material.

The cult of uniqueness has a large membership. It includes too many who fought in Vietnam and have since written about it. The danger of this membership is that it prevents one from seeing that the Vietnam War and its aftermath are merely symptoms of a systemic dysfunction, neglect, and abuse. Blind to "deep history" and the real wages of all wars, what's to prevent a nation from being condemned to yet another repetition? How can America learn, as Robert A. Pastor puts it, "to avoid being repeatedly bitten by the same snake?" (xi). The search for an antidote should begin with *The Wages of War*.

Believing that the Vietnam War was unique, and that the country's disregard, and even scorn, for its veterans is unique is not only a mistake based on ignorance; it is a mistake that paralyzes people within the same mythic force field they only *think* Vietnam destroyed. It is a mistake that makes people victims of a romantic optimism merely delayed or denied but still possible in better wars. Because of this paralysis, the roots of the mythic process, whereby warriors are validated for participating in insensate savagery, remain uninvestigated. Let there be no mistake: many vets either secretly or openly still want this validation. To think otherwise is to be naive about the whole prospect of healing from the war. As we've seen, Starkmann's psychiatrist in Caputo's *Indian Country* correctly diagnoses the mythic trap his patient is caught in: he can't admit that he was never so alive and fulfilled as when he was participating in the violence of the Vietnam War. Paradoxically, then, embittered Vietnam vets are not victims of unpleasant facts; they're victims of suppressed facts in American history and in their own psyches—namely, the fantasy that one can be regenerated through violence. Lacking the power of historical knowledge before they went to Vietnam, many veterans therefore experienced both the war and its aftermath as the rotten apple. The toxicity of the barrel itself remains suppressed by the pervasive power of myth.

In "Prospero Goes to Vietnam," I say that the myth of uniqueness came through the war intact. Perhaps I understated its ability to survive. In fact, rather than merely surviving the war, maybe it was recreated by it. In his book *The Captain America Complex*, Robert Jewett concurs. It is extremely difficult to escape what he calls the "Deuteronomic Principle" (181): if America had won the Vietnam War, that would be proof that the nation was pleasing to God; having lost it simply proved that God was displeased. Putting the defeat in the context of the whole history of "zealous nationalism," Jewett sees a vicious cycle: "The naive resolve that we will 'Never make a mistake like Vietnam again' simply lock[s] us into the very complacent dogmas which got us there in the first place" (190). So the "Captain America" myth didn't let America down; an apostate, enervated America let the myth down. In the 1980s that very message was sounded repeatedly by Captain America's real-life lieutenant, Jerry Falwell. Falwell did not gain national notoriety despite the Vietnam War—far from it. As Walter H. Capps argues, the war actually created this mythmonger and his zealous message to America (145). In his

215

hands, instead of losing power, the myth was tapped into with renewed hysteria.

It's likely that, because Americans are so used to getting their way and imposing their will on all forms of recalcitrance, they don't even know how to gather the bad news that they should divest themselves of mythic claims to uniqueness. Even when they're in a particularly deconstructive mood, maybe they're parting with less than they think. Maybe they're fooling themselves into thinking that rearranging the furniture will change the floor plan. Perhaps I'm doing that myself even as I write these words. As we saw with Kopit's *Indians*, just when one would think that the mythic Buffalo Bill had shot himself and his country in both feet, the fanfare begins again and up he pops, fully resurrected. There always seems to be a Jerry Falwell around to make sure of this.

Walter Truett Anderson also talks about this staying power of myth:

Certainly the death of society as everyone had known it was reported frequently enough. But the reports—such as Scott Fitzgerald's proclamation that his generation had returned from World War I to find all gods dead and all wars fought—turned out to be somehow premature. Throughout World War II America appeared to be a nation with all its gods, all its myths, all its old beliefs and symbols still in excellent condition. (43)

Similarly, ". . . the sixties left a legacy of doubt about the public reality—about all public realities—that has not been dispelled by later retreats into familiar beliefs and behavior. It was a time of transition from which there is no turning back" (48). Yet, says Anderson, the sixties revolutionaries ". . . massively underestimated the staying power of cultural myths . . ." (48).

Addressing this seemingly indestructible nature of myth, Todd Gitlin writes, "Anybody who went to sleep in 1968, with Eldridge Cleaver's *Soul on Ice* leading the bestseller list and *The Graduate* first at the box office, and woke up in 1985 to behold *Iacocca* and *Rambo*, and Cleaver as an apostle of the fire-breathing anti-Communist Unification Church, would be entitled to some astonishment" (272). Imagine the astonishment in store if one didn't wake up until 1991. One then saw an epidemic of moist-eyed, righteous patriotism, which

George Bush easily resurrected with the ever reliable good versus evil mythic scenario. For the most part, even "higher" education didn't seem to offer any defense against the spread of a renewed "Zealous Nationalism." In fact, it often was used to defend the return to mythic unity and solidarity (as it was in Nazi Germany in the 1930s). Teachers who dared to speak out against the Gulf War found themselves in free fire zone classrooms with a new generation of nineteen-year-olds eager to go on offense. As a university professor I worry that Loren Baritz may be right when he says, ". . . hoping that education can be the counterweight to dangerous cultural assumptions is not facing the miserable facts: the universities can't and the people won't" (327). Observing their country as it re-fired the old bellicose myths, some Americans felt that it wasn't so much that the Gulf War was scripted as being different from the war in Vietnam as that Vietnam had never happened. Aside from not losing again, no lessons apparently had been learned. Captain America was back in the saddle.

One of the more unpleasant facts about zealous nationalism that Americans need to face is that it precludes intellectual and ethical development. If we condense William Perry's nine-stage scheme of intellectual and ethical development to three stages, we see in American culture a preponderance of edgy bouncing back and forth between the first two stages, namely, the naive dualism of "Authority-right-we" versus "illegitimate-wrong-others" (59), and the vague, relativistic nihilism expressed by the Doors as "This is the End." Stage one would be represented by the man whose fire-trap attic is loaded with stuff he treasures, but hasn't looked at in years. Stage two is the man who believes he should junk all of it, but then somehow he doesn't follow through, as he slides imperceptibly—Eldridge Cleaver-wise—back to stage one. In stage three we see a man who throws a lot out but saves a few items, and maybe even finds new uses for others. Translated, he has a responsible commitment to ". . . the truth of the limits of man's certainty" (56). Perry says he has a tolerance, even a love (56), for complexity and paradox. He understands that reality is a social creation, so he is watchful; but he has learned to embrace limitations. In Paul Tillich's words, he has "the courage to be."

At its best, John Hellmann's *American Myth and the Legacy of Viet-*

217

nam does a masterful job of achieving the power of facing the unpleasant facts inherent in stage three. But Hellmann, perhaps like all of us Euroamericans, can't seem to resist the urge to bounce between stages one and two. One moment he declares American mythology to be unsalvagable; the next moment, it's back in the attic. For example, on page 200 we're told that the "American self-concept of a unique national virtue and destiny" is a "fraud" and an "essential lie." On page 223 we're told, "Surely America should not give up its sense of uniqueness and see itself as an ordinary country."

Actually, more often than not we see instances where the culture doesn't even manage to develop to stage two; it simply stays at stage one by inverting it, by switching sides. This is precisely what happened after Americans began hearing about the My Lai massacre. Almost overnight "Authority-right-we" versus "illegitimate-wrong-others" was converted to "Authority-right-they" (the massacred villagers) versus "illegitimate-wrong-we" (U.S. soldiers). Either position is a flight from complexity and complicity; the inverted form is merely an escape to the myth one seemingly was escaping from. Richard Slotkin addresses this tautological determinism:

> Mylai thus became the central trope of the "counter-myth" through which Americans expressed their growing disillusionment and disgust with the myth/ideology of counterinsurgency. But it is vital to note that this counter-myth merely reproduced, in inverted form, the moral/political symbolism of the original myth. The appeal of the counter-myth hinges on a misrepresentation of Mylai's politics that exactly reproduces—albeit with an *opposite* political intention—the original fallacy of counterinsurgency in Vietnam. (590)

Although many of the massacred were no doubt VC sympathizers, the American public simply replaced one simplification with another. They merely "rearranged the furniture" of the stage-one captivity narrative. The questionable structure of the cultural edifice never was inspected. This oversight led to the belief that now it was the totally innocent "Indian" *other* that needed to be rescued. Those who protested against the war after the My Lai news broke may have thought they were engaged in a fundamental revolt against the establishment's propaganda-maintained naive dualism; but, as Walter Truett

218

Anderson reminds us, notice how quickly they ". . . became caught up in a good-guy/bad-guy fantasy of their own" (175).

To this day, the thinking of millions of Americans regarding Vietnam has locked them into a stage-one paralysis, except that the country is now back to we versus them. The phenomenon that has maintained this arrested development since 1969 is the POW/MIA issue. Again, to the cognizant this issue should lead to the question "So what else is old?" Our search for its prototype takes us back to colonial America and its popular captivity narratives. Little has changed in the myth since the first published account by Mary Rowlandson in 1682. The following words by Bruce Franklin apply equally to the seventeenth- and eighteenth-century captivity narratives and to the plot of *Rambo: First Blood, Part Two*, as well as to at least a dozen other POW rescue films: "The foundation of American culture is the mythic frontier, with its central images of white captives tortured by cruel non-white savages until they can be rescued by the . . . great American hero, the lone frontiersman who abandons civilized society to merge with the wilderness" (*Progressive*, 25). That certainly is the story of John Rambo's quest, including his knack for merging with rocks, trees, mud, and water—to the point of being indistinguishable from them. So, rather than a new wrinkle in American history, the POW/MIA phenomenon is an old mythic response to what Franklin calls the "profound depths" of "psychocultural cravings" (*Progressive*, 24).

Captivity scenarios are not just one room in America's mythic superstructure; they make up its very foundation. Thus Richard Slotkin says, "Rescuing . . . captives is the strongest of mythical imperatives, a self-evident 'higher law' " (361). Elsewhere he calls them "the most sacred of the Frontier myths" (621). Slotkin's use of the word "sacred" is apt; for, as he and others have pointed out, captivity has long been viewed in Puritan America as a religious test to see if one can remain uncorrupted by the savage *other*. In contemporary, secularized America, the theological ramifications of captivity and rescue are gone, but the intensity of belief remains. Thus, incorruptibility lives on in the secular myth of the U.S. soldier enduring endless torture without granting more than his name, rank, and serial number. Having made a long list of films on this theme, Hollywood rarely, if ever, deconstructs the myth (see *The Hanoi Hilton*, for example). Similarly incontrovertible to zealots is the quasi-religious belief that these incorruptible soldiers still exist in Indochina. Notice how Bruce Franklin concludes the following passage:

> The belief in live POWs . . . [is] based not just on political rhetoric, rumors, and the POW rescue movies, but also on a sizable body of books, pamphlets, and articles that have promulgated a coherent and superficially plausible pseudohistory compounded of self-deception, amateur research, anecdotes, half-truths, phony evidence, slick political and media manipulation, downright lies, and near-religious fervor. (*M.I.A.*, xii)

The very subtitle of Franklin's *M.I.A.* (1992) leaves no doubt as to his concern that the whole POW/MIA issue is the work of "near-religious fervor" rooted in "the closest thing we have to a national religion" (*M.I.A.*, 7). Contrary to what we first assume, "M.I.A." does not stand for "Missing in Action," but for "*Mythmaking in America*." What puzzled Franklin as he began his study is the amazing power the POW/MIA myth has over the American imagination. Otherwise intelligent people who would scoff at Elvis or UFO sightings, or *National Enquirer* stories elevate, without a trace of doubt, the fantasy of live POWs to the status of fact. Actual facts wither in the face of these mythic facts, "documented" by grainy photographs. It makes no difference to believers that relative to other wars, the number of missing in Vietnam—1,172—is eight times less than in the Korean War, seventy-eight times less than in World War II. Nor does it seem to matter that the Vietnamese have more than 200,000 MIAs—in their own country. Nor do believers want to factor in the complication of what happened to the half million U.S. soldiers who deserted during the war.

Franklin gives a recent example of how real facts wilt. In 1992 a photograph of three live POWs was discovered. This led to a flurry of patriotic activity in Washington, including a House resolution to designate a "National POW/MIA Recognition Day." Everyone was for it. As Franklin points out, attraction to the captivity myth cuts across political lines; liberals and progressives are just as enamored as conservatives and reactionaries. As was the case in 1964, when all but two senators voted for the Tonkin Gulf Resolution to strike back at the "Indians" for firing at our "wagon train" on the South China Sea, so in 1992 the House passed the resolution unanimously. What makes this vote so astonishing is that two months before, the photograph had been exposed as a phony. Franklin tells us that "the picture of the three 'U.S. pilots' was actually a doctored version of a 1923 photo reproduced in a 1989 Soviet magazine; the three men were holding a sign proclaiming the glories of collective farming; mustaches had been added and a picture of Stalin subtracted" (*Progressive*, 24). Were people properly embarrassed by this revelation of the hoax, which Ned Buntline would have labeled "sissyshit?" Franklin's one-word answer: "Hardly." It would appear that the addiction to the myth is so acute that any honest whistle-blowing effort is viewed as being self-prophesied—a conspiracy to discredit the truth. Rather than make one think twice, the effort to discredit invariably reconfirms the rightness of thinking once, or of not even thinking at all.

Acute, the addiction also is widespread, as is exemplified by the House vote. But Franklin gives another, even more astonishing, example, a 1985 *60 Minutes* segment entitled "Dead or Alive." According to Franklin, its producer

> claimed that the show was designed to present the "two sides" of the issue. One side was the official position of the Reagan administration: there might be live POWs in Southeast Asia; when and if their existence were proved, the government would use all necessary means to recover them. And what was the other side? That live POWs were merely a myth that had now become a distinctive feature of American culture? No, the other side was the position of the "Rambo faction": the government itself was engaged in a vast conspiracy to conceal its own certain evidence of the existence of dozens if not hundreds of live POWs. (*M.I.A.*, 157–58)

The two sides here are like two related ones during the war: the generals, politicians, and editors who lied; and the occasional journalist who congratulated himself on trying to tell the limited truth of ethnographic realism. But even the side that finds fault with the government sees only the corruption of the system; the toxicity of the system itself goes undetected.

If the "near-religious fervor" were limited to the years following the war, that would be tragic enough, for we shouldn't forget that, until Clinton, every president since the war ended has used the POW/MIA issue as a weapon to keep Vietnam out of the UN, to deter nor-

221

malization, to forestall the reparations promised in the Paris Peace
Accords, and to maintain an embargo that has kept this country one
of the poorest on earth. But worse than this, in one of the most infamous chapters of American history, starting in 1969, Richard Nixon
cynically tapped into the captivity myth in order to galvanize public
support for the aimless continuation of the war. Americans took to it
like a bull to a red cape. In an act unprecedented in the history of
peace negotiations, he made the POW/MIA issue the central bargaining chip in the Paris Peace Talks. The result was four more years of
war, with absolutely no advantage gained by the United States. It was
just four more years of killing and destruction, after which Nixon
declared that now we had gained "peace with honor."

Franklin wonders,

> How is it possible to comprehend . . . [Nixon's] truly astonishing position,
> which seemed ready to trade countless American and Vietnamese lives for
> several hundred prisoners who would presumably be released anyhow at
> the conclusion of the war? Looking backward from decades later, we can
> comprehend such posturing only in the light of the dramatic transforma-
> tion in consciousness wrought by the POW/MIA campaign for the public
> mind. Even from the vantage point of 1975, the year Saigon finally fell,
> this consciousness seemed strangely aberrant. As Jonathan Schell then as-
> tutely observed, by 1972 "many people were persuaded that the United
> States was fighting in Vietnam in order to get its prisoners back," and the
> nation's main sympathy was no longer for "the men fighting and dying on
> the front," who "went virtually unnoticed as attention was focussed on
> the prisoners of war," "the objects of a virtual cult": "Following the Presi-
> dent's lead, people began to speak as though the North Vietnamese had
> kidnapped four hundred Americans and the United States had gone to war
> to retrieve them." (60)

In a 1993 piece for the *New Yorker*, Neil Sheehan refers to this continued distortion of the war and its aftermath as "the last fantasy of
the war" (51) and judges it "morally obscene" (46). In the same
spirit, as Franklin nears the end of his study, he observes: "In the
final analysis, the POW/MIA myth must be understood not just as a
convenient political gimmick for rationalizing various kinds of warfare and jingoism but also as a symptom of a profound psychological
sickness in American culture. One path back toward mental health
would be through an honest self-examination of how and why a so-

ciety could have been so possessed by such a grotesque myth" (170). That self-examination would require the society to face an unpleasant fact: it actually prefers and enjoys stage-one paralysis. But why? Because it protects the illusion of guiltlessness. Because the myth reduces complexity to "simple sets of paired antagonists" (655), in Richard Slotkin's language,

> it enables the believer to make sure he always is the antagonist on the "right" side. By refocussing and revising the war exclusively in terms of the captivity myth, Americans became the good guys. The "Trojans" took our Helen, which is all the proof we need. As in the response to the My Lai Massacre, victims and victimizers are forced to trade places to protect the guilty. Every Vietnam War captivity myth film has taken the distortions and reductions of the "grotesque myth" to the bank. "The basic technique" in all of these films, Franklin says, "was to take images of the war that had become deeply embedded in America's consciousness and transform them into their opposite." (133)

The "basic technique" reminds me of a newspaper story I read a few years ago, about a brazen burglar who sued the homeowners because during the commission of his crime he was bitten by the family dog. Ignoring their primary crime, Americans have denied their own inured violent treatment of prisoners, which then gets projected onto the other antagonist. I don't mean to suggest that some of the violence shouldn't be projected. But considering the intense U.S. bombing over the North, the restraint shown by the Vietnamese people is remarkable. As for how remarkable, anyone reading this should ask: "What would I have done to a captured pilot who had just destroyed my village and killed my family?" An amply documented fact of the war is that a prisoner of North Vietnam was far more likely to survive than a prisoner of the ARVN or the United States. But in stage-one thinking this neatly becomes inverted. The pervasive failure to gather this kind of bad news utterly wastes the suffering endured by the Vietnamese and the Americans.

Stage-one thinking inevitably is violent because it imposes extremely simplistic caricatures on reality. According to the epistemological paradigm of these caricatures, everything is what it is because it is not something else. Slotkin's "simple sets of paired antagonists" reduces the complexity of the world, its multiple ideologies and its peoples,

223

to binary boundaries. But, as Ken Wilber says in *No Boundaries,* "Every boundary line, remember, is also a battle line" (10). He explains this:

> The point is that as an individual draws up the boundaries of his soul, he establishes at the same time the battles of his soul. The boundaries of an individual's identity mark off what aspects of the universe are to be considered "self" and what aspects are to be considered "not-self." So at each level of the spectrum, different aspects of the world appear to be not-self, alien, and foreign. Each level sees different processes of the universe as *strangers* to it. And since, as Freud once remarked, every stranger seems an enemy, every level is potentially engaged in different conflicts with various enemies. (10)

Wilber is talking about humanity as a whole, but boundaried, stage-one thinking seems particularly endemic in America. Separated from the "not-selves" of Europe and Asia by two oceans, we seem especially prone to the solipsism of stage one. Being separated by two real boundaries has resulted in the imposition of false boundaries that are used in defense of American uniqueness. Loren Baritz addresses this very contention:

> The great ocean that defended us throughout our history also kept us from knowing others. The less one knows of the world, the more appalling the local customs of others may seem. The other side of that is also true: The less one knows of the world, the more one's own little daily rituals seem to have been decreed either by God or nature. (16)

In other words, the less one knows of the world, the less one sees Doc Peret's mediating filters in those rituals.

The "enabling ignorance" (Baritz, 17) of this binary paralysis leads to appalling arrogance as well, an "agent oranging" of real complexity and diversity. Baritz claims that, "Because of its Puritan roots, it is not surprising that America's nationalism is more Protestant than that of other countries. It is more missionary in its impulses, more evangelical. It typically seeks to correct the way other people think . . ." (22). This missionary impulse is exquisitely exemplified—because exquisitely thwarted—in a scene from *Catch-22,* a book that the Vietnam Veteran writer John Clark Pratt rightly calls "a paradigm for the Vietnam War itself" ("Yossarian's Legacy," 89).

224

The scene is set in a brothel in Rome and involves a confrontation between the puritanical Nately and a world-weary old Italian man sitting with great pleasure between two naked prostitutes. As if to emphasize that Americans put oceans between themselves and others, so that these others remain utterly not-self, Heller assembles what is perhaps the longest catalog of deprecating adjectives ever ascribed to one person in literary history. Projecting his own Jungian shadow on the old man, the all-American Nately regards him as being evil, debauched, ugly, Satanic, hedonistic, wicked, depraved, unpatriotic, traitorous, sly, sinful, sordid, vulturous, diabolical, uncouth, fickle, licentious, repellant, profane, villainous, shameful, unscrupulous, fiendish, unregenerate, abominable, sacrilegious, treacherous, corrupt, and immoral (247–57).

Given only one adjective, Nately no doubt would describe the man simply as "un-American." Ironically, the adjective is perfect. For, in lacking the propensity of Americans to reduce complexity to bellicose sets of antagonists, he *is* un-American. Heller makes this explicit. To Nately, one's country—especially if it is America—is sacred, and therefore worth dying for. To the old man, "A country is a piece of land surrounded on all sides by boundaries, usually unnatural" (253), and, therefore, "certainly worth living for." As far as Nately is concerned, the old Italian talks "like a madman." Because the man is speaking from the vantage point of Perry's third stage (the ninth, in his actual scheme), he does sound like a madman to the paralyzed Nately. The "uncouth bum" makes no sense to him because he is perfectly comfortable with tolerance, complexity, irony, and paradox. Thus, to Nately's accusation, "You talk like a madman," he responds: "But I live like a sane one." We do no harm to the "argument" of Heller's novel if we change "But" to "therefore."

This is beyond Nately's comprehension. In "stuttering dismay" he listens to the old man make a mockery of his boundaried worldview:

Italy . . . is one of the least prosperous nations on earth. And the Italian fighting man is probably second to all. And that's exactly why my country is doing so well in this war while your country is doing so poorly. . . . Italy is really a very poor and weak country, and that's what makes us so strong. . . . The real trick lies in *losing* wars. . . . [W]e will certainly come out on top again if we succeed in being defeated. (248–51)

Each of these stage-three paradoxes causes Nately to "gape . . . at him in undisguised befuddlement."

One thing vexes him more than any other. By comparison to Nately's father, who "believed in honor and knew the answer to everything . . . this old man believed in nothing and had only questions" (250). Actually, the interrogative old man does believe in something; unlike Nately and his father, he believes in not believing in belief: he doesn't trust it. That's why when Nately accuses him of having no principles, he responds with "Of course not" (252). Comfortable with tolerance, complexity, irony, and paradox, he is perfectly uncomfortable with the abstract principles that Nately clings to. His reason for this discomfort is quite likely the same one Hemingway's Frederick Henry discovers while fighting in Italy: they are "obscene." They are propaganda that makes each antagonist feel righteously and tough-mindedly realistic about the battle lines of their boundaries. Knowing that this is how the binary game tricks people, the old man admits to being unprincipled, but then turns right around and insists ". . . I am a very moral man" (252).

If Heller's old Italian makes any sense when he says, "we will certainly come out on top . . . if we succeed in being defeated" (after all, Italy did reap the benefits of the Marshall Plan), then maybe we can find a way to view Vietnam as our best war. Considering the near-unanimity of conviction that the Vietnam War was the very nadir of U.S. history, this statement may strike some readers as a sick leg-puller. My contention, however, is that it was a "good" war *because* it was a descent into hell. It was a war that blew the whistle on hollow pretentions. It called America's and Prospero's bluff. In ten years it compressed the three-hundred-year dark side of U.S. history so that everyone could see it. It exposed the childish dangers of dividing the world into sinners and saints, victimizers and victims, damned and chosen, Calibans and Prosperos. Because so-called good wars do none of this, they are the wars we really need to fear, for they lead only to violence-perpetuating answers, not bewildering, liberating questions. There is a sorely needed book that has yet to be written, as far as I know. It would analyze what happens to soldiers—such as those who fought in World War II—who participate in mass savagery and then return to a hero-worshipping welcome. What kind of crippling moral schizophrenia occurs when a person performs terrible evils and then is told he "done good"? What species of violence, ten, twenty, thirty years later, does this engender? What happens when, instead of having the opportunity to work through natural guilt for having killed and ravaged, one has to endure secret shame for having been lionized? What kind of topsy-turvy universe does this force the combatant of a "good" war to live in? Perhaps this is what one veteran of that war, the multi-faceted writer Donald Murray, had in mind when he said the official victory parade down Fifth Avenue ". . . was one of the worst days of my life" (45).

The Vietnam vet does not have to negotiate this morally discontinuous short circuit; he did evil and he was told he did evil. To an extent, Vietnam *was* unique, because for once, a dirty war was called a dirty war. For once, the during-and-after pictures match, and the rhetoric bears some resemblance to the reality. This offers Vietnam veterans an opportunity unprecedented in American wars. Contrary to just about everything one hears and reads about this war, its veterans could be the first and only "war heroes" in the history of this nation if only they could learn to live with an understood confusion. But they usually squander this opportunity. One can squander the rest of one's life, reiterating "We never lost a battle, but the government wouldn't let us win the war"; or, "We won the war, the government lost the peace." Or one can waste a life in perpetual disillusionment because Heller's old man was right. In other words, one can be used by the war, or one can use it. As a nation we can turn bad news into good news if we gather it, face it, and make new use of it.

We can do this only if we stop viewing the war as having caused a breakdown in the American psyche, when in fact it laid the groundwork for a breakthrough. As Kenneth R. Pelletier, a professor of psychiatry, says, we can make new use of bad news if we view "physical and psychological illness as potentially regenerative rather than necessarily degenerative" (33). The problem is that, instead of using the illness of the war, people often either fight it or sedate it. Either way, they squander rather than scrounge; the war then wins and sustains the breakdown. Speaking both physiologically and metaphorically, Lewis Thomas says, "Our arsenals for fighting off bacteria are so powerful, and involve so many different defense mechanisms, that we are in more danger from them than from the invaders. We live in the midst of explosive devices; we are mined" (92). Again, we have "paired sets of antagonists," the self and the not-self that attacks from the outside. Thomas calls our defenses against the perceived attackers "well-intentioned but lethal errors." They are responses to "propaganda" (93). Speaking now in a highly metaphorical way, Thomas says: "We tear ourselves to pieces because of symbols, and we are more vulnerable to this than to any host of predators. We are, in effect, at the mercy of our own Pentagons . . ." (94).

The way out of this self-destructiveness, according to Pelletier, is to recognize that "Symptoms may be an indication of the individual's [or nation's] attempt to undergo a self-healing process. . . . Certain forms of psychosis may be usefully left to run their course, rather than be sedated, because the person may be engaged in a deep . . . transformation" (33). The problem is that America has never been the kind of country to let any bad news run its course. It would rather wage war on it; so it responds with a war on cancer, a war on poverty, a war on drugs, a war on AIDs—all of which end up being as counterproductive as the war on Vietnam or the war on the bad memories it created. "Just Say No to Drugs" is another way of saying "Let's feel good about being forcefully simple-minded."

Our soldiers did a lot of unlearning in Vietnam; now, if they only would use their freedom from false knowledge—their disillusionment—in a constructive way, as an opportunity for a "painful birth" (Anderson, 4). Seen in this way, perhaps post traumatic stress disorder is not so much a sickness as it is a sign of health. Perhaps, like Leslie Marmon Silko's Tayo, the World War II veteran in *Ceremony*, the sickness stems from the fear of accepting real health *as* health. Perhaps veterans suffering from PTSD can be encouraged to see that the real order of their minds has been merely masquerading as disorder (Gleick, 22).

It may seem odd that I have quoted from Anderson's *Reality Isn't What it Used to Be* so often. After all, for the most part, Anderson doesn't even address the Vietnam War; but he does discuss a postmodern epistemology that Vietnam should have led us to. What happens, he asks, when we discover that human reality is a mere social construction? When this happens to us, we encounter a void; we come face to face with a sense of nothingness, very likely, the great distance between the end of Magellan's rope and the floor of the ocean. The word both Heidegger and the Vietnam veteran psychologist Arthur Egendorf use to describe the feeling that accompanies the encounter is "dread." Egendorf contends:

> To appreciate the nature of nothingness we must relax our impulse to turn away from it, for nothingness first comes upon us in the experience of dread. Dread is distinct from anxiety and worry, which are concerns about something specific. Dread . . . is the sense of everything falling apart, the ground slipping from under our feet, or the entire structure of our lives being whisked away. . . . That is what overwhelms us: the experience of being in the presence of nothingness itself. (166)

Precisely my experience with *Tracers*.

Egendorf believes that this feeling must be left to run its course:

> We do not heal ourselves from war or trauma by treating symptoms, memories, bad feelings, or underlying fears, just as it dosn't work to turn away from them. Healing must involve an alternative principle, a fundamental stance that turns us toward and includes all that's there, a posture that allows us to be at home in the world, rather than being rigid, antagonistic, and threatened. (163)

Vietnam veterans can teach their country how to be "at home," without the pretenses of a map masquerading as the territory. They have had the painful opportunity, as Egendorf says, to discover that war "is a mass ritual to exorcise the nothingness . . . [and] to defend our rigidly defined selves and battle our enemies firmly believing they alone threaten our security" (166). Living without false boundaries, the veterans can ask Heidegger's question, "What is being?" meaningfully; for being then no longer means a unique self apart from, but a part of the mysteriousness we all need to call home. Once we are at home, Egendorf says, "Nothingness then appears without any negative quality. What emerges is a welcoming presence" (166).

Memorials to War

I didn't want a monument,
not even one as sober as that
vast black wall of broken lives.
I didn't want a postage stamp.
I didn't want a road beside the Delaware
River with a sign proclaiming:
—"Vietnam Veterans Memorial Highway."

What I wanted was a simple recognition
of the limits of our power as a nation
to inflict our will on others.
What I wanted was an understanding
that the world is neither black-and-white
nor ours.

What I wanted
was an end to monuments.
—Bill Ehrhart, "The Invasion of Grenada"

Well, my own design for a memorial is somewhat more theatrical,
and fragrant.
—Jesse, *Paco's Story*

Since there was so much bitter debate about what the Vietnam Veterans Memorial should look like and express, and there still is with

regard to what we ended up with (a most unwelcoming presence, some feel), I thought it germane to this chapter to share two other "designs"—one that Jesse, a minor character in *Paco's Story*, thinks would be appropriate, and one that he fears will be built instead. The first would surely bring "an end to monuments" of war; the second would perpetuate James Webb's "glory in them fields." The memorial he would like to see constructed would befoul apathetic, greedy Americans in order to implicate them in a dirty war. A white marble slab with the names of the dead

"Arrange[d] . . . any goddamned way you've a mind to . . ." (158) would be placed on top of a grassy knoll. The grass leading up to the slab would be hosed down to make it "good and soggy; nice and mucky" (159). In the middle of the marble would be a big granite bowl filled knee-deep with "thousands of hundred-dollar bills" mixed together with . . . every sort of "egregious" excretion that can be transported across state lines from far and wide—chickenshit, bull shit, bloody fecal goop, radioactive dioxin sludge, kepone paste, tubercular spit, abortions murdered at every stage of fetal development—I don't know what and all. . . . Then advertise. "Come one! Come all! Any and all comers may fish around in that bowl of shit and keep any and all hundred-dollar bills they come across," bare-handed, but first they must take off their shoes, roll up their trousers, slug through that knee-deep muck, and wind up slopping it all over that marble. (159)

The memorial he fears will be built is some sort of traditional "horse's ass of a hero's statue" (157) of a

half-hacked Boy Scout Lieutenant ("all my life I've wanted to lead *brave* men to *victory* in a *desperate* battle!"). . . . He'll pose, fucking-new-guy-fashion, with his cheerleader, frat-boy grin on his face, as much as to say, "Hi, Mom! I'm fucking-A *proud* to be dead. . . . And you got to know that statue will be some dipped-in-shit, John Wayne crapola. . . . They'll mount that John Wayne-looking thing on a high pedestal and set it out by the road so the lifers and gun nuts can cruise by in their Jeep campers and Caddies and see it good and plain. Or they can park and stand real close (dressed in their K-Mart cammies), and get a lump in their throats and all creamy between the thighs, feeling sad and sorrowful, remembering and admiring the old days. (157–58)

As it turned out, Maya Lin's design won the competition, and it resembles neither of Jesse's models. However, because of the bitter

231

design debate, Frederick Hart's traditional sculpture of three soldiers was added just yards away from the VVM, and, to some degree, it does participate in a tradition of memorializing war that Jesse (and Heinemann) despises. (Maya Lin once compared what Hart's memorial does to her design to painting a moustache on the Mona Lisa.) The debate that resulted in the compromise memorial was fought between those who wanted something that would honor the warriors and those who wanted Lin's design because it elicited a thoughtful and complicating remembering of the war and its human cost. It was fought between those who wanted to replace bad news with good news and those who wanted to make new use of the bad news. That is, it was fought between the squanderers and the scroungers.

Refusing to heal "from the bottom up and the outside in," many vociferous, stage-one veterans and nonveterans heaped insults on the design. In the *Wall Street Journal*, Andrew Ferguson says it's "a trough of mawkish self-pity, a teenage sulk tarted up in black granite." In "Vietnam: Memorials of Misfortune," Elizabeth Hess quotes many other displeased people. Tom Carhart, a member of the Vietnam Veterans Memorial Fund, was especially outraged. He called it "the most insulting and demeaning memorial to our experience that was possible" (265), a "degrading ditch," a "black gash of shame and sorrow," and a "black spot in American history." Demanding a white memorial, he claimed "Black is the universal color of shame, sorrow, and degradation." Reflecting the self-serving solipsism that marked the entire war with Vietnam, Carhart neither cares nor knows that in Vietnam *white* is the color of sorrow.

Carhart had allies. Tom Wolfe considers the design abstract and elitist—a "perverse prank" (269). James Webb designated it a "wailing wall for anti-draft demonstrators" (266). Ross Perot called it "a slap in the face" (265); in a classic stage-one maneuver, he brought people in from all over the United States to Washington, and had them, according to Lin, plant the rumor that she was a leftist and that all the jurors were Communists, "and people believed it" (271). Even Phyllis Schlafly got in on the action, calling the VVM a "tribute to Jane Fonda" (266). Furthermore, although I can't verify the frequency, I've heard (and heard of) vets refer to the Wall as "the gook wall."

Frederick Hart has entered the fray as well, somewhat unprofessionally it would seem. In an interview with Hess, he claims that "Lin's memorial is intentionally not meaningful," and that it "is contemptuous of life" (273) and "nihilistic" (274). In what seems like professional jealousy he asserts: "there is nothing more powerful than an ingenue. If she had been a professional, the design would have been sacked." In view of the fact that all submissions to the design contest were "blind," this is a puzzling statement. Hart concludes the interview with a sarcastic put-down: "People say you can bring what you want to Lin's memorial. But I call that brown bag aesthetics. I mean, you better bring something, because there ain't nothing being served" (274).

Finally, Bill Ehrhart, whose poem against memorials begins this chapter, has added his name to the detractors. In "Who's Responsible," he claims that because the VVM is an "intoxicating," "inarticulate substitute for accountability," it is "an awful cliché" that "precludes discussion or critique or wisdom." Ehrhart would also seem to concur with Hart's brown-bag accusation, for he claims the memorial ". . . tells us only what each of us chooses to hear" (96). In some ways, Ehrhart is the last person in the world who would ever put up with replacing bad news with good news. He's made a literary career of deconstructing the textbooks of America's feel-good "reader's digest." In his poetry and speeches, he argues—both implicitly and explicitly—that Americans need to study their culture's history and icons and not be gullible cheerleaders. He challenges us to become better literary critics of our national narrative. Yet his criticism of the VVM, though refreshingly different from that of Carhart, Webb, and Perot, is not very studied.

The point that needs to be made is that these embittered reactions exemplify the refusal to face up to Snowden's serious wound. Rather than being "contemptuous of life," or an "inarticulate substitute for accountability," Lin's memorial courageously, brilliantly, and literally gathers, faces, and makes new use of more than 58,000 unpleasant facts. The problem Lin had to face is the same one faced by any memorialist of any war: how to commemorate the war without conferring dignity on it, how to elicit thought, rather than goose bumps and sentimental tears. As I said in the chapter on drama, simple irony doesn't work. When the subject is war and combat, irony is like pits in a watermelon: you spit irony out—or even swallow it—to get at

233

the seductive power of nihilistic splendor. And then you start talking in patriotic, either-or drivel. The nation saw this happen at a VVM ceremony on Memorial Day 1993. Operating with a Dick-and-Jane epistemology, vets shouted at President Clinton, "We fought, you ran," then turned their backs on him and, suffering from a basic training hangover, stood at parade rest. Others chanted "Go home!" "coward," and "shame." In the context of the actual VVM, these stage-one actions were the result of prolonged adolescence, and they were utterly incongruous, representing as they did a total misappropriation of the Wall's intent.

But intent often is damned. This is precisely what happened in 1992 when "Historial," the deconstructive memorial to World War I, was dedicated in Péronne, France. According to Madeleine Bunting, despite the fact that "Historial is a demanding, intellectual museum which attempts to illustrate complex historical ideas," the assembled diplomats somehow "spat that out" and launched into an insane rhetoric that has been with us for millenia:

> "From their sacrifice, a new era of fraternity was born" (US); "Their self-sacrifice and heroism will never be forgotten" (Canada); "They gave their lives so that we could live in freedom with dignity" (New Zealand); and the South African ambassador, speaking in Afrikaans, wished "to remind everyone that we fought with the free world for peace and justice." The international committee of historians who have guided the project through its gestation, winced; this rhetoric was exactly what the museum has set out to challenge.

In the early autumn of 1993, I witnessed a similar misappropriation of another monument—Glenna Goodacre's Vietnam Women's Memorial. In the middle of its 23-city tour, before being permanently placed 300 feet from the VVM on November 11, it stopped off in Minnesota. It was put on display in a bizarrely incongruous setting—the Mall of America. It was surrounded by high-tech, spend-your-money-now glitz and hype. That situation couldn't be helped; the Mall generously donated the space of one of its rotundas.

But that unavoidable logistic compromise was a blood relative of the war "consumerism" demonstrated during the ceremony. Diane Carlson Evans, a former Vietnam nurse and founder and pusher of the project that led to the funding and creation of the VWM, spoke inclusively and pacifically to all women who participated in the war or demonstrated against it. Unfortunately, her voice was drowned out by the Military Mythological Complex, which soon took over. It would seem that none of its members in attendance had actually studied Goodacre's work of art. Although realistically cast in bronze, it lends itself in no way to the conventional validation of war. The faces of the four figures say it all. A nurse holding a dying soldier looks on him tenderly, but she is saddened beyond language. The soldier himself has a Goya-like expression of terror and pain. The compress on his forehead will be as helpful as the M & Ms Doc Peret gives to dying squad members in *Cacciato*. Instead of protecting him from "incoming," the sandbags he lies on will likely be his death bed. Another woman looks off to the horizon, mouth agape, as if screaming for help that won't help the soldier even if it comes. Behind these three figures—invisible, from a unidimensional perspective—a third woman kneels prayerfully; but, in view of the memorial's totality, these would seem to be unanswerable prayers. Goodacre's memorial shows care and commitment, but it also shows pain and anguish without the conventional redemptory compensations. At the ground-breaking ceremony in Washington D.C., General Colin Powell, Chairman of the Joint Chiefs of Staff, said, "The nurses saw the bleakest, most terrifying face of war." The VWM captures that terrifying face. Finally, because it is circular, the women's memorial has no "finish." At whatever point one decides to walk away from it, there is a sense of having left things undone.

To my disappointment, at the ceremony in Bloomington, Minnesota, there were "watermelon pits" everywhere, although many were likely swallowed unnoticed by the intoxicated warriors—closet and otherwise. There were color guards, the singing of the national anthem by a hip eight-year-old girl, the Pledge of Allegiance, the playing of the Marine, Army, Navy, Air Force, and Coast Guard hymns; there were lots of those words despised by Frederick Henry—words like "duty," "honor," "courage," "sacrifice," and "God." Finally, there was the regional VA director telling vets stuck at stage one that "we vets know we won that war." Self-irony was M.I.A., as was any mature, grown-up attentiveness to Goodacre's sculpture.

235

Quite likely, one of the reasons some veterans remain unhappy with Maya Lin's memorial is that they have to misappropriate it more radically than Goodacre's in order to engage in that kind of rhetoric and inattentiveness. Without a "smoking gun," as it were, the Wall is too abstracted from the essentials of war. In fact, it is a quiet symbol, not of war but of 58,000 people who are no longer with us because of war. What makes the VVM a great piece of art, though, is not just what it precludes (or tries to), but the ways in which it provokes the visitor to attain Perry's third stage of interrogative affirmation. The iconography of the memorial is well known to almost everyone; so I will reiterate and interpret only those aspects of its design that are pertinent to this book. I've already mentioned that the memorial both "begins" and "ends" in 1968, during the heart of the war. This lack of closure makes the interaction of viewer and monument a dynamic event—almost a mobile experience. When we try to make an end to our visit, we are pulled back into the war's insane middle. Further, as we approach the vortex of the two wings, we are whiplashed either forward or backward sixteen years, always moving in a 1959–75/1975–59 interface. Regardless of the direction we choose to move in, the flashbacks and flashforwards force us into a much more complex relationship with time and history than our future-oriented, narrative-obsessed sensibilities are used to.

But more needs to be said about the "beginning," "middle," and "end" of this memorial. It is peculiar not only that the beginning and end of our walk represent the middle of the war, but that those representations are at first so small—just inches high. Yet, at the vortex of 1959–75, two seemingly unimportant dates, because almost no killing was taking place, the Wall reaches its greatest height—ten feet. One explanation for this, if I may return to Severo and Milford, is that Lin's "text" is "parenthetical." Like *The Wages of War*, the VVM turns parenthetical material into main clauses. In a sense, 1959 and 1975 *are* the Wall's two most important dates: in 1959 almost no one had started to pay any attention to the dangerously myopic, solipsistic thinking of U.S. military and political leaders; in 1975, heavily into denial, almost everyone stopped paying attention. Drawing our attention to these two dates, the VVM, as Charles L. Griswold reminds us, is a "monument" in the true sense of the word, derived as it is from the Latin *monere*, meaning "to admonish," "warn," "advise," "instruct" (691).

There are other ways in which the VVM is "parenthetical," thereby warning us to pay attention to details. First, its very location seems "bracketed" by the landscape. If one were to approach it from the north, one would almost literally have to fall into it to see it. Even from the standard approach routes, it is so inconspicuous that one can nearly miss it. People often do. By contrast, the Washington Memorial is visible from many miles away. Does this mean the VVM lacks power? Yes and no. When asked by Elizabeth Hess if the memorial has a female sensibility, Lin answered: "In a world of phallic memorials that rise upward, it certainly does. I didn't set out to conquer the earth, or overpower it, the way Western man usually does. I don't think I've made a passive piece, but neither is it a memorial to the idea of war" (Hess, 272).

Actually, the memorial is anything but passive and powerless. Grant F. Scott comments: "Whereas the other monuments are eerily self-sufficient, boasting forms that are clearly closed, the VVM necessitates our existence and our gaze for the completion of its aesthetic. Its form is wonderfully open and unfinished" (39). Scott also refers to the monument's "choreography" and to the fact that it "makes us work." Again, we see that sense of the granite's "mobility." This is due in part, as we've seen, to the Wall's nonlinearity and lack of temporal closure. As many people have noted, it also is due to Lin's decision not to arrange the names alphabetically, but instead, according to the date of death. This requires the visitor to search, ask for help, even get up on a ladder to find a name. Like a postmodern novel, Lin's text doesn't offer a completed plot to entertain the passive reader. Its power thereby resides in what it engenders, not in what it is.

The power also resides in the scope of what it embraces. Its polished black granite reflects its surroundings—visitors, grass, trees, water, clouds, airplanes taking off overhead, and both the Washington and Lincoln memorials. In other words, it integrates the visitor in a complex mobile collage in which the viewer watches himself look as others watch him look at names of the dead, which are conjoined by the landscape and a compression of history stretching from the

Revolutionary War to the Civil War to the Vietnam War. In this sense, the VVM is a metamemorial, a metafictional reflexive text compelling us to check out Doc Peret's wires and circuits and filters.

I should add that the Wall is *self*-reflexive as well, particularly at night. It watches itself. Standing at the vortex, one notices that the two wings not only reflect each other but that the footlights along each wing place one in the middle of a lighted runway, an eerie corridor that seems both to rise and descend to those two troubling dates when America didn't pay and stopped paying—stopped paying and didn't pay—attention. The effect is overwhelming. Still standing at the vortex, the viewer's metamemorial experience is further enriched by a slight movement of the head to the left or the right. An inch to the right brings the Lincoln Memorial into view; an inch to the left produces the Washington Monument. The effect transforms linear history into a spatial collage that almost gently reminds us to contextualize and interrogate our history, not to celebrate certain parts in isolation.

There is much debate regarding Lin's intentions in having the Memorial reflect the Washington and the Lincoln. For example, Charles Griswold feels that their inclusion in the Wall's black surface should rekindle love of country and its ideals. He believes the reflections give the viewer "a firm sense of both the value of human life and the still higher value of the American principles [what would Heller's old Italian say?] so eloquently articulated by Washington and Lincoln . . ." (173). This high-minded thinking leads Griswold to conclude his reflections on the monument's meaning with the words, "America is still like a ray of the sun in a somber world," and ". . . in spite of everything, America remains fundamentally good" (714).

Grant Scott responds acerbically to Griswold's assumptions, calling them "naive" (38). In a footnote he adds,

> Although I am greatly indebted to [Griswold's] essay, I wonder about the rosy optimism of its conclusions. On closer scrutiny many of Griswold's assumptions seem to issue from the emotionally charged atmosphere of the Memorial's dedication; his desire to celebrate the Wall's patriotic and therapeutic function thus seems to cloud his discussion of its fundamentally "interrogative" character. (40)

Scott's point seems well taken. At the end of his essay, Griswold does return a lot of stuff to the attic. Plus, the very degree to which Lin's design is utterly different from, say, that of the Washington Monument would seem to lend credence to Scott's thinking. By descending into the earth horizontally rather than thrusting upward, by being yonic rather than phallic, it would seem to make a political statement (although contest rules prohibited that): "I am different from you, and I don't share your assumptions regarding power, militarism, and war." Scott certainly believes the VVM makes that statement: ". . . the wings of the memorial point [at the Washington and the Lincoln] rather than encompass, indict rather than include or meliorate. Coming out of the shallow dark cleft in the landscape, it is impossible not to sense the Washington Monument's arrogance, or the tomb-like stolidity of the Lincoln Memorial" (38).

Scott seems so sure and so right. Indeed, if we allow the VVM to transform future-oriented history into a spatial collage, we see an omnipresent leitmotif of "Indian-hating" in American history that culminated in the Vietnam War. If we look between the parentheses, we see an Indian-hating Washington, who refered to them as "beasts of ye forest," who are like wolves, "both being beasts of prey, tho' they differ in shape" (Drinnon, 65). Between another set of parentheses we see Lincoln enlisting to fight in the ignominious Black Hawk War "at the first tap of the drum" (Drinnon, 199). Between another set we see him, in 1862, issue the direct order to hang thirty-eight Sioux in Mankato, Minnesota, for not taking kindly to being defrauded and starved by white Minnesotans. This massacre was the first domino to fall in the long, vicious Plains Wars (the last was at Wounded Knee in 1890). That is quite a legacy, and it's one that the VVM seems to ask us to dig for as we ask ourselves what possible relationship there could be between all these names of dead people and eighteenth- or nineteenth-century presidents.

But to point fingers, to indict, is to impose an exit on the Memorial. It is to rearrange the furniture of stage one. It is to forget our own reflection in the Wall. If Washington and Lincoln are implicated in the march to Vietnam, then so are we. We're all family—an extremely dysfunctional one, to be sure. And, indicting two different old uncles

239

named Sam won't change that fact, unless we indict ourselves along with them. At his best moments, when he doesn't succumb to patriotic fervor, Griswold seems to grasp the complex, dialectical nature of our experience with the VVM. In a perfect expression of stage-three thinking, he says that the Wall urges us to avoid "the false muses of intoxicating propaganda and nihilism" (713). Like all the other texts looked at in this book, the point of Maya Lin's is not just to dig up unpleasant facts that get you off the hook; instead, it is to create from them a more responsible self and nation.

Only one thing is wrong about the VVM; but it's a big wrong, which is shared to one degree or another by almost all of the literature we've considered in this book. Where is any recognition of the millions of dead and maimed Indochinese? Why isn't it even possible to trace the Vietnamese people onto a piece of paper and take that home? Lady Borton, a frequent visitor to Vietnam and the author of *Sensing the Enemy: An American Woman Among the Boat People of Vietnam*, has asked this question many times for many years. In an *Akron Beacon Journal* editorial, she said,

> It was years before I could visit the Wall. In the early '80s, I often read about the Vietnam Wall. . . . I would read by my living room stove, surrounded by photographs I had taken during the war. The photos were faces of Vietnamese civilians—mostly children—who had lost legs or arms. Surrounded by those photos, I felt angry about the Wall.

The combat veteran Dan Reeves seems instinctively to have recognized that the Vietnamese are missing on the VVM. He both begins and nears the end of his video *Smothering Dreams* (a phrase from Wilfred Owen's poem "Dulce et Decorum Est") being interviewed by Susan Stamberg by the Wall. The film surrealistically replays, over and over, both the games and the rhetoric that send eager boys to war and the actual horrors of a platoon almost wiped out in an ambush. After he replays the ambush for the final time, ending it with an off-camera soldier, desperately trying to stay alive without squares and rectangles, screaming "Which way?" he displays the kind of graphic missing from Maya Lin's memorial: "This work is dedicated to the men of the 2nd Platoon Company A 1st Amtrac Battalion and the North Vietnamese soldiers who died on January 20, 1969 along the Cua

Viet River." In a simple yet powerful gesture, Reeves takes the first step in carrying out what Borton called for this nation to do in her editorial: "It seemed to me that stories behind the names etched into that granite must someday press through the earth to Vietnam itself. Perhaps only then, when we reach through with our own wall of sorrow to theirs, can we all be healed."

I started this book by expressing my worry over our habit of tracing surfaces. As we've seen, the best writers to come out of the war dig down into the unexamined parentheses of American culture. Their work isn't finished, however; nor is ours. We all need to join Lady Borton and utilize the most fundamental bad news of the war: we didn't just lose it, we found out who we always have been. But this news will never be processed until we fighters, writers, and readers agree that it is not only possible but preferable to live—humbly and penitently—in a new understanding of our confusion. This decision has an even more primary prerequisite: we must press through those names of the dead to that point where America and Vietnam become hyphenated and bleed into each other, like a palimpsest.

In *American Myth and the Legacy of Vietnam*, John Hellmann approvingly quotes from David Brudnoy's 1977 review of *Star Wars*. Seeing a nation immobilized by post-Vietnam disillusionment, Brudnoy says "... America appears sated with reality ..." (Hellmann, 210). Conversely, in this book, I contend that America was and is sated with the unreality of its own intractable paradigms. As we've seen, the only legacies of the war imprinted on the culture are, one, we lost it, and, two, we won't repeat such a mistake again. Unscathed by the war are the myths of America's unique mandate to manifest its destiny, namely to impose its brand of Puritan order on geopolitical chaos and epistemological ambiguity. The war did very little to deconstruct Jewitt's *Captain America Complex*. The situation will remain unchanged as long as the nation clings to the myth of the war's uniqueness. Until this myth is shown to be fraudulent, only the application of American values—not the "values" themselves—will be viewed with suspicion. As long as people lock themselves into thinking of the war as a mere one-time mistake, misjudgment, or miscalculation, instead of another descent into moral turpitude, they will continue to throw out the rotten apple and save the toxic barrel.

I have shown that this leaves America with a whole series of unexamined, dangerous gut feelings. Convincingly, the gut keeps telling us: wars can work; they provide validation for men; you lose if you do not win; the soldiers won the war, and the politicians, media, and protestors lost the peace; the most aggressive technology will ensure victory; Vietnam was unique in American history; the warrior narrative of realism is objective and natural; menus are edible; maps are the territory and symbols are objects; sense-making is an indisputable mandate; confusion and chaos must be eradicated; what, not how, we think is all we need concern ourselves with; metafiction is an irresponsible, academic game. These all are gut feelings that continue to sate Americans. All of them should have been reexamined following the war; none of them were—at least not on any significant scale.

I have argued that the only way out of the tautological trap reinforced by these confident gut feelings is a guerrilla metaconsciousness that snipes at Doc Peret's filters, which caricature our perceptions and our memories of the Vietnam War. Most of the time, most of us don't even know this is happening. I recently had this fact driven home to me while looking at a 3-D poster called "Stealth Bomber." All I saw was a non-representational, arabesque mosaic of computer-generated images, repeated over and over—until, that is, I *looked again*, and squinted, peering out of the corners and tops of my eyes. Suddenly, there was the totally obvious Stealth Bomber. How could I not have seen it? But, after a long blink, I no longer could. The experience reminded me of how limited and adjustable are our perceptions. We can't trust them any more than we can trust our culturally inculcated memories of Vietnam. The subject of the poster is appropriate, for, like Snowden's mortal wound, the deadly airplane stealthily hides from our view.

The "fighting writers" we can learn from are wary of the cultural filters that prevent us from seeing the obvious. They are like pilots flying in bad weather. As Ornstein and Ehrlich say, surrounded by clouds, pilots must learn "to override gut feelings" (263). Failure to do so will result in a crash. Like instrument-rated bush pilots, the

Vietnam writers that need to be paid attention to consciously rely on "artificial horizons." Knowing that "being in the clouds" (a newly understood confusion) is a permanent condition, they make postmodernism a way of life, not just a literary style studied in the academy. Metafictions and metamemorials are strategies for survival; they can help save us from our own blindness and excess. But the alternative way of "seeing," one clung to by far too many, is the unconscious and unreliable artificial horizon of self-aggrandizing myth.

And so we return to our options: do we squander the waste of Vietnam or do we scrounge from it? Let us hope that we do the latter with urgent resolve, for it is my belief that we will fight less if we learn to write better.

WORKS CITED

Anderson, Walter Truett. *Reality Isn't What It Used to Be*. New York: Harper Collins, 1990.

Arden, John. *Serjeant Musgrave's Dance. Plays: One*. New York: Grove, 1977.

Balaban, John. *Words For My Daughter*. Port Townsend: Copper Canyon Press, 1991.

Baldwin, James. "Sonny's Blues." In *The Story and Its Writer*, edited by Ann Charters. Boston: St. Martin's Press, 1991.

Baritz, Loren. *Backfire: Vietnam—The Myths that Made Us Fight, The Illusions that Helped Us Lose, The Legacy that Haunts Us Today*. 1985. New York: Ballantine, 1986.

Barry, Jan. "Green Hell, Green Death." In *Unaccustomed Mercy*, edited by W. D. Ehrhart, 28–29. Lubbock: Texas Tech University Press, 1989.

Basinger, Janine. *The World War II Combat Film: Anatomy of a Genre*. New York: Columbia University Press, 1986.

Beidler, Philip. *American Literature and the Experience of Vietnam*. Athens: University of Georgia Press, 1982.

———. *Re-Writing America: Vietnam Authors in Their Generation*. Athens: University of Georgia Press, 1991.

———. "Bad Business: Vietnam and Recent Mass-Market Fiction." *College English* 54:1 (1992): 64–75.

Bell, Pearl K. "Writing about Vietnam." *Commentary*, October 1978, 74–77.

Benson, Steve. "Language Lines." In *The Line in Postmodern Poetry*, edited by Charles Bernstein and Bruce Andrews, 195–97. Urbana: University of Illinois Press, 1988.

Bly, Robert. "Knots of Wild Energy: An Interview with Wayne Dodd." In *American Poetry: Wildness and Domesticity*. New York: Harper & Row, 1990.

Borton, Lady. *Sensing the Enemy. An American Woman Among the Boat People of Vietnam*. New York: Dial Press, 1984.

―――. "Deep Inside the Vietnam Wall of Sorrows." *Akron Beacon Journal,* 11 Nov. 1992, A:18.

Brecht, Bertolt. "Theatre for Pleasure or Theatre for Learning?" Trans. Edith Anderson. *Mainstream* 12:2 (1958): 3.

Brook, Peter. *The Empty Space.* New York: Atheneum, 1969.

Brown, David, and W. Richard Bruner, eds. *How I Got That Story.* New York: Dutton, 1967.

Brown, D. F. *Returning Fire.* San Francisco: San Francisco State University Press, 1984.

Broyles, William, Jr. "Why Men Love War." *Esquire,* November 1984, 55–65.

Brustein, Robert. *The Theatre of Revolt.* 1962. Boston: Little, Brown, 1964.

Bryan, C. D. B. "Barely Suppressed Screams." *Harpers,* June 1984, 72.

Bunting, Madeleine. "All Quiet on the Tourist Front." *Guardian* 24, July 1992.

Butler, Robert Olen. *A Good Scent From a Strange Mountain.* 1992. New York: Penguin, 1993.

Capps, Walter H. *The Unfinished War.* Boston: Beacon Press, 1982.

Capra, Fritjof. *The Tao of Physics.* Boston: Shambhala, 1991.

―――. *The Turning Point.* 1982. New York: Bantam, 1983.

Caputo, Philip. *Indian Country.* 1987. New York: Harpers, 1991.

―――. *A Rumor of War.* New York: Ballantine, 1977.

Chomsky, Noam. "Visions of Righteousness." In *Unwinding the Vietnam War,* edited by Reese Williams, 288–315. Seattle, Wash.: Real Comet Press, 1987.

Coffey, Michael. Interview with Tim O'Brien. *Publishers Weekly,* 16 February 1990, 60–61.

Conrad, Joseph. *Heart of Darkness* and *The Secret Sharer.* New York: New American Library, 1950.

Coppola, Francis Ford. *Apocalypse Now.* Zoetrope Studios, 1979.

Crane, Stephen. *The Red Badge of Courage.* New York: Bantam, 1981.

Cross, Frank A., Jr. "Rice Will Grow Again." In *Carrying the Darkness,* edited by W. D. Ehrhart, 77–79. Lubbock: Texas Tech University Press, 1989.

Del Vecchio, John M. *The 13th Valley.* New York: Bantam, 1982.

Didion, Joan. *A Book of Common Prayer.* New York: Simon and Schuster, 1977.

―――. *The White Album.* New York: Simon and Schuster, 1979.

DiFusco, John, et. al. *Tracers.* New York: Hill & Wang, 1986.

Drinnon, Richard. *Facing West: The Metaphysics of Indian-Hating and Empire-Building.* New York: New American Library, 1980.

Works Cited

Durden, Charles. *No Bugles, No Drums.* 1976. New York: Avon, 1984.

Dürrenmatt, Friedrich. *Problems of the Theatre.* Trans. Gerhard Nellhaus. New York: Grove, 1964.

Eason, David. "The New Journalism and the Image-World: Two Modes of Organizing Experience." *Critical Studies in Mass Communication* (1984): 1:51–65.

Eastlake, William. Participant, Vietnam Writers Conference. Audio cassette. St. Paul, Minn.: Macalester College, 1978.

———. *The Bamboo Bed.* 1969. New York: Avon, 1985.

Egendorf, Arthur. *Healing From the War.* Boston: Houghton Mifflin, 1985.

Ehrhart, W.D., and Jan Barry, eds. *Demilitarized Zones.* Perkasie, Pa.: East River Anthology, 1976.

Ehrhart, W. D., ed. *Carrying the Darkness.* Lubbock: Texas Tech University Press, 1989.

———. *Unaccustomed Mercy.* Edited by W. D. Ehrhart. 1985. Lubbock: Texas Tech University Press, 1989.

———. "The Invasion of Grenada." In *Unwinding the Vietnam War,* edited by Reese Williams, 282. Seattle, Wash.: Real Comet Press, 1987.

———. "Who's Responsible." *Viet Nam Generation* 4.1–2 (1992). 95–100.

Ellis, Joseph R. "Memory Bomb." In *Demilitarized Zones,* edited by Jan Barry and W. D. Ehrhart, 14. Perkasie, Pa.: East River Anthology, 1976.

Engelmann, Larry. *Tears Before the Rain: An Oral History of the Fall of South Vietnam.* New York: Oxford University Press, 1990. Excerpted in program brochure of *Miss Saigon.* New York: Dewynters, 1991.

Eoyang, Eugene. "Chaos Misread: Or, There's Wonton in My Soup!" *Comparative Literature Studies* 26 (1989): 271–84.

Ferguson, Andrew. "When Bad Is BAD." *Wall Street Journal,* 20 September 1991.

Fish, Stanley E. *Self-Consuming Artifacts.* Berkeley: University of California Press, 1974.

Fitzgerald, Frances. *Fire in the Lake.* New York: Random House, 1972.

Foucault, Michel. *The Archaeology of Knowledge.* New York: Pantheon, 1972.

Franklin, Bruce H. *M.I.A. or Mythmaking in America.* New York: Lawrence Hill, 1992.

———. "The Myth of the Missing." *The Progressive* 22, January 1993, 22–25.

Frye, Northrop. *Anatomy of Criticism.* New York: Atheneum, 1969.

Fuentes, Carlos. *Myself With Others.* 1981. New York: Farrar, Straus & Giroux, 1988.

———. "Central and Eccentric Writing." In *Lives on the Line,* edited by Dorris Meyer, 113–25. Berkeley: University of California Press, 1988.

247

Fuller, Jack. *Fragments*. New York: William Morrow, 1984.

Fussell, Paul. *The Great War and Modern Memory*, New York: Oxford University Press, 1975.

———. *Thank God For the Atom Bomb*. New York: Ballantine Books, 1988.

———. *Wartime*. New York: Oxford University Press, 1989.

García Lorca, Federico. "Theory and Function of the *Duende*." In *The Poetics of the New American Poetry*, edited by Donald M. Allen and Warren Tallman, 91–103. New York: Grove Press, 1973.

Gibson, James William. *The Perfect War*. New York: Random House, 1986.

Gilman. Owen W., Jr. *Vietnam and the Southern Imagination*. Jackson: University Press of Mississippi, 1992.

Ginsberg, Allen. *Planet News*. San Francisco: City Lights, 1968.

Gitlin, Todd. *The Sixties: Years of Hope, Days of Rage*. New York: Bantam, 1989.

Gleick, James. *Chaos*. New York: Viking, 1987.

Gotera, Vince. *Radical Visions: Poetry by Vietnam Veterans*. Athens: University of Georgia Press, 1994.

———. "Depending on the Light." In *America Rediscovered: Critical Essays on Literature and Film of the Vietnam War*, edited by Lorrie Smith and Owen W. Gilman, Jr., 282–300. New York: Garland Publishing, 1990.

Graves, Robert. *But Still It Goes On*. New York, 1931.

———. *Collected Poems, 1975*. Oxford: Oxford University Press, 1988.

Gray, Amlin. *How I Got That Story*. In *Coming to Terms: American Plays and the Vietnam War*, 77–118. New York: Theatre Communications Group, 1985.

Greene, Graham. *The Quiet American*. New York: Viking, 1955.

Griswold, Charles L. "The Vietnam Veterans Memorial and the Washington Mall: Philosophical Thoughts on Political Iconography." *Critical Inquiry* 12 (1986): 688–719.

Groom, Winston. *Better Times Than These*. 1978. New York: Berkley Books, 1984.

Grotowski, Jerzy. *Towards a Poor Theatre*. Trans. T. K. Wiewiorowski. New York: Simon and Schuster, 1968.

Halberstam, David. *One Very Hot Day*. 1967. New York: Warner, 1984.

Hall, Donald. *The Pleasures of Poetry*. New York: Harper & Row, 1971.

Hallin, Daniel C. *The "Uncensored War."* Oxford: Oxford University Press, 1986.

Hanley, Lynne. *Writing War*. Amherst: University of Massachusetts Press, 1991.

Hansen, J. Vincent. *Blessed Are the Piecemakers*. Saint Cloud, Minn.: North Star Press, 1989.

Hasford, Gustav. *The Short-Timers*. 1979. New York: Bantam, 1980.

Works Cited

Hassett, Steve. "And what would you do, Ma" (untitled). In *Carrying the Darkness*, edited by W.D. Ehrhart, 131. 1985. Lubbock: Texas Tech University Press, 1989.

Hayles, N. Katherine, ed. *Chaos and Order*. Chicago: University of Chicago Press, 1991.

Heinemann, Larry. *Paco's Story*. New York: Penguin, 1987.

Hejinian, Lyn. "Line." In *The Line in Postmodern Poetry*, edited by Charles Bernstein and Bruce Andrews, 191–92. Urbana: University of Illinois Press, 1988.

Heller, Joseph. *Catch-22.* 1955. New York: Dell, 1979.

Hellmann, John. "The New Journalism and Vietnam: Memory as Structure in Michael Herr's *Dispatches.*" *South Atlantic Quarterly* 79 (1980): 141–151.

———. *American Myth and the Legacy of Vietnam*. New York: Columbia University Press, 1986.

Hemingway, Ernest. *A Farewell to Arms*. New York: Scribner's, 1986.

Herr, Michael. *Dispatches*. 1977. New York: Avon, 1978.

Herzog, Tobey, C. *Vietnam War Stories: Innocence Lost*. New York: Routledge, 1992.

Hess, Elizabeth. "Vietnam: Memorials of Misfortune." In *Unwinding the Vietnam War*, edited by Reese Williams, 262–81. Seattle, Wash.: Real Comet Press, 1987.

Hoover, Paul. *Saigon, Illinois*. New York: Random House, 1988.

Horne, A. D., ed. *The Wounded Generation: America After Vietnam*. Englewood Cliffs: Prentice-Hall, 1981.

Howe, Irving. "Writing and the Holocaust." *New Republic*, October 1986, 27–39.

Jeffords, Susan. *The Remasculinization of America: Gender and the Vietnam War*. Bloomington: Indiana University Press, 1989.

Jennings, Francis. *The Invasion of America*. Chapel Hill: University of North Carolina Press, 1975.

Jewett, Robert. *The Captain America Complex*. Santa Fe: Bear and Company, 1984.

Just, Ward. *Stringer*. Port Townsend, Wash.: Graywolf, 1974.

Karl, Frederick, R. *American Fictions, 1940–1950*. New York: Harper & Row, 1983.

Kesey, Ken. *One Flew Over the Cuckoo's Nest*. 1962. New York: Signet, 1976.

Kinnell, Galway. *The Book of Nightmares*. Boston: Houghton Mifflin, 1971.

Knightley, Philip. *The First Casualty*. New York: Harcourt Brace and Jovanovich, 1975.

Kissinger, Henry A. *American Foreign Policy*. New York: W. W. Norton, 1974.

Komunyakaa, Yusef. *Dien Cai Dau*. Middletown: Wesleyan University Press, 1988.

Kopit, Arthur. *Indians*. New York: Hill & Wang, 1969.

Kovic, Ron. *Born on the Fourth of July*. New York: Pocket, 1976.

Kowit, Steve. *The Maverick Poets*. Santee, Cal.: Gorilla Press, 1988.

Kroll, Jack. Rev. of *How I Got That Story* by Amlin Gray. *Newsweek*, 1 March 1982, 68.

Lomperis, Timothy J. *Reading the Wind: The Literature of the Vietnam War*. Durham, N.C.: Duke University Press, 1987.

McDonald, Walter. "Once You've Been to War." In *Carrying the Darkness*, edited by W.D. Ehrhart, 193–94. 1985. Lubbock: Texas Tech University Press, 1989.

McMahon, Marilyn. "Wounds of War." In *Visions of War, Dreams of Peace*, edited by Lynda Van Devanter and Joan A. Furey, 84–87. 1988. New York: Warner Books, 1991.

Mailer, Norman. *Why Are We in Vietnam?* New York: Putnam, 1967.

———. *The Armies of the Night*. New York: New American Library, 1968.

Mann, Emily. *Still Life*. In *Coming to Terms: American Plays and the Vietnam War*, 213–74. New York: Theatre Communications Group, 1985.

Marin, Peter. "Coming to Terms with Vietnam." *Harpers*, December 1980, 41–56.

———. "Living in Moral Pain." In *The Vietnam Reader*, edited by Walter Capps, 40–53. New York: Routledge, 1991.

Martin, Andrew. *Receptions of War*. Norman: University of Oklahoma Press, 1993.

Mason, Bobbie Ann. *In Country*. New York: Harper & Row, 1985.

Mersmann, James F. *Out of the Vietnam Vortex*. Lawrence: University of Kansas Press, 1974.

Murray, Donald M. *The Craft of Revision*. Fort Worth, Tex.: Holt, Rinehart & Winston, 1991.

Myers, Thomas. *Walking Point: American Narratives of Vietnam*. New York: Oxford University Press, 1988.

Nelson, Cary. *Our Last First Poets*. Urbana: University of Illinois Press, 1981.

O'Brien, Tim. *If I Die in a Combat Zone, Box Me Up and Ship Me Home*. 1969. New York: Delacorte Press, 1975.

———. *Going After Cacciato*. 1975. New York: Dell, 1978.

———. *The Things They Carried*. 1990. New York: Penguin, 1991.

Olson, James S., and Randy Roberts. *Where the Domino Fell*. New York: St. Martin's Press, 1991.

Ornstein, Robert, and Paul Ehrlich. *New World, New Mind*. New York: Simon and Schuster, 1989.

Works Cited

Paquet, Basil T. "Morning—A Death." In *Carrying the Darkness*, edited by W. D. Ehrhart, 218–19. 1985. Lubbock: Texas Tech University Press, 1989.

Pastor, Robert A. *Condemned to Repetition*. Princeton, N.J.: Princeton University Press, 1987.

Pelletier, Kenneth. *Mind as Healer, Mind as Slayer: A Holistic Approach to Preventing Stress Disorders*. New York: Delta, 1977.

Perry, William G., Jr. *Forms of Intellectual and Ethical Development in the College Years: A Scheme*. New York: Holt, Rinehart & Winston, 1968.

Pirandello, Luigi. *Naked Masks*. New York: Dutton, 1952.

Postman, Neil. *Amusing Ourselves to Death*. New York: Penguin, 1986.

Pratt, John Clark. Preface. *Unaccustomed Mercy*. Edited by W. D. Ehrhart, vii–xvi. Lubbock: Texas Tech University Press, 1989.

———. Panelist. *Back in the World: Writing after Vietnam*. Audiotape. New York: American Arts Project, 1984.

———. *The Laotian Fragments*. 1974. New York: Avon, 1985.

———. "Yossarian's Legacy: *Catch-22* and the Vietnam War." In *Fourteen Landing Zones: Approaches to Vietnam War Literature*, edited by Philip K. Jason, 88–110. Iowa City: University of Iowa Press, 1991.

Rabe, David. *The Basic Training of Pavlo Hummel* and *Sticks and Bones*. 1973. New York: Penguin, 1978.

———. *Streamers*. New York: Knopf, 1982.

———. *Hurlyburly*. New York: Grove, 1985.

Rand, Ayn. *Atlas Shrugged*. New York: New American Library, 1957.

Remarque, Erich Maria. *All Quiet on the Western Front*. 1928. New York: Fawcett, 1990.

Reston, James. Introduction. *Coming to Terms: American Plays and the Vietnam War*, vii–xi. New York: Theatre Communications Group, 1985.

Rimbaud, Arthur. *Rimbaud*. Trans. and ed. Wallace Fowlie. Chicago: University of Chicago Press, 1966.

Rottmann, Larry, Jan Barry, and Basil Paquet, eds. *Winning Hearts and Minds*. Brooklyn: 1st Casualty Press, 1972.

Sack, John. *Lieutenant Calley: His Own Story*. New York: Viking, 1974.

Said, Edward W. *Culture and Imperialism*. New York: Knopf, 1993.

Scholes, Robert. *Fabulation and Metafiction*. Urbana: University of Illinois Press, 1979.

Schönberg, Claude-Michel, and Alain Boublil. *Miss Saigon*. New York: Broadway Theatre, 1991.

Schroeder, Eric James. *Vietnam, We've All Been There: Interviews with American Writers*. Westport, Conn.: Praeger, 1992.

Scott, Grant F. "The Vietnam Veterans Memorial." *Journal of American Culture* 13:3 (1990): 37–40.

Works Cited

Severo, Richard, and Lewis Milford. *The Wages of War*. New York: Simon & Schuster, 1989.

Sheehan, Neil. *A Bright Shining Lie*. New York: Random House, 1988.

——. "Letter From Vietnam: Prisoners of the Past." *New Yorker*, 24 May 1993, 44–51.

Silko, Leslie Marmon. *Ceremony*. 1977. New York: Penguin, 1986.

Silliman, Ron. "Terms of Enjambment." In *The Line in Postmodern Poetry*, edited by Charles Bernstein and Bruce Andrews, 183–84. Urbana: University of Illinois Press, 1988.

Sloan, James Park. *War Games*. Boston: Houghton Mifflin, 1971.

Slotkin, Richard. *Gunfighter Nation*. New York: Atheneum, 1992.

Smith, Lorrie. "Resistance and Revision in Poetry by Vietnam War Veterans." In *Fourteen Landing Zones: Approaches to Vietnam War Literature*, edited by Philip K. Jason, 49–66. Iowa City: University of Iowa Press, 1991.

Smith, Steven Philip. *American Boys*. 1975. New York: Avon, 1984.

Steffens, Lincoln. *The Autobiography of Lincoln Steffens*. New York, 1931.

Stevens, Wallace. *Opus Posthumous: Poems, Plays, Prose*. Ed. S. F. Morse. New York: Random House, 1982.

Stoicheff, Peter. "The Chaos of Metafiction." In *Chaos and Order*, edited by N. Katherine Hayles. Chicago: University of Chicago Press, 1991.

Stone, Robert. *Dog Soldiers*. Boston: Houghton Mifflin Company, 1974.

Straub, Peter. *Koko*. New York: E. P. Dutton, 1988.

Summers, Harry G., Jr. *On Strategy: A Critical Analysis of the Vietnam War*. 1982. New York: Dell, 1984.

Swain, Daniel M. "Brothers in Arms." In *Unwinding the Vietnam War*, edited by Reese Williams, 107–110. Seattle, Wash.: The Real Comet Press, 1987.

Tang, Truong Nhu. *A Vietcong Memoir*. New York: Harcourt Brace Jovanovich, 1985.

Terry, Wallace. *Bloods*. New York: Ballantine, 1984.

Tesich, Steve. *The Speed of Darkness*. 1989. New York: Fireside Theatre, 1991.

Thomas, Lewis. *The Lives of a Cell*. 1974. New York: Bantam, 1975.

Turkel, Studs. *"The Good War."* New York: Ballantine, 1985.

Van Devanter, Lynda, and Joan A. Furey, eds. *Visions of War, Dreams of Peace*. New York: Warner, 1991.

Vonnegut, Kurt. *Hocus Pocus*. New York: G. P. Putnam, 1990.

Walter, Krista. "Charlie Is a She: Kubrick's *Full Metal Jacket* and the Female Spectacle of Vietnam." *CineAction!* (Spring 1988): 19–22.

Watts, Alan. *The Essence of Alan Watts*. Millibrae, Cal.: Celestial Arts, 1974.

Webb, James. *Fields of Fire*. 1978. New York: Bantam, 1979.

Weigl, Bruce. *Song of Napalm*. New York: Atlantic Monthly Press, 1988.

Works Cited

————. *What Saves Us*. Evanston, Ill.: TriQuarterly Books, 1992.
Weil, Simone. *The Simone Weil Reader*. New York: McKay, 1977.
Wilber, Ken. *No Boundary*. Boulder: Shambhala, 1981.
Woolf, Virginia. *Three Guineas*. New York: 1938.
Wright, Stephen. *Meditations in Green*. New York: Bantam, 1984.
Zinn, Howard. *Declarations of Independence: Cross-Examining American Ideology*.
  New York: Harper Collins, 1990.

INDEX

Index

256

Index

Index

Index

Index

Library of Congress Cataloging-in-Publication Data

Ringnalda, Don.
    Fighting and writing the Vietnam War / Don Ringnalda.
        p.   cm.
    Includes bibliographical references and index.
    ISBN 0-87805-730-7 (alk. paper)
    1. American literature—20th century—History and criti-
cism.   2. Vietnamese Conflict, 1961–1975—Literature and the
conflict.   3. Vietnamese Conflict, 1961–1975—United States—
Moral & ethical aspects.   4. Vietnamese Conflict, 1961–1975—
United States—Philosophy.   I. Title.
PS228.V5R56   1994
810.9'358—dc20   94-16059
                                                        CIP